CW01368025

My Dancing Life

Praise for previous books by Marina Grut

The History of Ballet in South Africa, 1981.

"A wonderful book for the balletically inquisitive to browse around in. … The fascination of Grut's book makes one long for similarly detailed accounts of activities in other places"

Jack Anderson, American ballet critic, in Dance Chronicle

The Bolero School. An illustrated history of the Bolero, the Seguidillas and the Escuela Bolera: syllabus and dances, 2002.

"It would be very important for the community of university teachers, researchers and Escuela Bolera dancers if your stupendous [estupenda] work could be translated into Spanish, for its effect not only here but also in other Spanish-speaking countries".

Antonio Álvarez Cañibano, director of the Centre for Documentation of Music and Dance in the Spanish Ministry of Education and Culture.

"I liked your book very much, it is a real jewel. ... I have recommended it to all my pupils and professionals."

Eloy Pericet, Escuela Bolera teacher, Madrid.

Royal Swedish Ballet. History from 1592 to 1962, 2007.

"A masterpiece about the Royal Swedish Ballet in Stockholm. ... A great and important work. ... A colossal amount of knowledge."

Anders Jörlén, Swedish dance critic, in Dansportalen 26.8.2008

"Your wonderful book".

Stephanie Jordan, Dance Research Professor, University of Roehampton, London.

My Dancing Life

Spanish and Ballet Across Three Continents

Marina Grut

The Book Guild Ltd

First published in Great Britain in 2017 by
The Book Guild Ltd
9 Priory Business Park
Wistow Road, Kibworth
Leicestershire, LE8 0RX
Freephone: 0800 999 2982
www.bookguild.co.uk
Email: info@bookguild.co.uk
Twitter: @bookguild

Typeset in Aldine401 BT

Printed and bound in Great Britain by CPI Group (UK) Ltd, Croydon, CR0 4YY

ISBN 978 1912083 541

British Library Cataloguing in Publication Data.
A catalogue record for this book is available from the British Library.

This book is dedicated to
my wonderful husband, our three children,
their spouses, my eight grandchildren,
and all the remarkable people in this book who shared my happy life

The cover photograph shows the author performing
a Spanish dance at the age of 21.
Cover graphics and photo editing: Nicolai Grut

Contents

More information is available on the website www.grutbooks.com, and then click on "Books by Marina Grut" or the sites below it.

Acknowledgements

I am extremely grateful to the following:

– The Carina Ari Memorial Foundation (*Stiftelsen Carina Aris Minnesfond*) in Stockholm whose generous grant made this publication possible;

– Professor Nancy Heller in Philadelphia for recording the information about members and repertoires of the Spanish Dance Society's Spanish Dance Theatre in Washington DC, USA;

– Ivy Salvage in London who helped me so uncomplainingly with the proofreading;

– The editors: Brenda Kirsch, Sally Brigham and my husband Mikael Grut;

– Eleanor Fitzpatrick, Archives and Records Manager, Royal Academy of Dance, for assistance with information through the years;

– David Leonard of Dance Books Ltd for his good advice;

– In South Africa: Von Schele Lottering, Wilcarina Yeates and Fiona Rodel.

– All the other people who have assisted me in various ways with this book.

Every effort has been made to trace the owners of copyright of texts, illustrations and any other materials quoted or used.

The early part of Chapter 3, 'Student Life in Stellenbosch and Cape Town', was published in the book *Om Hennie Aucamp te Onthou* (*To Remember Hennie Aucamp*, Protea Boekhuis publisher, Pretoria, 2015).

Abbreviations

CAPAB	Cape Performing Arts Board (KRUIK in Afrikaans)
CDET	Council for Dance Education and Training
DC	District of Columbia
GWU	George Washington University in Washington DC
ISTD	Imperial Society of Teachers of Dance
NAPAC	Natal Performing Arts Council
PACOFS	Performing Arts Council of the Orange Free State
PACT	Performing Arts Council of the Transvaal
RAD	Royal Academy of Dance (originally '… Dancing')
SDS	Spanish Dance Society
UCT	University of Cape Town

Introduction

Our youngest son Nicolai lay stretched across the bottom of my bed in Washington DC listening to family stories and anecdotes. He said, 'I hope you are going to write all this down. I can *never* remember it all'. I thought it a valid request. I wish that I had asked more questions when I still had my parents around. I did pump my brother Quintus's memory. There was a great age difference between us and he remembered things I could not possibly have known about.

Someone switched me on and no one allows me to switch off. I have worked steadily and ceaselessly all my life and never expected any rewards, but I have been singularly blessed that these have come, not least in the relationship that I have with my family, with my past pupils and the dancers I have trained all over the world. The first honour of my career in Spanish dance came in Washington DC in America in 1989. A letter arrived from the Spanish Embassy informing me that King Juan Carlos I of Spain had honoured me with the title of Dame of the Order of Queen Isabel of Spain, the *Lazo de Dama de la Orden de Isabel la Católica*, for my preservation and presentation of Spanish dance. A description which accompanied the medal explained that it was the highest decoration bestowed on a foreign national by the government of that time.

I had hurriedly opened the letter from the Spanish Embassy before leaving to teach at George Washington University's Theatre and Dance Department. My husband Mikael was arriving from his work at the World Bank. He saw me standing in the hallway, holding the letter in my hand, with the colour drained from my face. He asked, 'What's wrong? What has happened? Tell me, tell me'. I replied, 'It's nothing bad. In fact it is something rather wonderful'. I told him what had happened. He hugged me and said, 'Congratulations, you deserve it'.

When the medal was presented to me by the Spanish Ambassador Julián Santamaría, Luisillo and his Spanish Dance Theatre company happened to be in Washington DC performing his ballets at the Kennedy Center's Concert Hall. He came to the presentation. After the ambassador's impressive speech, telling my entire life story in detail, Luisillo said some very kind words of congratulation. He later turned to me saying, 'You realise that you are now above me'. I asked whatever he meant by that. He thought for a while and then he said, 'If the king has a dinner party, you will sit next to him and I will be at the other end of the room'. We both laughed. Nothing could have been further from the truth but very soon afterwards he too was presented with that award, assuring his place at the table!

The Spanish Ambassador to the United States Julián Santamaría presenting Marina with the Lazo de Dama de la Orden de Isabel la Católica in Washington DC in February 1989. Photo: Roslyn Arington.

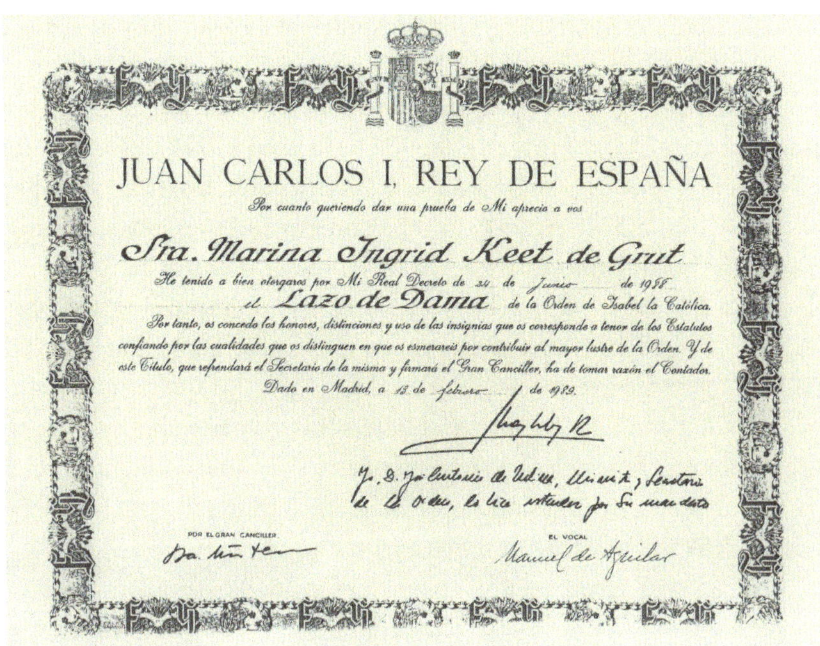

JUAN CARLOS I, REY DE ESPAÑA

Por cuanto queriendo dar una prueba de Mi aprecio a vos

Sra. Marina Ingrid Keet de Grut

*He tenido a bien otorgaros por Mi Real Decreto de 24 de Junio de 1988 el **Lazo de Dama** de la Orden de Isabel la Católica. Por tanto, os concedo los honores, distinciones y uso de las insignias que os corresponde a tenor de los Estatutos confiando por las cualidades que os distinguen en que os esmeraréis por contribuir al mayor lustre de la Orden. Y de este Título, que refrendará el Secretario de la misma y firmará el Gran Canciller, ha de tomar razón el Contador.*

Dado en Madrid, a 13 de febrero de 1989.

POR EL GRAN CANCILLER

EL VOCAL

Manuel de Aguilar

Medal certificate.

Congratulatory speech by Luisillo (Luis Pérez-Dávila) to Marina at medal presentation. Photo: Roslyn Arington.

My husband has always given me his full support for all my activities. His love of dance is as great as mine, especially for Spanish dance's rich variety, and he thinks very highly of our Spanish Dance Society. I said in my reply to the ambassador Julián Santamaría when he pinned on my medal that Spain's culture is the richest and most varied in the world. Its music and dance was my first love from an early age, and my husband who at that time was at the other end of the world in Sweden, was gripped by its literature and poetry. After my little speech, the Spanish ladies from the embassy rushed up and embraced and thanked me.

Luisillo's company came to join in the party once they had changed from their costumes. He was devastated by his presentation in the poor dance venue which the impresario had booked for him at the Kennedy Center. He had no way of creating a theatrical presentation, which was his strength. It was all so tragic. The concert hall had no wings for entrances, no backcloth, not enough lighting. Luisillo, who was a man of the theatre, was frustrated in that forum in which his way of presenting Spanish dance was impossible.

He was beside himself with anguish as he stood beside me at the back of the auditorium. Suddenly he rent his shirtfront with anger and agony. I watched as the buttons flew in all directions. Backstage, while pinning his shirt together, his wardrobe mistress said, 'What are you thinking of, doing a thing like this? You are about to meet the Spanish Ambassador'. He arrived at the medal ceremony with pins in his shirtfront, partly hidden by his tie. If one looks very carefully at the photograph, there is one pin to be seen exposed next to his tie. He had every right to sue the impresario because he had expected all the facilities of the big Kennedy Center opera stage, not the poor facilities of the concert hall. This came after a gruelling tour of one-night stands, with the dancers often sleeping on the bus while travelling to the next venue and never having a chance to do their washing properly or get a decent rest in a bed. When he sent me the tour schedule he had written on it, 'Our cruel agenda'.

Inspired by his work and his dance company, I had named the company that I established in Washington DC the 'Spanish Dance Theatre', after his. What the Spaniards at the embassy appreciated was the range of dances from Spain which we presented, not just flamenco as others did. The embassy staff always attended our performances. One night at the embassy a stage had been built for us over the fountain in the room that represented an Andalusian patio. The room was decorated with coloured tiles and tall white columns. There was a wonderful atmosphere. On that occasion the Minister for Culture, a Valencian, came up to me and said, 'Look at your dancers, their costumes are so beautiful and representative. They are so well kept and spotlessly clean, with not a crease in sight. Their shoes are highly polished. The men's shirts are pure white. And above all, they dance with such dedication and joy, sweeping us along with them. You can feel so proud. We appreciate very much that you represent Spanish culture so beautifully in all its richness and variety and not just flamenco'. That was the key to our success with the public because flamenco is really very limited to a 'lay' audience. Our beautiful costumes were researched and made by Caroline Weinberg and Professor Bill Pucilowsky. When I asked Professor Bradley Sabelli from the Theatre Department at George Washington University (GWU), 'How do you spell Pucilowsky?' He replied, 'You don't. You just accept it'.

The musicians whom I had gathered around us to accompany our performances used the instruments from the various regions. The two types of bagpipes and drums from Galicia and Asturias were played by Eric Rice-Johnson, whom I had hijacked at a folk festival where he was playing Scottish bagpipes; I persuaded him to learn the Spanish ones. Mary Anne's brother, Paul Shelton, played the large Celtic drum, John O'Loughlin played the Basque *txistu* flute and tabor, Larry Robinson and Juan Pagán played the *bandurrias* and the lute, and the guitarists were led by our faithful, knowledgeable Ralph Pemberton, who became our music administrator. He found us from his World Bank connection with my husband Mikael. Other guitarists who joined him were Margarita Jova's brother Henry Jova, when he was in town, Tom Stefanic and sometimes Paco de Malaga. The famous elderly *cantaor* (singer) Manolo Leiva graced us with his regal presence on many occasions.

We had surprised the Basque President when he visited Washington. As he stepped out of his car he saw all the dancers in Basque costumes welcoming him with the Basque dance used in greeting dignitaries,

Erreberenzia (reverence), and also performing for him other Basque dances as taught to me in San Sebastian by the revered maestro Juan Urbeltz.

Marina, John O'Loughlin and Ralph Pemberton.

None of this would have been possible without the support of two remarkable women, both of them professors at the GWU Theatre and Dance Department. First, Nancy Diers Johnson, the skilled chairperson who steered the joining together of theatre and dance into one department. No easy task, but done so successfully, with tact and sincerity and great 'people skills'. The Spanish dance course, including the summer schools that we organised together, yielded credits for the GWU students and for other students who also attended, from the USA and abroad. It was great fun working with her because of her easy style and genuine interest. Then there was the inspirational and intrepid Professor Maida Withers who teaches students with incredible vitality and knowledge, whilst also steering her contemporary 'Dance Construction Company' into fascinating choreographies. She is still being creative with them on all sorts of modern-age projects, such as using laser lights to Philip Glass's music running on two tracks, which changes from one to the other as the dancers cut through the beams. No two performances are the same. She tackles environmental themes and emotionally moving ballets such as *Families are Forever*. Her inventiveness is still strong in 2016, as I write. What a department to work in and what support I received from these two unselfish women, who never spared themselves. Their magnanimity extended to awarding me the title of professorial lecturer, with the right to the title of professor. Students were given such care and personal attention.

Nancy Diers Johnson, Chair of the Department of Theatre and Dance, GWU.

Marina with Professor Maida Withers of the GWU Department of Dance.

My most faithful supporter was Joanne Petrie, our chairman, otherwise known in the government as 'Mother Time' because she was involved in setting the time zones for the Department of Transport. She, with the help of friends, managed to get us registered as a society at a minimal cost. This enabled us to be awarded grants. She valiantly did all the grant-writing and all the follow-up paperwork after receiving the grant money. There was a lot of form-filling and report-writing. One day we were all sitting around a table to assist her. She read out, 'How many South Sea Islanders were in the audience?' She firmly filled in – 'Two'. 'Do you really know that?' I asked. She looked up, saying very convincingly, 'There must have been at least that number'. I said, 'I'm beginning to believe you', and her rejoinder was, 'So am I'. To the one question about members with disabilities, Mary Ann piped up, 'You can put me down', and Joanne said, 'I already have. And I was down last year because I was pregnant'. Her death has left me bereft of my wise, most faithful, knowledgeable and beloved companion.

Joanne Petrie, Chair of the Spanish Dance Society (SDS) in America.

In London, where I live now, the audiences are fed only flamenco and it would be so good to be able to show the riches of Spanish folklore. Proof of how it is appreciated when audiences are able to see this amazing variety, the most diverse in the world, is that we performed to sold-out houses with each new programme we presented in Washington DC. The Kennedy Center asked us to allow them to present us each year, and the National Geographic Society asked us to do a programme specifically for them, without flamenco. I persuaded them that a balanced programme should include that dance form as well. One needs so many resources for a company: a venue to work in, a lot of money and above all – energy. Now, in 2017, the spirit is still willing but the money is not there and the flesh, ah the flesh, is very weak.

This idyllically happy period of my life in the USA was really the end of my theatrical career. At the end of 1993 I retired together with my husband to London where our daughter and her family live. I have presented lecture-demonstrations for the Cecchetti Society, the Royal Academy of Dance, the Lilian Baylis theatre at Sadler's Wells, and in July 2000 the Covent Garden's Clore Studio Theatre at the Royal Opera House. The Royal Ballet's Artistic Director Dame Monica Mason had introduced us to Deborah Bull who was in charge of the performances at the Clore Studio. Also, in 2012 there was a fascinating collaboration with Flemming Ryberg of the Royal Danish Ballet, and Richard Glasstone of the Cecchetti Society. This, and my presentation of the classical school of Spanish Dance, the *Escuela Bolera,* brought together the three styles that flourished in the same period in the 19th century.

In 2008 it came as a great surprise and joy when the Carina Ari Foundation's Board of Directors awarded me the Carina Ari Gold Medal for that year for my book *Royal Swedish Ballet: History from 1592 to 1962,* published in 2007. The Carina Ari Foundation has played a great role in my life. My books on classical Spanish dance and on the history of the Royal Swedish Ballet (see Bibliography) would not have appeared in print had it not been for the Carina Ari publication grants. That foundation understands the preservation of things that are precious in the dance world. The Stockholm ballet writer and critic Anders Jörlén wrote as follows about my book, in the Swedish *Dance*

Portal on 26.8.2008: 'A masterpiece about the Royal Swedish Ballet in Stockholm'; 'A great and important work'; 'A colossal amount of knowledge'; and 'A well-written work crammed full of facts'. For this trust in me I thank the Carina Ari Foundation and treasure the Carina Ari Gold Medal 2008, received from the hand of Princess Christina, a great balletomane. As we walked together later, she said quietly and kindly to me, 'You have performed a great service to ballet in Sweden'. For that memory I shall be eternally grateful. It made all the gruellingly hard work so worthwhile.

Someone once asked me why I had written my books on classical Spanish dance[1] and on the Royal Swedish Ballet[2], as well as an earlier book on the history of ballet in South Africa[3]. I replied, 'Because no one seemed to want to do it and it needed to be done'.

This autobiography, the account of my life in dance on three continents, was made possible by a generous Carina Ari publication grant. It explains and records many ballet and dance facts that are not well known to the wider world.

If you are only interested in my dance career, please go directly to Chapter 2 because Chapter 1 describes my childhood, my immediate family and the area where I grew up.

---

1 *The Bolero School, an Illustrated History of the Bolero, the Seguidillas and the Escuela Bolera: Syllabus and Dances.* Dance Books, London, 2002, ISBN 1-85273-081-1.

2 *Royal Swedish Ballet History from 1592 to 1962.* Olms Verlag, Hildesheim, 2007. ISBN 978-3-487-13494-9.

3 *The History of Ballet in South Africa.* Human & Rousseau, Cape Town, 1981. ISBN 0-7981-1089-9.

1

My Childhood in Calvinia in the Karoo

Before I start my saga, I should set the stage. How can one describe the Karoo where my mother, brother and I were born? That vast expanse of nothingness, a semi-desert with bush-like growths that are the only vegetation for miles. Humps of hills called 'sugar loaves' and flat-topped 'table mountains' stretch out across the horizon. It is sheep country, too dry for agriculture. One of the bushes gives the mutton of that area its distinctive flavour.

I was born in 1934 in Calvinia, a small Karoo town named after the French/Swiss reformer Jean Calvin. It is situated in what is today the Northern Cape Province, about halfway between Cape Town and the Namibian border. I was the first baby born in the hospital there. Calvinia is different. It lies like a green oasis in that vast hard-packed earth. It is surrounded by table-like mountains, but the highest one goes to a point and is called Ribuni, a San (Bushman) word meaning 'don't ask me'. My parents often climbed it and made tea at the summit with the snow that lay there. That was the habitat of the baboons and for a while we looked after an orphan baboon baby. What struck me when I visited my birthplace Calvinia almost sixty years later was the pure, clear air. The brightness and clarity were stunning.

I love the Karoo. The rocks are red and in spring a blanket of flowers that defies description appears as if by magic, after the first rains. The flowers fill the barren area with endless colour, but oh so briefly. People come each year from hundreds of miles away, and even from overseas, to see this feast of beauty. The people of the town are rightfully proud of this lovely area. This is their barren but beautiful land.

I remember the picnics my parents took me on where, as a small child, I got lost in the tall golden *gousblom* flowers, which some years grew high enough to hide me. We played hide-and-seek among the mustard-coloured blooms. I now see them sold in florists and garden centres in London.

Marina and her cousin Joan Wagner in Calvinia.

Marina by the river in Calvinia.

The only danger was the sparsely growing prickly pear with one large flat paddle-shaped leaf growing out of the next in a zigzag crazy way. Like dominoes placed together by a blind man, they make their ridiculous way skyward. They have delicate flowers that look like a child's paper cuttings, with myriads of lemon-coloured petals. These turn into the prickly pears that cling carbuncle-like to the higgledy-piggledy plant. It can be invasive. If the multitudinous seeds in these plants fall, they produce more and more of this not-so-popular plant. Because the fruit is covered in prickles, one has to eat it with a knife and fork, opening the tough skin to expose the deliciously cool, orange-coloured and delicately flavoured flesh. Unfortunately there is very little flesh, and the pips do get in the way and between one's teeth. But they are somehow part of my childhood as is the fruit of another desert succulent, the *vygie* (fig), or *hotnotsvy* (Hottentot Fig). These are an acquired taste as they leave your mouth puckered up at times – and yet the memory is sweet. But they look dreadful. When ripe, they are about an inch long, deep reddish-brown, hard, crinkled and with small fig-shaped fruits growing close to the ground on the succulent plant. If cut open they divide into compartments, in which the sweet pips lie dripping in a sticky juice. The desert is sparing with its treats, so there is not much to be gleaned from each fruit. It is the outside cover that gives it the tart taste, as you suck out the meagre delight. *Vygies* were there all year round and on my travels I see these succulents also in other countries, for example Malta. The climate, and thus the vegetation, in Malta is actually very Karoo-like.

My father walked with me each evening across the barren veld. We studied the plants and myriad insects in the coolness as the sun went down behind the hills, fascinated by the dung beetle rolling his ball of dung backwards to his lair and the 'tok-tokkie' beetle clicking his way home. The lion ant's trap was an inverted sand cone down which unsuspecting ants tumbled into his waiting claws. There are plenty of ants in the Karoo. The 'Argentine' ants, for example, were brought into the country in the bedding imported with the horses from South America during the Boer War.

Then there are the 'elephant's foot' plants, where one lies on one's stomach to suck the sweet nectar from the tight knot of minute yellow flowers that are surrounded by two large flat leaves spreading on the ground. The deliciously scented, tasty and rare *koekemakranka* (pronounced 'kookuhmuhkraanka') is a delicate bright-yellow sheath filled with seeds. It stands up from a plant that has a string-like curly leaf coming out of the ground. The leaf comes before the fruit, as the autumn crocus's leaf comes after the flower, never existing at the same time. After squeezing out the seeds into one's mouth, the sheath was saved and dried to a see-through film between the pages of a book and used as a scented bookmark. It is red when ripe; the different colours of red, orange or yellow before it ripens give variations on the theme. It is extremely delicate at this stage. I wonder whether this delicacy has survived the avid searches by the local San-like people who were a part of my childhood.

The names *toktokkie* (tapping-beetle), *koekemakranka* and *tjienkerientjee* are San names from the original inhabitants of the area. *Tjienkerientjee* (chinkerinchee) is the name given to the white flower of a bulb now called, among other things, the Star of Bethlehem. In some areas a very beautiful bright orange variety exists and I am amazed that this has not been cultivated for sale. It is far more beautiful than the white one and I remember it from the Riversdale district. Linnaeus's pupil Thunberg wrote about it when he visited the Cape in the 1700s. The name was given to it by the San for the sound made when the stems are rubbed together.

On the way home from the walks with my father, I was careful not to look back over my shoulder when we crossed the dry riverbed. My grandparents' tiny maid, Sannie, said that the devil kept those who looked back and saw him in the sunset. His eyes were said to be as red as the setting sun and one should not look into them. This is probably a San legend serving to stop children burning their retinas by looking into the sun.

Once or twice a year the water rushed into the riverbed. You could smell the wet earth from afar and we used to run to see this phenomenon. The grey earth slowly turned black as the water wended its way down over the dry sand. Then came the exciting rush of the torrent as it filled the river for a brief stay. Water has its own magic.

To my surprise I found recently in the book *South African Wild Flower Guide No. 6, Karoo* that of the two plants most associated with my cousin Joan's and my childhood games, one was an interloper. This was the Australian saltbush, *Atriplex lindleyi*, a dwarf shrub up to 30 cm high, with blue-green leaves and with sponge-like capsules close to its stem. We used these as cabbages for our dolls but we never served the other plant to our dolls because its bunches of miniscule shiny red berries were delicious to eat. A small flower that I loved was the *Discus capsular* with its delicate deep-pink flower which is rather like a columbine, with two little horns underneath.

The so-called 'pepper trees' (*Schinus molle)*, with their beautiful feathery leaves and bunches of pink 'peppercorns' hanging in clusters, are also part of the Karoo of my childhood. These made good toy-food. I see this tree also in south Europe but it is actually of Peruvian origin. The other trees are the cypresses, with their knobbly seeds which actually resemble the markings on the backs of tortoises, of which there were many in the veld. I had one exceedingly large tortoise and could ride on its back. One day someone left the garden gate open and it escaped to freedom – I hope.

Strangely enough, willows, which need plenty of water, also featured in the dry Karoo of my childhood. These were to be found on the farms, around dams that had been artificially laid out. In De Aar I also saw iguanas swimming around in these dams.

My great-grandfather – christened John Henry but called Harry on his grave in Calvinia – was a builder who came to the Cape in 1860 from Kent in England, where he was born in 1838; he was to die in faraway Calvinia. I believe that my allergies come from his genes and that he moved to the Karoo for health reasons. He married Elizabeth Catharina Lerm and built many of Calvinia's homes, especially on Water Street near the river. Water Street runs down the side of the *Moederkerk* (Mother Church) or Dutch Reformed Church, which is the centre point in the town. My grandfather also built and lived in several of the beautiful houses on Water Street at different times. I believe some of them are now protected historical monuments.

My grandfather was George Benjamin Buck, born on 10 June 1872 in Calvinia, where he died in 1944. He too was a builder. The name George never featured. He was called '*Oom* (Uncle) Bennie' by the locals and '*Oupa* (Grandpa) Ben' by the family. He was a quiet, self-effacing man. I found no photographs of him. He married Anna Maria Louw Stofberg, daughter of a well-to-do shop owner in the town. The river ran behind his house.

Marina's great-grandfather's house in Water Street, Calvinia.

Marina's maternal grandmother Anna Maria Louw Stofberg, Marina's mother Helen, and Marina's uncle Harry.

Marina's mother Helen, née Buck.

Oupa Ben suddenly decided to stop his work as a builder and was always pottering around in the garden among his beloved fruit trees. He did not have a strong physique and was frequently coughing. He always wore an unbuttoned waistcoat, summer and winter, and kept bees at the bottom of the garden. My cousin Joan and I, his grandchildren, loved to chew the warm honeycombs after the honey had dripped into the big dish that he placed beneath them. We were happy to be around him.

The Bucks were a close-knit, very happy family and when my parents were married it meant that my father took my mother away to towns all over the Cape each time he received a promotion, which was every two years. Helen was my mother's name. However, in the Buck family, no one was ever called by their given names but by their nicknames, hers being Nellie. It was deplored by my father who believed that your given name should remain constant.

My mother was very wise, and her wisdom wide-ranging. She believed in avoiding overdressing young children. Once they were sweating, she maintained, and rightly so, they were more prone to catch chills while they cooled down, especially if a wind was blowing. She always washed eggs before using them. The British health service recently suggested this to protect against salmonella. In Canada the eggs are washed before being sold. This does mean that they don't last as long as unwashed eggs but the public is protected. My mother did it automatically. She also washed a tin before opening it. It is inevitable that some liquid leaks over onto the lid as you open it and from there back into the can. Germs from storehouses which had gathered on them thus entered their contents.

She considered the sun dangerous, something which again is only being recognised now. I always had to wear a hat and she carried a sunshade. She felt that children who were loved were contented children and that it was wrong to equate love with spoiling. In her view, no one could ever get too much love, but also that no should mean no, without backtracking. Once understood by a child, this saves endless strife.

My father's father, a SAPA (South African Press Association)-Reuter reporter with *The Star* in Johannesburg, in 1899 broke the news of the Boer ultimatum which triggered off the Boer War. To be able to 'scoop' this news, he cycled the 58 km (36 miles) from Pretoria to his newspaper in Johannesburg with the news which he had heard in the parliament of the Transvaal Republic. After that he was a hunted man in the Transvaal and he fled to the Cape. He had a stroke at a very young age which made him unable to work, although he lived for many more years, leaving it to my grandmother to support the family. She was a pianist and tried to support her family by playing for church services and giving piano lessons in the Strand where they lived, near Cape Town.

My father, being the oldest of the four children, had to leave school early to earn money to help his mother. He joined the post office as a humble clerk and he funded one of his brothers through university, at Brasenose College, Oxford. He always had a complex that further education had been denied him but he read voraciously and became very erudite. He and my husband had a firm bond when they discussed world events, politics or literature. My father spent the war years listening each lunchtime to the news. He had a large map of the world pinned up on the dining room wall, where he marked events with coloured pins as they occurred. I have to this day a dislike for the endless talking from a radio.

Marina's father.

Marina's father Pieter Quartus Keet, "Quartie", with his parents Pieter Gerhard Jacob Keet and Maria Elizabeth de Wet.

While we were living in Calvinia, a very important occasion was the eclipse of the sun. Calvinia was the best place from which to view it, and there was no pollution. Still today you see so many stars in the night sky. The eclipse brought hundreds of people to this little town, which suddenly had the attention of the world focused on it. As well as the telescopes and the scientists came news teams from all over the world to report the event.

My father became the centre of their universe, sending messages out all over the world by teleprinter. Words were tapped out by him at an incredible speed in Morse code. He was busy night and day. I remember being taken to look through those powerful telescopes and seeing the morning star. An eclipse is always very brief. In those days people used sooted glass to look at the sun, to see the eclipse and not be blinded. The 'feathered' community of Calvinia were extremely annoyed by this event. As the sun gradually disappeared, all the chickens and doves went to roost, tucking their heads beneath their wings. Then, a few moments later, it became light again. They were outraged at this deception and a cacophony broke out as they clucked and cooed in disgust. It was all fascinating to a six-year-old like me.

In 1995 when we revisited Calvinia, the postmistress took us to her house, my former home when I was six years old. She told us that although Calvinia had been an exclusively English-speaking town when we had lived there, it was now Afrikaans-speaking. First the Jews had left, having closed down the synagogue when there were not ten men, a 'minion', to have a service. There had been a large Jewish community there in the 1930s and the 1940s. Mr and Mrs Rosenblatt, who were our neighbours, owned the local store. The Helfet family had two sons of whom Arthur became a famous surgeon in Cape Town. It was said that he had secretly been taken to Washington to operate on President Kennedy; it would always be denied, we were told. What I do know is that a book by an American author stated that Arthur Helfet had been flown from Cape Town to Washington to give forensic advice in a murder case there, and that is perhaps nearer to the truth. I also know that when I had a severe dance-related injury – breaking bones in my foot while exiting barefoot from the stage and hitting a lightstand in the dark – all the consultants wanted to operate and put me in iron splints. My mother said, 'Go to Arthur'. To Arthur I went. He took some sticking plaster and showed me how to bandage my metatarsals, lifting up the injured bones for support. It worked like a miracle.

There was 'high society' in little Calvinia. The important people of the town were the officials, the judge, the magistrate and the postmaster. Bridge games and dances were the entertainment of this small community. Long ballgowns and tuxedos were worn, the men fitted out with white gloves, all the way out there in the semi-desert. You went 'calling' and visited people formally. If the person was not 'at home', a calling card was left to show that you had been there. Few people had telephones then, to call in advance of their visit, but because my father was the postmaster we owned one. The women dressed up on these occasions with hat and gloves. But mostly neighbours just popped in to chat. Once a week there were cinema shows.

The author Uys Krige asked me why my brother spoke English with an Afrikaans accent and I spoke Afrikaans with an English accent. My father was determined that I would not speak English with an Afrikaans accent like my brother, who was fourteen years older than I was. He considered it an important passport to the world. Everyone was instructed to speak only English to me and then, once the first language was secure, when I was seven years old, I was sent to an Afrikaans school to learn that language.

My Uncle Harry, unlike my father and his moving from town to town, refused his promotion each time in order to stay on in his beloved Calvinia. The people all knew each other and the farmers were generous with gifts. My uncle was loath to leave this big-hearted community for others less forthcoming. There was a wonderful community spirit.

Throughout her whole married life, until we came to Stellenbosch in 1944, my mother had moved every two years, each time my father was promoted to a higher office. From their first years in Calvinia, where my father was a young postal clerk, they moved to Mooreesberg where he was postmaster, then Riversdale, back to Calvinia, George and De Aar, and finally arriving in Stellenbosch, where my mother fell in love with this beautiful town and refused to go elsewhere. My father spent some time in Worcester, commuting over weekends, and finally commuting to the head office in Cape Town, an hour away, where he reached the high post of Chief Superintendent of Post, before being struck down with blindness. He could add up a row of figures by just running his fingers along them.

The Coloured people at the Cape are mostly Calvinists and Afrikaans-speaking, whereas the Black tribes have their own languages: Xhosa, Zulu, etc. It is not generally known – not even in South Africa – that there are more Coloured than White Afrikaans-speakers. They are gentle people and because of that they are ignored. The Blacks have the political power, the Whites the economic power and the Coloureds fall in between the cracks. In 1924 the South African writer Sarah Gertrude Millin wrote a book about these people called *God's Stepchildren,* and that is how it still is.

They are descended from San (Bushmen), Khoikhoin (Hottentots), Malays, Malagasy (from Madagascar), Blacks, Indians (the last four groups came as slaves during the Dutch time) and Europeans. In Cape Town the Malay ancestry is noticeable, in the Karoo the San ancestry dominates. Today there are no longer pure San people in the Karoo. In colonial times they were appallingly treated by both the Whites and the Blacks, as they still are in some African countries, forced off their land in favour of wildlife and tourism.

2

Dancing 'Under the Tablecloth'

My ballet life unfolded in the stunningly beautiful Western Cape Province of South Africa, more specifically in Cape Town under the imposing Table Mountain with the white cloth of mist caused by the fierce summer wind called the 'south-easter', the cloth at times covering the flat-topped mountain and rolling over its edge – the 'tablecloth' of the above title. Table Mountain, and the Russian artist Tretchikoff who settled in Cape Town, are both so famous that a postcard reached him from overseas addressed merely 'Tretchikoff, Table Mountain'! His work was so sought-after in Britain that when the Sadler's Wells Theatre Ballet visited South Africa in 1957 some of the dancers bought up any card or print of his paintings that they could find.

This is really an area very different from the rest of the country. Being the oldest and most settled part of South Africa, it is steeped in culture and has a rich history. The University of Cape Town (UCT) Ballet School, where I went to study, was always multiracial, something forgotten today. Johaar Mosaval and David Poole, who were principal dancers in the Royal Ballet in London, are prime examples of this fact. They were trained at the UCT Ballet School on the slopes of Table Mountain.

I was ten years old when we moved to the idyllic second oldest town in the Cape, Stellenbosch, 30 miles (50 km) from Cape Town. The name was created from the two surnames of the first governor of the Cape, Simon van der Stel, and that of his wife whose surname was Bosch. In South Africa it is sometimes known as the 'Oak Town' (*Eikestad*) because its streets are lined by oaks. There was a ballet studio in the Plum Tree nursery school in Louw Street next door to our home. I awoke the first morning to doves cooing in the lush oaks outside my window, water running down the street in the irrigation furrow in front of the house, and a river at the end of the road. All of my childhood had been a blissfully happy one but this was paradise. I saw the children dancing in the ballet school across the road and my fate was sealed.

My decision, encouraged by my ballet teacher Cecily Robinson, was to go to the UCT Ballet School, founded by the principal Dulcie Howes, situated in Rosebank, a suburb of Cape Town. My mother was very supportive because she was artistic but had never had a chance to follow her talent. My father was not against my decision as such but against entering a very precarious world without having another career to fall back on.

My father had persuaded my brother to go to university, when all he wanted to do was art. Quintus suffered through three years of a BA course and then suddenly, just before getting his degree, he wrote home and said that he had enrolled in a commercial art course in a well-known art school in Cape Town run by Budapest-born Arthur Podolini[1]. My father was devastated and angry. My mother lived for months off the fruit of her guava tree in the garden of our home in George to save money from her household allowance to send to my brother. She ate them fresh from the tree in summer or made them into preserves for the winter.

Three people in particular helped with my education: Ruth Denman, my father, and Dulcie Howes. Denman, the principal of Rhenish School in Stellenbosch, supported my wish to go to the ballet school. She said wisely, 'If that is what you really wish to do, then do it. I can give you a reading list that will give you a better education than any school can give you'. My father had educated himself and understood the wisdom of that advice which was remarkable coming from a school principal. She followed it up with a list discussed with my father. My brother fetched the books from the library and my father and I read them together. Unfortunately he smoked all the time, and my bad lungs (bronchiectasis) today may stem from that time.

1 1891-1946; in 1961 there was an exhibition of his art in Eugene, Oregon.

Marina's brother Quintus Keet.

Next, my parents went to consult Dulcie Howes because I would be studying dancing under her at the university ballet school in Rosebank in the mornings and teaching in Stellenbosch in the afternoons, an hour and a half's journey each way. Dulcie, another enlightened woman, said that she would help me. I was to do the written work in my own time and she would mark it for me. That placated my father. She gave me an amazing assessment afterwards. So I launched into a very exciting but stressful time. I was to thrive on it in one way and suffer in another. But I was young and headstrong. My father worriedly gave way to the pressure from all these women. Today I celebrate being part of a method in Spanish dance teaching that recently celebrated its 50th anniversary internationally: the right to the title of professor, and two medals, as I mentioned in the Introduction. I was also awarded a day in my name by the Mayor of Washington DC, a Lifetime Achievement Award from my Spanish Dance Society (SDS) members in America, a Special Achievement Award from the Hispanic Institute for the Performing Arts, an Outstanding Service Award from the International Association of Blacks in Dance (USA), a Certificate of Appreciation from the George Washington University, and others. From my esteemed colleagues came the title of Honorary Lifetime President of the Spanish Dance Society internationally. How I wish my father could have experienced the results of his trust in me.

Some parents used to educate their children at home. Nowadays children are put into school at five years of age. I was lucky, mine started at seven years, so I had many years to play and be creative on my own before being stifled and frightened at school. Mary Skeaping (Chapters 11 and 12) was entirely educated at home and became the artistic director of the Royal Swedish Ballet, among many other prestigious appointments. Teaching should be exciting and approached as an adventure. Encouragement is very important. American children are taught through encouragement, which gives them huge self-confidence.

In 1950, when it became known in Stellenbosch that I had decided on a career in dance, to our surprise the Dutch Reformed *dominee* (parson) visited us, asking to speak to my mother in my presence. He dared to say, 'Are you aware of what your daughter is going to do?' My mother, sitting with her hands crossed demurely on her lap, speaking quietly with her usual mellow voice replied, 'Yes I am. She is going to work harder than you ever have in your entire life'. He rose to his feet and departed. We were Anglicans and yet he dared to confront her.

The *dominee's* wife was in her garden one Sunday while my mother was watering our garden next door. The hedge parted and his wife peered at my mother saying, 'It is a sin to work on a Sunday'. She departed hurriedly. However, my mother was to give our neighbour her comeuppance. Late that night she heard someone watering the next door garden; it was the *dominee's* wife. My mother parted the hedge and said, 'God can see in the dark!'

The very first dance teacher at the Cape was Helen Webb, who at first taught 'fancy dancing' – to teach the upper-class children deportment. Helen was the daughter of Matthew Webb, the first man to swim the English Channel. She had come to visit her brother who had settled in Cape Town. She was so happy there that she decided to stay and teach 'fancy dancing'. Later Webb returned to London to further her dance studies. She then came back to teach ballet in Cape Town, where she was joined from time to time by her former pupil Maude Lloyd who had advanced her standard by studying in London where she then performed in the Rambert company.

Lloyd raised the standard of ballet at the Cape, and dancers like Cecily Robinson and Frank Staff were to emerge. They left to join the greater dance world in London. Almost immediately, Robinson joined the Woizikowsky ballet from Rambert, and Staff was to choreograph for the Ballet Rambert. Other dance teachers were to emerge. The Cape Town Eisteddfod took place annually. Miss Harrison was the organiser and I recall her, always present day after day, wearing a long black tunic, like those of the Preobrajenskaya[2] era (Chapter 7). The day's schedule was clutched in her hand. She was calm and soft-spoken. She needed to be able to control matters when feelings ran high on the announcement of the awards. In another city during an Eisteddfod, there was near pandemonium when David Poole was judging a Spanish dance section where entrants were shouting out during their performance and where while reading out his results Poole said, 'Sa! Sa! Sa! and Si! Si! Si! means nothing to you, still less to me!'

Many years later, when Webb was adjudicating in Cape Town, she awarded the cup for the best choreography at the Eisteddfod to a very surprised me. I loathed competitions but had entered at that time on the spur of the moment to give my pupils from Stellenbosch a chance to perform on stage in the big city. Webb was most complimentary and had genuinely enjoyed my entry. The cup must still be around there somewhere, with my name engraved on it.

There were two intensely competing ballet 'sects'. The method of the Royal Academy of Dance (RAD) was taught by the teachers living on the western side of Table Mountain by the sea at Sea Point. On the eastern side Dulcie Howes founded the UCT Ballet School and its company at Rosebank, which I attended when old enough to do so, and there they taught the Cecchetti method. Fascinatingly, the climate was as diverse as the teaching. By the sea on the western side it was dry and hot, while by the university on the eastern side it was often rainy and damp. The British favoured the eastern side, while the Greek and Jewish communities were drawn to the sea and sun on the western side.

2 For the Russian names in this book I have adopted the spelling used by Horst Koegler in *The Concise Oxford Dictionary of Ballet,* 1977, which is still the definitive dictionary of ballet. The ending '-skaya' as in 'Preobrajenskaya' is also written '-ska'; it is pronounced '-skja'.

Cecily Robinson and Frank Staff as Columbine and Harlequin in the pas de deux produced by Maude Lloyd, 1932.

At the start there was a sharing of dancers in the performances of the UCT Ballet and the Ballet Club started by Cecily Robinson, based on the one in London founded by Marie Rambert. When Markova and Dolin came to Cape Town in 1949 to perform in the full-length *Giselle,* Dolin was impressed by 'one of the finest *corps de ballet* that Markova and I have ever danced with'. He also wrote: 'I would like to state that Cecily Robinson's rehearsals and production of *Le Lac des Cygnes* (*Swan Lake*) were as fine as anything I have seen'. This was the ballet standard that was to be my heritage.

My first teacher was Katherine (Kay) Zaymes. She was of Greek descent and came from the suburb of Sea Point, where the sea and sun reign. She was a lovely dancer and teacher and had been dancing in, and ballet mistress of, the Sadler's Wells Opera Company. She shared her Sea Point studio with her sisters Dorothea (Dolly) and Felicia (Filly), also from the Wells. They had all been trained by Cecily Robinson. Katherine had returned from London and I became a pupil when she came once a week to her Stellenbosch studio. So my good ballet foundation was secure.

At that time, individual RAD and Cecchetti teachers produced excellent dancers but we at the University Ballet School felt vastly superior because we had several teachers training us, not only in ballet but in other dance styles as well, and we also had a company. There was very little communication between the two sides, so we rarely came across each other.

I was sent to audition in Cape Town for a performance that was to be arranged by the ballet teachers. It was my first sally into the wider world. I was fourteen, 'green and cabbage looking', as the saying goes. Totally unworldly I was suddenly to get my first taste of what lay out there in the wider world. For the first time I experienced bullying from the Sea Point dancers. It occurred after I was chosen by Eve Borland, later ballet critic of the *Cape Times*, to dance in her ballet to von Weber's music *Invitation to the Waltz*. Arriving early from Stellenbosch I installed myself in the only dressing room for all the cast. Three girls chased me out saying, 'What do you think YOU are doing here?' In the passage the kind orchestra members found a chair and table for me and hung my costume over the double-bass case. On arrival Eve Borland asked, 'What on earth are you doing HERE?'

Kay Zaymes then handed over the Stellenbosch studio to Amelia Conn. She too had been a pupil of Cecily Robinson's, who taught both the Cecchetti and the RAD syllabus. After the Woizikowsky Company, Robinson had entered the De Basil Russian companies as Cécilé Zonova. All this gave her a beautiful, sweeping Russian style. When not on tour, rehearsing with the company in Paris, she studied with Olga Preobrajenskaya. Her career was short-lived. She tore the cruciate ligament while being lifted by her partner André Eglevsky, who she said was very, very lazy! She was carried into the hospital in full ballet costume and make-up to the amazement of the nursing staff. The ligament healed badly after an operation and she could not rise up

Marina, 12, in Hungarian costume.

on pointe. She returned to Cape Town saddened by this hard blow to a brilliant career, missing a tour to Australia. Her misfortune was Cape Town's fortune. She was to start the Ballet Club where the Cape Town dancers could take classes and dance in performances of the ballet classics in her repertoire.

Earlier, studying with Robinson at Rambert's, the South African Frank Staff was so talented that he became easily bored, appearing to be lazy and skipping classes with Rambert and Maude Lloyd. I wrote in my book *Ballet in South Africa* of the two young dancers lunching with Lloyd and of Staff telling wild imaginative tall stories about why he had missed classes, while Cecily kicked him under the table to admonish him. He was an amazingly talented choreographer, almost suffering choreographic diarrhoea. During the war the Russian composer Prokofiev visited London and saw a ballet by Frank. He was impressed, and he gave him the score of his *Peter and the Wolf*. It had been presented in Russia as a puppet show, as a play, and in other forms, but never as a ballet. It has been forgotten that its first performance was by Frank Staff for Ballet Rambert. Elsewhere it is often credited to other choreographers. Frank's version is so intelligently presented with subtle wit. Also unseen outside South Africa are his other brilliant choreographies showcasing his delightful humorous touches and his dramatic storytelling ability, as in *Transfigured Night* to music by Schoenberg. It was his last choreography before his death. He created for the company of the Performing Arts Council of the Orange Free State (PACOF) in Bloemfontein, where he was artistic director. He had a rare inborn gift, as had Antony Tudor. Many of Frank's ballets used to be, and probably still are, in the repertoire of the Cape Town Ballet. His most modern masterpiece was *Raka* based on the epic Afrikaans poem of the same name by NP van Wyk Louw. More about that later.

Years later in Stockholm, the Swedish impresario Professor Bengt Häger told me of how he had marvelled at the choreographic talent of Frank Staff. The young Häger was working in London as manager for the Metropolitan Ballet with Celia Franca as ballet master. In 1948 he met Frank Staff, who had choreographed *Fanciulla delle Rose* to music by Arensky. It was the first ballet choreographed for Beriosova in London, drawing attention to her talent.

Robinson brought with her to Cape Town the ballets in which

she had danced – *Les Sylphides*, the *Polovtsian Dances* and *Spectre de la Rose* from Fokine, plus *Swan Lake* and *The Sleeping Beauty.* She had fascinating stories to tell of her travels through Europe just before the Second World War broke out. On tour with the Ballets Russes in Spanish train compartments, they shared them with chickens and goats. In Germany she experienced the fear among the passengers as the police came through the coaches asking for passports.

Years later I watched other dancers being asked to restage *Les Sylphides* in Cape Town, while Robinson, the fount of the original staging there, was sitting ignored in the audience. How she must have suffered, and what a loss to the younger generations not to make more use of her in her old age. We gained from her training with Preobrajenskaya in Paris. She had the glorious extension of the style in the upper back, so typical of the Russian training. I thrived on that and on her intense interest in her pupils, and the excitement with which she imparted the steps. These were no ordinary classes. She taught us to – dance.

Joining in her classes in a church hall in Rondebosch were Patricia Miller and Dudley Davies. They had recently returned from their overseas careers, Patricia as ballerina with the Wells, dancing in all the Cranko ballets, partnered by David Poole. Cranko was another student from the UCT Ballet, as was the other choreographic talent Alfred Rodrigues. Both were to gravitate to Sadler's Wells in London. Dudley Davies's professional excellence terrified me when he partnered me in the *pas de deux* classes with Cecily. I was learning the two White and Black Swan *pas de deux* from *Swan Lake*, the *Bluebird pas de deux*, and those from *Giselle,* including the peasant *pas de deux*, *Les Sylphides* and *Spectre de la Rose.* These were all among other ballets which we were later to perform with the UCT Ballet Company.

In 1960 in Moscow, Mikael and I witnessed an unforgettable performance in the Bolshoi Theatre, with Struchkova and Fadeyechev. A very young Yekaterina Maximova danced brilliantly in the peasant *pas de deux*, bringing the house down when all the visiting foreigners applauded. Everyone turned to look at the Royal Box where we had been seated and had jumped to our feet applauding, recognising her talent. The surprised Russians were sticking to Struchkova; Maximova had not yet 'arrived'. The audience rushed up to the orchestra pit at the end to laud Strutchkova. In the late 1970s, Maximova and her husband

Vladimir Vasiliev came many times to dance in Rome, thrilling us in the open-air theatre at the Baths of Caracalla. She had a bad fall once, when blinded by a photographer's flashing light, although photography was forbidden. Vasiliev, her husband and partner, rushed across the enormous stage and in one sweeping gesture scooped her into his arms and ran straight off into the wings.

After experiencing Maximova's dancing, I wrote to Robinson saying that it had been like watching her dance and what a privilege it had been to experience her talent, which had also transported and inspired us in her own uplifting classes. She wrote thanking me, saying how depressed she had been until my letter arrived. She claimed that the younger generation no longer wanted her classes and that I had no idea what my letter had meant to her. Youth is often dismissive of history.

Because my teacher in Stellenbosch, Amelia Conn, was getting married, she suggested that I should take over her studio. It was on my doorstep; if someone else came to take it over, it could be lost to me forever. What a quandary. The watershed of my life came when I sat at the dinner table and said, 'I am going to buy the studio next door'. The price of the studio was the so-called 'goodwill payment' for taking over a going concern. One had no idea whether the pupils would stay on with the purchaser but that was the way it was done. My father put down his knife and fork in shock and said, 'Where are you getting the money for this purchase?' I replied forthrightly, but rather scared, 'From you of course'. He argued that at the age of 16, apart from being too young and lacking in experience and knowledge, I knew nothing about life and that it would be too hard for me. Better to first acquire a stable profession. But I was stubborn and my mother supported the idea, understanding that it might be 'now or never'. I was determined and wanted it my way. In a way I had no choice.

My father, of course, was right. The strain on me was terrible and I cried myself to sleep many a night. However, I would never admit it and gradually I matured into it, with my mother's sterling support; she took the strain of the running of the studio off my shoulders while I was still studying. She also stitched away at the hundreds of costumes for all the shows that I staged with my pupils. Tap dancing had been part of the curriculum but I gradually replaced this with Spanish dance.

Robinson was very humble and had sent me to join the University Ballet School to study further. There Howes reigned supreme and the Cecchetti method was taught, up there on the mountainside in a disused aeroplane hangar. Her ballet school had become part of the university's College of Music.

Professor Bell, the head of the college, had been impressed by Howes' achievements in her studio in the next-door suburb of Rondebosch. He approached her to move her school to the College of Music in Rosebank. They both admired each other and it was a great working relationship. As a tribute, he composed the music for one of her ballets. Bell was probably in love with Howes but she had a solid marriage to Guy Cronwright who was managing director of Cape Times Ltd, publisher of the morning English newspaper.

This next period of the UCT Ballet School is described in great detail in my book *The History of Ballet in South Africa*. This was a correspondingly great period in ballet in Britain. Ninette de Valois was creating her school and forming her Sadler's Wells company, and Marie Rambert was teaching in Notting Hill Gate and staging ballets in her own small theatre that had been a church. They inspired dancers abroad, not least in Cape Town. This juxtaposing of two creative forces was to be echoed in Cape Town with Howes mirroring de Valois, and Robinson creating the Ballet Club by following Rambert's example. These two rivalled each other and created endless opportunities for dancers and choreographers.

Cape Town became the cradle of ballet in South Africa. During the Second World War years Dulcie built an audience for British ballet. The troop ships inevitably stopped at the Cape, where the entertainments at hand were the ballet performances. The troops attended the performances while on shore leave, enlarging the audience attendance for the local ballet scene. They returned to Britain bitten by the ballet bug – or maybe taken with the pretty girls – and swelled London audiences.

Howes became principal of the UCT Ballet School and later director of the company that she founded there. She had not only danced in Pavlova's company and played cards with her husband but had also studied the Cecchetti method with Margaret Craske and various national folk dances from Derra de Moroda. Pamela Chrimes, who was trained at the UCT Ballet School at the same time as John Cranko and Alfred Rodrigues, had also attended classes with Robinson. Pamela had become a soloist at the Sadler's Wells Theatre Ballet company in 1945, becoming ballet mistress at the Sadler's Wells Opera Ballet in 1948, before returning to South Africa. Another Howes-trained student, Jasmine Honoré, who was also taught by Cecily Robinson and Yvonne Blake, had danced with the Rambert company in London and had studied Spanish dance with Elsa Brunelleschi in London. Her studies had included piano at the College of Music. Robinson also taught at the UCT after her Ballet Club folded, because the wise Howes was clever enough to invite her there. Later Chrimes was to study Russian folk dance with the Moiseyev company in Moscow, as well as ballet at the Bolshoi, and Kirov. So the school had a vast repertoire to impart to the students.

The UCT ballet classes were taught by several teachers at the school including Howes, whose classes contained slightly too long repeats in the exercises. From her I learned theatre skills, how to organise, plan lighting, rehearsing and, in fact, how to manage and produce performances and manage a company. She was also the major influence in my life in many other ways. Although she was careful with money, in other ways she was extremely generous. When we returned to visit South Africa with our family of three children, she moved and gave us her house in Bishopscourt to live in, with its wonderful garden and swimming pool. Her staff stayed on to look after us.

Pamela Chrimes was married to the very likeable journalist John Worrall who wrote the first book on *Ballet in South Africa,* from which I quoted earlier in connection with Dolin's visit to Cape Town. Sadly, because of her heavy workload, the marriage broke down. Pamela was astonishingly rude but well-meaning, loyal and always ready to help students in every way she could. I admired her very much. She also taught Russian, Hungarian and Polish dancing, which featured in the full-length classics. Jasmine Honoré, who taught history of ballet, theory, and Spanish dance, was very busy with her large family. She had converted to Catholicism and Susan Collins and Karen Langerman, who were both very religious, found a link with her. Karen used to call me 'Merrilegs'.

Gentle Mary Suckling was another of the ballet teachers who also had a large family. I remember one amusing story, when she and her husband Dr Peter Suckling were called to an emergency meeting at their youngest child's school. It was suggested that there was something deeply psychologically wrong with the child and they met together with the teachers and child. The teacher said, 'Tell us, why do you only draw with black crayon?' The little girl said, very simply, 'Because everyone else always takes all the colours before I can get there'. End of interview!

I had made my life unbelievably hard by trying to study while teaching. There seemed to be no other way. Conn had said to me, 'If you let this studio go to someone else, then when you are ready to teach the door will not be open for you to teach in Stellenbosch'. She was right. I had to grit my teeth and bear it.

At six in the morning I would rise at home in Stellenbosch, cycle to the station and take the train to Cape Town, changing to a branch line for a train to Rosebank. The hill up to the university ballet school on the slope of Table Mountain was a steep walk; there was no shuttle bus. Class started at 8:30am. We then did other classes such as Spanish or character dancing, and rehearsed the ballets we were to perform. I then went home and taught in Stellenbosch until catching the 6pm train back to Cape Town. We rehearsed again until I caught the train arriving back in Stellenbosch at 11pm. The conductors on the train all knew me and checked to see if I was awake when we reached Stellenbosch. I then cycled uphill home again. Sometimes, with a wind against me I could barely make it, with tears of exhaustion running down my cheeks. At 6am I had to start again. If there were performances, my brother would meet me halfway by car afterwards, at Bellville, and drive me home. The trains ran no later than 11pm, long before I could get to the station after a performance.

Soon the strain began to tell on me and Ursulene Rose-Innes suggested that I stay over with her after performances, at her parents' home. This was wonderful. She was often paired together as a dancer with Sheila Chisholm, both being tall. Sheila went on to become a ballet teacher and then dance citic for the *Cape Times.* Her father , the director of the College of Music, conducted the orchestra for some of our performances.

Later Karen Langerman suggested that I should stay over with her, and we had a lot of fun together. Karen's parents were very good to me. They lay awake until we crept in after a rehearsal or performance and wanted to hear everything that had happened. Her father always said, laughing, as we moaned about all the trials of the ballet scene, 'You two do take your pleasures sadly!' Mr Langerman, a lecturer in mathematics at UCT, thought the ballet students were the only ones who were able to do research properly, as our theoretical classes always went by the board when we had performances and yet the essays had to be handed in, so everyone did their own research to complete them.

It was only recently that I found out about another reason for my perpetual tiredness: I was 78 years old before a blood test showed that I had inherited 'thalassaemia trait' or 'Mediterranean anaemia', a genetic condition which reduces the blood's ability to absorb oxygen. I probably inherited it from my numerous Huguenot ancestors who came to the Cape from the south of France at the end of the 17th century. My friend since 1951 Susan Collins said of me at the UCT Ballet School, 'You were always tired but you were always laughing'. My brother and I inherited laughter from our father. They were always laughing, joking and teasing me.

Music appreciation at the UCT Ballet School was taught by a member of the College of Music staff. At one stage this was Arnold van Wyk, 'South Africa's first best composer on my side of the street' as he styled himself when answering the phone. Like me, he was born in the Calvinia district. He is well known in the world of music, features in music encyclopaedias, and his compositions are played internationally. He had a wicked sense of humour and regaled me with stories of the gaffes in the ballet students' essays. I regret that the only one I remember is: 'Tchaikovsky was a lesbian and it made him very sad'.

When I was teaching at the ballet school, Arnold gave me the use of his music *Primavera,* and I had an idea to use it for a ballet based on NP van Wyk Louw's above-mentioned epic poem *Raka*. I went to Dulcie Howes' office to discuss this project with her. Her office door was always open so that anyone could come to consult her – whatever it was, joys or problems. While I was explaining my idea for the ballet I saw that she was distracted and suddenly she said, 'Your ballet is not your ballet anymore. That was Frank Staff who was standing in the doorway, listening to every word you said'. I realised that Frank would do an excellent ballet but I was determined to choreograph my idea. However, I did not get around to it and we soon left for Rome, so it never came to fruition. Years later Frank did choreograph *Raka,* not to Arnold van Wyk's music but to Newcater's. It was very different from my idea, which would have been more folk-orientated. His version was rather remarkable and that epic poem by NP van Wyk Louw needed to be created for the theatre.

During the 1950s I choreographed many children's ballets for my Stellenbosch pupils: in 1952 *Peter and the Wolf* and *The Sorcerer's Apprentice*, using the actor Limpie Basson in the title role; and in 1953 a programme for a children's arts festival. In 1957 I was working with the talented Coloured EOAN Group in Cape Town. Several of their students were accepted into the UCT Ballet School. I remember them well. That year I also produced a lecture-demonstration at the Beattie Theatre together with Deanna Blacher. In the 1950s I was also involved in other shows at the Little Theater, the Baxter and the Beattie.

UCT Ballet School students in Peter and the Wolf (Prokofiev).

Choreographic Group

It was at the UCT Ballet School that I was to find true friends who shared my interests. Karen Langerman and Susan Collins have been my lifelong friends, Karen later living in the Cape Town suburb Fish Hoek and Susan in Spain. Richard Glasstone and I were to share an intense interest in choreography when he joined the ballet school from what was then Elisabethville in the Belgian Congo. We were, I suppose, a couple of rebels determined to 'do our own thing'. My friend and fellow student Susan Collins later said, 'You and Richard were always different from the rest of us'. I was not aware of that, but it was because of our intense interest in choreography.

We went to ask Howes if we could use the students for our trial choreographies. She was not pleased. Undaunted, Richard and I went to Professor Inskip who ran the Little Theatre of the university, a charming, small, intimate and well-run theatre where fascinating plays were presented. He was intrigued. His suggestion was that provided we did not ask for financial support from the university, we could go ahead. There were stipulations. We could have the theatre for free but the lighting and stage staff were to be paid, and we also had to pay for programmes. I think the stage staff were supportive and probably hardly charged us anything. So we were set to start our choreographic group. Fools rush in! We actually had the nerve to invite the critics of the two morning newspapers to give us private 'crits'. The gall of it. They too must have been bemused. Denis Hatfield, an Englishman who had settled in Cape Town, was the dance critic of the *Cape Times*. From the Afrikaans *Die Burger* newspaper came WEG Louw, their arts editor and theatre and dance critic. Nothing ventured, nothing gained. They not only came to the shows but gave us their serious opinions, all typed up and posted to us. Most impressive aid for two upstarts! We were so eager, we were unstoppable.

I quote from page 88 of my book *The History of Ballet in South Africa*:

> 'The Little Theatre was run by Cecil Pym, who built all the scenery himself. A dour ancient-looking little Cockney

The Little Theatre, Cape Town.

Denis Hatfield, Cape Times ballet critic. Caricature by John Dronsfield.

> with a forbidding manner and a cigarette always dangling from the corner of his mouth. Generations of students always marvelled at his ability to talk without ever having to remove it. His bark was worse than his bite and he was always helpful and kind. Today, two beautiful chairs stand in the foyer to commemorate his many years of selfless service. The temporary controller at this time was Leonard Schach, standing in for Inskip'.

The chairs represent Inskip's thoughtfulness. Theatres in South Africa were filled with selfless, talented backstagers. Emile Aucamp was another such treasure at the HB Thom Theatre in Stellenbosch, an artist at lighting. I always included this talent into my ballets.

Howes was not encouraging. She refused to lend me an ancient scratched wooden table and bench for our Little Theatre performances. Unfazed, I requested to borrow garden chairs and tables from a large furniture shop, promising an advert in our programmes. They even delivered and fetched them back. We were on our way in style.

Howes had to admit defeat, but Richard insists it was her way of making us do it ourselves. At a Sunday morning rehearsal after our first show she said triumphantly, 'Now you see what a success this venture was. Marina showed initiative and it was a learning curve. Had I lent the table set, this would not have been such a success'. The furniture was a charming, white-painted wrought-iron group, much nicer than the dilapidated table and bench. Howes used this ballet on a programme at a university arts festival. It was light and fun with pretty costumes made by my mother. It was to music by Offenbach. Richard made an apt suggestion for the title, *Comme Ci, Comme Ça* – in English, *Like This, Like That*. The costumes for his ballet to Ravel's *La Valse* were reconstituted from existing ones from the UCT costume cupboard by Mary Suckling and Jasmine Honoré. He says that Robinson told him afterwards she was amazed as he had hardly learned to *plié* and yet there he was choreographing a ballet.

Who knows what gave us the courage to tackle all that at our stage of development, in 1954, three years after starting our course. I had done a lot of shows with my pupils at Stellenbosch but to stand up to

Dulcie Howes in that way, when I was a real 'scaredy-cat', just amazes me. It shows how determined we were.

At first only the two of us were 'gung-ho' but gradually from the students emerged Peter Cazalet, who was later to design magnificent sets and costumes professionally. From the dancers who were performing in our ballets came Len Martin, Yvonne Lakier, Susan Collins, Deirdre Betts and Robyn Potter; and there emerged the choreographic talent of Rose Kinsey and Chris van Niekerk. Chris arranged a charming, humorous 1920s item titled *L'Enfant Terrible* in which I was a 'flapper'. It was a delight to perform it to Wolf-Ferrari's music. Louise Lombard was The Child, and The Dandy was Ken Martynne. Both this ballet and my *Comme Ci, Comme Ça* were chosen to be performed at the university's arts festival at the Little Theatre on 4 September 1958.

The main item on the programme was the director of the College of Music conducting the only opera of the Hungarian composer Béla Bartók, *Duke Bluebeard's Castle* – with disastrous results. It was a small theatre and the dressing room was attached to the stage. We were told on pain of death that the lavatory was not to be flushed during the performance. The stage set was one room, with doors leading off it. The Duke, sung by Gregorio Fiasconaro, proceeded to victimise his poor wife, Desirée Talbot, with horror after horror revealed as each door was opened. It came to the final denouement. He sang, 'And behind this door', long pause, 'And behind this door' – another long pause and as the door was flung open, a clunk and rush of water was heard as some culprit flushed the loo. We dancers just fled out of the stage door. I have no idea what happened either on stage or in the auditorium. However, the opening night review said, 'Great opera and refreshing ballets'.

Before Richard departed to study in London in 1956 we were given the amazing 'bounty' of ballets when the Sadler's Wells Theatre Ballet visited Cape Town with an incredible repertoire including choreography by former UCT Ballet-trained dancers such as John Cranko and Alfred Rodrigues, and dancers such as David Poole performing in them. Nowhere else could one get ballet history at such a glance, at such a level or with such a range of styles from Frederick Ashton, Ninette de Valois and Walter Gore, to Andrée

Howard. We were treated to a perfection of sensitive artistry in performance by dancers who could not only dance but who could also act. That was a real learning experience and we revelled in such an unexpectedly rich gift. What a choreographic overview for ballet lovers and students.

3

Student Life in Stellenbosch and Cape Town in the 1950s

My youth was divided between Cape Town where I studied ballet and Spanish dance at the University of Cape Town (UCT) Ballet School and performed in their company, and Stellenbosch where my university friends and I had a wonderful social life. I worked hard but I also played hard.

My friend Karen Langerman used to say, 'I am Marina's only girlfriend. The others are all men!' The 'boys', as I shall call them, were Enrique Breytenbach, Paul Roux and Hennie Aucamp. They often passed my house in Dorp Street, where we all lived, in the dead of night. Seeing the light on in my room, they would knock on my window and ask me to go for a walk or for an 'illegal' swim, climbing over the wall of the university pool. The walk up the oak-lined avenue *Die Laan*, running alongside the river, was always magical. The world belonged to us, as there was never another soul to be seen. In winter the stark leafless boughs of the oaks made dramatic patterns against the moonlit sky. In the spring their leafy boughs let thin streams of dappled moonlight slip through on us as we walked along the riverbank. Nasturtiums covered the banks, and after day trips to the river we went home with bouquets of their red, orange and yellow flowers.

I felt very blessed, and life was sweet. The 1950s were such an innocent era, filled with music from excellent musicals featuring Fred

Astaire, whose dancing we assiduously copied, amongst many others. The world was tired of war, and from America came those clever musicals and other films of entertainment, with which the present American violence that streams out at us cannot compare. The world was ready to laugh and play and we were the beneficiaries.

I was usually accompanied to the local dances by Enrique, who would sit down every now and again next to Limpie Basson, another friend of ours, who earned money playing the piano for the dancing. At the piano they would play together with great results. Then Enrique would give Limpie a rest and take over the playing while Limpie danced with me. I was often so tired that I could hardly walk home afterwards. Enrique and I always won the competitions and we would place the prizes of chocolates or champagne on the table and invariably find that the others had polished them off in our absence, while we were on the dance floor. We never learned our lesson. We could not bear to stop dancing and they knew it and would wave a chocolate or glass of champagne at us as we danced by.

My friends all flourished. Enrique later taught music at the teachers' training college, Limpie became a well-loved actor, Paul Roux became a journalist at the Afrikaans paper *Die Burger*, and Hennie Aucamp became a well-known writer of short stories, plays and musicals. Mikael, a student from Sweden whom I met in 1955, translated one of Hennie's short stories into Swedish and it was eagerly snapped up by one of the most prestigious newspapers in Sweden. When Mikael's letter proposing marriage to me arrived one morning, I saw Hennie pass by going to class on his bicycle. I rushed out and shouted to him, 'I'm going to marry Mikael!' He fell off his bike in surprise.

In the 1960s, when Mikael taught at the University of Stellenbosch, we invited Hennie, Paul and the well-known author Uys Krige to lunch in Clifton, by the sea where Uys then lived. I had got to know him when I did the choreography for one of his plays. We asked him his age, and he stood up, stretched out his arms and replied dramatically, 'I span the centuries'. Well, almost, for he was actually born in 1910. Uys had a strong personality and he was very extrovert, very lovable. He said that I reminded him of a poplar tree as I was never still but always in motion like its leaves.

Later when we lived abroad, Hennie's books, beautifully inscribed, would be sent to us, and his stories, often with a twist at the end, were eagerly imbibed. They are so special, bringing to life the people where he lived among the farms of the Eastern Cape. He was one of the great storytellers of the world. I am pleased to see that he is mentioned in my copy of the *Encyclopædia Britannica,* in the article on 'South African literature'. Even when we lived abroad we were in close contact by phone or correspondence.

When our student days were over, we all continued to be in touch with each other, and when we met we picked up as though we had never been apart, Mikael fitting in beautifully. He had met Hennie even before he met me because they both used to go walking in the mountains with other members of the student mountain club. Years later when we visited South Africa in 1996 and gathered together at Enrique's home in Gordon's Bay, they called me aside and whispered, 'Limpie has a surprise for you'. They led me into the room with the piano, and Limpie sat down to play 'I Only Have Eyes for You', which had been my favourite tune to dance to. They had remembered. I loved the way Limpie crossed his hand over to play a syncopated section of the rhythm.

With friends at Gordon's Bay in 1996. From left: Limpie Basson, Mikael Grut, Paul Roux, Enrique Breytenbach, Marina Breytenbach, Hennie Aucamp and Marina Grut.

Limpie plays “I only have eyes for you” for Marina.

Back to my student days in the 1950s in Stellenbosch. One weekend my friend Karen came to stay with me. My room was at the front of the house and visible from the street. We were lying in our beds chatting till 2am. Suddenly there was a knock on the window. It was Paul. He said, ‘I thought you’d still be awake. I’ve found a Spaniard for you’. It was certainly surprising in Stellenbosch, especially at two o’clock in the morning. We let them in and Paul asked us to do a Spanish dance for the bemused visitor. We dived behind the open wardrobe door, donned my Spanish dresses and danced *Sevillanas* for him, music, castanets and all. He was stunned and Paul said happily, ‘He wouldn’t believe me'. Later Hennie wrote that one night when I was dancing a Spanish dance for them, at their request, he asked me why dancers frown when they do Spanish dancing. I said, 'That is not frowning, that's passion'. Hennie said that a blush flooded his cheeks and he felt that he was in the heart of decadence! But each one of us was as innocent as the other.

Sundays were spent in bed recovering. In the evening we would all troop to St Mary's, the Anglican church on The Braak, an open grassy area in the centre of the town, to hear the Reverend King preach marvellously 'tooled' sermons. He delivered them in a very theatrical way with special lighting. My friends were all from the Dutch Reformed Church. They claimed that when they were schoolboys they wickedly drank all the communion wine that they could get hold of, for the fun of it. A long plank with holes in it had glasses placed in the holes to steady them for the communion wine, served individually to each person. This plank was passed along the pew. They filled extra glasses for their row, which they then consumed. A long stick was passed along the pew with a pouch for the weekly contributions, which they dared someone each Sunday to take a penny or two out of, instead of putting in money. All really innocent fun but considered very daring at the time. Reverend King was so popular among the youth of the town that the church had to be enlarged twice to fit the swelling congregation. Afterwards we all trooped to his home, where his kind long-suffering wife served tea and biscuits to us hordes and we held 'intellectual' discussions with him. Then home to my equally long-suffering mother for a cold supper. She adored them, and they her.

Now Mikael and I are the last survivors of all the people in that photograph. Sadly, Marina, Enrique's wife, was the first of us to die – of cancer. Limpie was next, collapsing in the main street of Stellenbosch. Then Enrique from the anaesthetic when he was in hospital for a back operation. Paul and Hennie died in their own beds in their flats.

Years later on a return visit to Cape Town I was walking down the main street holding a bottle of wine. It was a gift from balletomane Sonny Cohen who had taken me to lunch. I did not know what to do with it as I was on my way to a radio interview at the South African Broadcasting Corporation. Suddenly I saw, coming towards me, the Reverend King who had now been promoted to Very Reverend and Dean of the Cape Town Cathedral. He said, 'Marina, how good to see you', and I said, 'Hello, could you perhaps use a bottle of wine?' He laughed and said, 'Only you, Marina'. This was a repeat of what he had said when, at the insistence of Susan and Karen, I was to be confirmed by him at Stellenbosch… but then it had to be with the very young children because I had a ballet performance when the seniors were scheduled!

I once went to discuss with him that I could not believe in God. He said, brushing it aside, 'Don't worry. Many people feel the same', and went on to discuss something else. My father, a very enlightened man, was an atheist, but he believed that I should find out about religion myself before I made up my mind. He also believed that there were important occasions in life which should be celebrated in special ways, especially birth, marriage and death. So he was a member of the Anglican church, which he thought was the most benign of religions and which carried out those ceremonies with dignity. He regularly supported them with donations. I became a mostly non-practising member of the church at the age of twelve. That seems to be a very thoughtful period in a child's life. I was lucky. As we see today, the indoctrination of the young can lead to terrible strife.

Our friend Hennie passed away in March 2014, the last of our merry group. The others had all died within weeks of each other by the end of 2012. By then even my Spanish dance friends were all gone. The 'greats, like Luisillo, José de Udaeta, Alberto Lorca, all my close friends, and others such as Antonio Gades, Pilar López, Mariemma, Juanjo Linares, Angel Pericet, as well as Joan (Juan) Fosas of my 'Spanish family'. His sister Rosa and her husband and children had 'adopted' me in Rubí, near Barcelona. I felt bereft and that I had lived too long. A whole wonderful era was gone and I was endlessly writing their obituaries for the *Dancing Times*. Mary Clarke was then the editor, a post now perfectly filled by her successor Jonathan Gray. I said to her, 'I think that I am the obituary queen'. She said, 'Oh no, I am'. It was happening to her too, and she was afraid to read her mail or answer her phone each morning. On her retirement at the age of 90, she said to me, 'Now you can be queen'. Neither of us enjoyed writing the obituaries. Then my closest cousin also died, and so did Mary, in 2015. Not only had I lost a dear friend but the UK dance world had lost its 'institutional memory' because she had an encyclopaedic and detailed knowledge of the recent history of British dance. Who could I share and discuss mutual experiences with now?

The worst blow came before all this, when my close friend Karen Langerman was brutally murdered in Fish Hoek in 2007 by three men. She owned nothing of value. They rolled her in a carpet and stabbed her repeatedly, leaving her bleeding to death. She had recently lost her invalid husband whom she had selflessly nursed for seventeen years, and she had experienced a 'life' again for only one year when she was struck down. She was found some days later by a family member who had a lunch appointment with her. The police apparently know who the murderers are but there has been no prosecution, although they left fingerprints and were known to the police. I had phoned her two days before her murder to beg her to move from her house to a flat. Her dog, which might have alerted her, had died, and the arrival of a new one was delayed. She had laughed at my concern and said that she had a high wall surrounding her home. I had said that it was no deterrent.

Back to my family in Stellenbosch. My mother was most hospitable and my friends loved coming to our house. Years later, when I had married Mikael and was living in Stockholm, they visited her regularly, Paul shouting down the passage to the maid, 'Tos, bring the tea', teasing my mother with her usual words on seeing them enter the house. In those days doors were never locked. There were always plates of food and drink waiting for us when we returned from the cinema or dancing. When my mother died, Mikael said quietly to me, 'In her way, your mother was a saint'. She had enough love and goodness to give to everyone. My friend Susan remembers her well.

4

The University of Cape Town (UCT) Ballet School's Company

During the mornings after class at the ballet school in Rosebank, the students rehearsed the ballet repertoire for performances with the UCT company at the City Hall or in the open-air Maynardville Park, or for one of its tours in South Africa, the Rhodesias or Mozambique. Coming out of that training, the students were well-equipped to not only run a school but also to prepare a rehearsal, place dancers rehearsing on stage, conduct a dress rehearsal with an orchestra and present a performance professionally. Everyone helped with setting the stage, lighting and costumes, etc., and all were able to join companies as professional performers, which so many of them did in Europe and the USA.

To have danced all my student career and afterwards to an orchestra was due to Howes' amazing organisational powers. The thrill of each orchestral rehearsal is embedded in my psyche and is with me still, seeming to enter my body and transport me when I hear the rich sounds of a symphony orchestra. Dancers who have not had that experience are much the poorer for it. That we, mere students, were able to dance the classics in large theatres, accompanied by orchestras conducted by superb conductors, is an unforgettable luxury. Professional dancers consider it normal but we revelled in the experience of each ballet season.

The rewards were great. Professional dancers such as David Poole, Patricia Miller, Dudley Davies and Frank Staff (as choreographer only) came from overseas to produce new ballets and to dance the leading roles, serving to give us a professional standard to aspire to. Nadia Nerina and Alexis Rassine came to dance *Giselle* with us. It was a wonderful experience and for Nerina it was a good dress rehearsal for the role which she was to dance in London. She was experiencing agonising back pain and was suffering greatly in the wings between entrances, doubled up in pain. I often held her in my arms trying to comfort her and relieve her pain.

Howes worked the students very hard. She wanted perfection. One night the Cape Town Municipal Orchestra, which accompanied the performances, were packing up and we had to continue rehearsing to a wire recorder. It shocked them. They suggested that the students form a union to get better working conditions and even receive some form of payment. One student said, 'If it means that we will dance the way you play, we would rather not, thank you'. Not a very gracious response. One night Howes' husband Guy Cronwright was seen shaking his head at all the heavy-breathing, sweaty dancers still rehearsing on stage at midnight. He quickly made his exit.

There were performances among the trees at the old open-air municipal garden of Maynardville in the suburb of Wynberg. Weeping willows framed our stage, a magical setting for ballets such as *Les Sylphides, Swan Lake* and *Giselle*, sylphs appearing and disappearing beneath the softly sighing stems. If it started to rain, the dancers continued dancing, the audience pulled raincoats over their heads and the orchestra members sneaked away one by one, protecting their smaller musical instruments under their jackets. What the cellists did, I cannot remember. The plucky pianist Leonard Hall remained to see it through to the end, with the piano protected from the downpour. Leonard was a real 'trooper'. He had a great sense of humour and tremendous enthusiasm. He was tubby and we thought that he was a 'couch potato'. Imagine our surprise when one day during a rehearsal, as though to dispel that idea, he suddenly leapt to his feet and did a complete somersault on the spot before our astounded eyes and returned to his playing as though nothing had happened.

Across from the ballet school in Rondebosch was the university swimming pool and also a group of temporary huts which had originally been constructed for returning soldiers resuming their studies. It was known, perhaps thoughtlessly, as Belsen. The girls were always 'going for a swim', when the real attractions were the boys from across the way. The attraction was mutual. Howes, innocent of all this, remonstrated with the dancers for this excessive swimming because they would tan and turn purple under the blue stage lights in ballets with sylphs or wilis. She did, however, approve of swimming as the only sport that did not distort their muscles. Howes was always on the search for male dancers to be partners and was not averse to sending someone over to the pool to ask the male students if they would like to come over and 'hold a girl' while we were doing double work in the *pas de deux* class. Not many fell for that one.

The University of Cape Town Ballet School.

Later, military service became compulsory and the male dancers were called up. But Howes was shrewd. She knew that if dancers did not have regular classes, their muscles would change, so she arranged for the dancers to be stationed in Cape Town and released to come to classes in Rondebosch at the UCT Ballet School. There was much teasing of the 'ballet boys' by the other soldiers. However, this came to an abrupt end when the drilling started and the ballet boys outstripped the other soldiers in strength and stamina, leaving their mates huffing and puffing. Then they were left in peace. It is not easy to lift a girl high.

When we were on tour, as can be imagined, the girls attracted much attention. There was a constant stream of admirers who followed by car alongside our train. We were gathered together and easy to find in the two coaches specially designated for us. There was one particularly attractive girl, Joan Bellairs, nicknamed 'Botty Bellairs' because of her beautiful bottom! At every stop she seemed to be met by another boy, enthusiastically welcoming each one with hugs and kisses. Howes felt very responsible for the safety of the girls, and hangers-on were frowned upon. When our manager, Betty Roscoe, remonstrated with Joan, her story was always, 'But that was my brother' – or cousin – or nephew – until Betty said in despair, 'You seem to have a very large family'. We did have a lot of fun, and even Howes was entertaining on the journeys with, what seemed to us, very risqué songs. I remember 'The foggy, foggy dew', 'He told her he loved her but oh how he lied' and 'The hills of West Virginia', which seemed particularly, deliciously wicked. We joined in with great gusto. It made the long train journeys seem less arduous. When Irma Dyer joined us, fresh from dancing in the musical *Oklahoma* in London, she taught us all the songs from it. She had one other, which must have referred to drugs, way beyond our understanding at that time, 'Butterflies wearing hob-nailed boots, dancing across my bed, and ten little men with feathers, hitting me on my head'.

Performance Glitches

Pamela Chrimes was always the principal dancer in our productions. I was placed one day in *Swan Lake* to lead the exit of the swans off the stage. It was not only not my usual place but totally different choreographically. In our version, some of the girls were lifted on to the men's shoulders and I was one of those. A girl called Anne Phillips suddenly had to be replaced. She departed without much warning. She was a kneeling swan, right in the front, and she led everyone off at the end. Howes looked at us and said, 'Who is musical? Ah, Marina', and put me down in the front. I did not realise the implication of that. We had the old wire recorders and they had a limited capacity, so we never actually rehearsed to music for the final exit because it ended before the exit music. Musical or not I really had no clue as to when to lead the girls off. I had been up on a man's shoulder before, and now I was on the floor, supposedly to start the exit of all the swans.

There I was in the front on my knee, with my toe pointed in front, not knowing when to go, and the whole cast behind me. I whispered over my shoulder *sotto voce* to the girl behind me, 'When do we go?' and she replied, what sounded like 'Gh, gh, uhn guh', which I took to mean we should already have left. I leapt to my feet and started the tragic *bourrées* off, waving my arms up and down. All sorts of gasps were heard from all over the stage. I looked over my shoulder and there were the girls still lifted on the men's shoulders, their eyes goggling down at my solitary passage across the stage. By now I had reached centre stage in my solitary flight and was blocking out Pamela Chrimes and her partner Ivan Baptie. She hissed, 'Get out of my way', and I hurried on, now a very worried swan. I had to go all the way upstage between the row of kneeling and lifted swans, my arm movements becoming more and more tragic as I went and the boys who were lifting the girls making all sorts of teasing remarks at me. I had reached centre stage back and was hovering until the others could catch up with me. In front in the wings stood Howes – waiting for me. I did not want to exit. Enough said. The aftermath was pure murder.

Another time when Dulcie glared at me from the wings was when we were in the open at Maynardville. It had rained the night before and the orchestra members had crept off while we had got soaked to the skin. The ladies who helped us the next day ironed the costumes to get them dry – and they had stretched. We were dancing *Les Sylphides*. I was standing with another girl, I think Deirdre Betts, in the classic position with one arm around each other, and the other arm in front. I noticed from the wings much sniggering from the stagehands. Unbeknown to me, my costume had stretched a lot with the ironing and I was standing there, full frontal nude as the dress's neckline had slipped down to my waist. I had been told never to move once in a position so I stood dead still. Howes came to the wings and said severely, 'MARINA, PULL UP YOUR DRESS'. It was easier said than done. But Deirdre and I squiggled it up to guffaws from the stagehands.

David Tidboald was our regular conductor. We had many other wonderful conductors, such as Christopher Fifield. The joke about one of them, a non-English-speaker, was that he had run up to a secretary with an urgent letter that needed to be posted, and said, 'Thees letter hhas a hhorry. Send it by fly'. One conductor never waited for the swans to gather across the back of the stage in a straight line before starting the coda. The audience certainly saw 'the flight of the swans', as they flew across from all angles, having to start dancing in mid-flight, before reaching their places across the back. He never learned.

One night, on tour, all manner of things went wrong. A three-legged dog ran onto the stage during *Les Sylphides*, in the *Nutcracker Suite.* Baart Saayman's headdress ended up round his neck; and in the finale, as the girls were lifted onto the men's shoulders, the partner of one girl who was very light, misjudged his strength and she was thrown right over his shoulder, crashing into the lights at the foot of the backcloth. A truly grand finale.

Howes was a clever businesswoman. To save money when we toured, she arranged for us to be billeted by the ballet clubs in the cities, where delighted 'ballet mothers' took care of us. On the tours Karen Langerman and I chose to be billeted together. At one town our hostess had '*bobotie*' put into sandwiches waiting for our supper each night. *Bobotie* is a light Cape Malay dish made of curried minced meat, not ideal for sandwiches as the fat congeals when cold. After a week of those we paled at the sight of them as we raised the silver lid of the salver that hid them. Years later Karen phoned me and said, 'I had a nightmare last night; guess what it was about – twenty-four bobotie sandwiches'.

Coppélia danced by the UCT Ballet School students in 1947, led by Joy Shearer, with John Dronsfield's décor, cleverly designed for touring.

In Durban Karen and I were once billeted with an artist and she did a painting of us in our *Mirliton* costumes from *Nutcracker*. It was large, at least 1.5 metres tall. After much deliberation we decided that we would ask to buy it. She had already sold it and we were so disappointed. So, somewhere is this painting of us, preserving a sweet moment of our lives. I just hope that it is not languishing in someone's attic or worse.

In Port Elizabeth the dancers went down with serious illnesses. The situation reached a crisis, where the next girl down meant cancelling the show. The lady with the sandwiches was a rather formidable medical doctor. When I accidentally broke my toe she said, 'You cannot dance'. I said I had to or the show would be cancelled. She said determinedly, '*I* will tell Miss Howes'. She was holding me by the arm as we came down the aisle at the rehearsal. Her courage drained away when the moment arrived. She stood facing the even more formidable Howes, whose motto was, 'Only death is an excuse'. So I danced, in a shoe two sizes larger, stuffed with glass wool, tears streaming down my cheeks. I said, 'I can do this, as long as nobody minds if I cry from the pain'. Nobody minded, least of all Howes. I really do not know how I got through that performance. My moment of glory was stolen by Yvonne

Lakier who fainted on stage. A doctor rushed up out of the audience and the next morning's newspaper reported: '… and the doctor took her home to bed'.

We learned our stagecraft the hard way, doing the setting up of black cloths, called 'wings', all round the stage, hanging the lights, ironing, etc. I remember once being handed a spade and a bag and being told, 'Fill it'. We were in the dry Karoo and the ground was like cement. This was one of the bags used to stabilise the light stands, the weight of the sandbag resting on the metal supports of the lights. I stood for hours hacking away at this hard soil and getting nowhere. A passer-by took pity on me and went to a building site to fill it. Howes looked surprised when I handed it to her. I also remember a girl called Robin Potter marching across the stage with one of the light stands singing 'Onward Christian Soldiers', while a shocked visiting parson watched.

Touring with the UCT company brought ballet to small towns where ballet had never been seen. Richard reported that the maid in the home where he was billeted went home to her employer after an evening at the ballet and said, 'Madam, those poor girls. They have no feet. Their legs end in points'. It was a labour of love for all. Nobody was paid a salary, except musicians, stage staff and the secretary-cum-manager. The first such manager in my time was Molly Goldthorpe, a former ballet teacher in India married to Colonel Goldthorpe (ex-Indian army). Betty Roscoe later followed as manager. Molly was given the nickname 'Golly', and when Karen left for Germany she suggested I stay over with her during performances in Cape Town. So kind and thoughtful of her.

Pip Marshall went along to set up and do the lighting. The students performed as part of their stage experience, and the girls all fell in love with Pip. One morning a student came running up to us saying, 'I had a nightmare. I was having Pip's baby'. It had been obvious for a long time that she was falling in love with the oblivious Pip. She kept her distance after that, but in any case it had been wishful thinking on her part because Pip was happily married with two children. Later, after his wife passed away, he and Pamela Chrimes were married.

It is interesting to compare the various productions of the classics. The first time I saw the all-male Trockadero company sending up *Swan Lake* and *Giselle*, I could appreciate it because they were using the same versions that we had danced. I remember that I always wanted to do a 'real' *Giselle*, with wilis looking as though they were all bedraggled from their tombs.

We always travelled by train. Sometimes our two coaches were unhitched and we were put into a siding until another engine came to fetch us. These waits were very tedious so Richard and I once entertained everyone on the platform by 'sending up' the company, the teachers and the ballets in Trockadero fashion, although that company did not yet exist in those days.

One hot summer when we waited in sweltering heat Richard Glasstone and I decided to take a chance and go to the hotel in the nearest little town and pay for each of us to have a bath. We sneaked out and walked across the veld to the town. It was a great risk as we had no idea how long we were to wait to be picked up, and we risked being left behind. The hotel manager was very kind and gave us towels and two bathrooms. We had hardly got dressed when we heard a train hooting its arrival. Panic-stricken, we ran all the way back to the train in the heat. Nobody knew what we had done and the company could have left without us. But it was not our engine. It rushed past without stopping and we were sweatier than before, waiting once more in that heat.

Throughout all this I was teaching and having shows with my pupils. Howes used to say, 'I don't know how you fill those performances but you have people hanging from the chandeliers'. I did a lot of charity work and raised thousands each year for the tuberculosis clinics. People who did such work usually took a cut of the profits for themselves, but I never did. Long-suffering Howes, Chrimes, Robinson and her husband Philly always came to see these performances. What dedication and love on their part. They were such loyal friends.

5

London and Spain, 1955: Rambert, Brunelleschi, Clarke, Llorens

Five years after joining the University Ballet and dancing with them and touring all over Southern Africa, I decided that I needed to study further. I was mainly interested in choreography. I had done many productions, including ballets, at my ballet school, and the choreographies at University Ballet.

Robinson suggested that I go to Ballet Rambert, where they had a choreographic group doing experimental work. I liked this idea, and armed with all sorts of letters of introduction I embarked on my first sea voyage from Cape Town to Southampton in 1955. Jasmine had suggested that I had a feel for Spanish dance and should study further with Elsa Brunelleschi. I could not understand her about this but she was proved right in the end.

After the ship had left Cape Town, I thought I was dying from seasickness because of the 'cape rollers', the big waves characteristic of the South Atlantic. The stewardess asked what she should do with all the flowers which I had been given. I was so sick that I could not have cared less, and I said, 'Throw them in the sea'. When we had passed the cape rollers and I felt better, I wanted them again, but they were nowhere to be found.

I turned twenty-one when we reached the Canary Islands. The celebrations never ended. They started early as people said, 'You never know with the weather'. So I actually had many parties each night. We went ashore at Las Palmas and we were all in a very festive mood. I was persuaded to dance in a tavern. I also leaned out of our taxi window and played castanets to a surprised policeman standing on a pedestal, and the people I had befriended on the boat bought me a beautiful Spanish doll wearing a dress with a train.

In London I was met at the train from Southampton by Len Martin, Ken Martynne, Brian Bayles and Ivan Baptie, the now London-based 'ballet boys' whom I knew from Cape Town. They helped with my baggage, but when I gave a tip to the porter he threw it angrily on the ground. I had not the vaguest idea of how much to give – I still over – or under-tip. The ballet boys shouted that they had done the work anyway and they picked up the coins. It was good to be met by people I knew. I was staying in Notting Hill Gate where Karen Langerman's cousins and her brother Rupert were staying. Again it is good to know people when you are a stranger in a big city.

I sallied forth to Ballet Rambert. At that time David Poole had left the Wells and was also taking classes with Marie Rambert. He said to me, 'She is desperately trying to turn me into a danseur noble'. I had come with the express purpose of joining her choreographic group, to do experimental work. She sat me down, held my hand and said, 'My dear, I am so sorry, I do not know what to say except that I am sorry, but the group has folded'. So I went for classes there instead. When I arrived she used to say, 'Ah, here comes the well-dressed South African'. I was. I wore Paris creations in those days.

With the Rambert group closed, I went to Elsa Brunelleschi for Spanish dancing classes as well as taking Rambert's ballet classes. I quaked that either would discover what I was doing, as they did not like each other. I loved Rambert's classes. She would choose a piece of music from the piles on the piano and then improvise the exercises to that. To me, music is always of the utmost importance, so I did enjoy it. Many years later I met her daughter at a Maude Lloyd memorial event at the Sadler's Wells in London.

Elsa Brunelleschi desperately tried to persuade me to do her ballet classes as well as Spanish dancing. She banged her chest with her palm

Elsa Brunelleschi.

and said, 'I am of royal blood. I am the pupil of Cecchetti. Not the pupil of the pupil of the pupil of Cecchetti. No, I am of royal blood, I am the PUPIL of Cecchetti'. She took me out to have a tomato juice at a pub. While I went to get the drinks, she arranged with people at the next table to hide my dance case. When we left I looked around and could not find it. She let me suffer for a while and then took it from the people at the next table, where she had hidden it saying, 'Lesson No.1: Trust no one, not even me'.

She suggested that I should live with her and her family in 1 Powis Square, Notting Hill, which I am told still exists today. She said that I could have the use of her library and her music. I went there, and in a way it was good, in another it was austere. I suffered very much from the cold. Those were the days of smog, when it hurt to breathe. One night I could only find my way home by feeling along the walls and knowing that the church on the corner, where I had to turn off, was made of stone. The bathroom had a window pane missing, so it was agony to bath. When the pipes froze and burst it was even worse and one had to lug kettles of boiling water up the stairs. The smog used to creep through the cracks of my bedroom window and I watched as it slithered in. My clothes were black until I could wash them again in Stellenbosch's pure water. I remember talking to the South African dancer Johaar Mosaval who had spent years as a principal dancer at the Royal Ballet, and asking him whether he would choose dancing as a career if he started again. He replied, 'No. When I think of being on tour and after performances breaking the ice on the water in a basin in my room to wash – no'.

Those were still hard days in Britain which had only recently emerged from a gruelling six-year war against fascism, and for much of that time she and the Commonwealth had stood alone in the struggle. Today Britain is a very different place, and in London a change of the fuels used for cooking and heating from coal to oil and gas has got rid of the smog, a great victory in the campaign against air pollution.

But life in London in those days also had many compensations. Elsa used to have viewing parties whenever there was dance on the telly. She invited interesting people to join us and it was there that I met Mary Clarke, soon to become the editor of the *Dancing Times* magazine, and Cyril Beaumont who owned the famous ballet bookshop on Charing Cross Road. When I went to visit him in his minute bookshop with the iron staircase, he was always very kind to me and had much of interest to tell about the books that I bought. Elsa's sister Leila used to do the cooking and we would all sit and watch the TV and munch Spanish paella. Afterwards there were interesting discussions. It is amazing that I was to attend the 100th birthday celebration of the *Dancing Times* when we retired to London. Mary Clarke, who has since died aged ninety-one, had then retired as its editor. At that time we frequently spoke to each other on the phone.

In 1955 at Elsa's, I used to write to my parents almost every day. One day she stood in my doorway and said, 'You write a lot. Do you know that writing is the occupation of the lonely?' She made me go to shows and report back to her on what I had seen. I got into the habit of sketching the costumes of shows because she drove me crazy asking for details. What she was teaching me was to look intelligently at these performances. After the first Spanish dance show she said, 'What steps have you learned?' Of course I had learned nothing. 'Go back,' she would encourage me. The next time I had learned some. 'Where are you looking?' she said, 'Those are male steps, Marina. I must say', she added, 'I can't blame you, they have such cute little bottoms'. She also took me backstage and I met Pilar López and the members of her cast, Dorita Ruiz and Elvira Real, and the very young El Farruco who has recently died. Elvira came to teach us a flamenco dance called *Alegrías*. This was a clever strategy of Elsa's. She got new material into her studio without having to travel or pay someone to come from Spain. We benefited because we had someone teaching us new dances.

We went to the Russian Moiseyev company. 'The Russians have spies everywhere', she said. Every time they did a stamp, she would clutch my arm and say in a stage whisper, 'You see, you see, that was a Spanish step. They have spies everywhere'.

One day there was a very bad smog and we were in the middle of a class, when she looked out at the dark green light outside and said, 'Hm. The end of the world'. She disappeared into her office. I took over the class and we continued. She did not return. I opened the door and there she was lying on her back on the floor, with a pillow under her head. She looked up. 'Tell them I can't sleep if they stamp', she said. 'But it's their class', I said, 'they've paid for it'. 'Well', she said, 'tell them it's bad for their kidneys – then they'll stop'. She was incorrigible.

She sent me off to Spain to study in Barcelona with Emma Maleras, in Madrid with La Quica and in Seville with Realito. I collected photos for her, for her book on Antonio Gades, whom she hero-worshipped. She also had close contact with Luisillo. On my return to London, she trained me day after day on the dances I had brought back with me. She took me to have photos taken with Duncan Melvin, which was torture. It took hours and he kept falling over the flex of the lamps as he adjusted the lights and Elsa would jump up and catch the lamps as they fell. At last it was done and we were both exhausted. She was always fighting with someone. She had obtained work for a group of her students in a film but they refused to give her a percentage of their fee. She was furious. When the film was being put together she found out that their roles were those of prostitutes, and she was delighted. 'Serves them right', she chuckled.

Luisillo and Teresa visiting Elsa's London studio.
Elsa kneeling, her sister Leila behind her.

I cannot remember why she was angry with another of her pupils but she sat watching her rehearse in the studio with lips curled back with distaste. 'She dances like the back of a bus', she said. But I knew that she appreciated the girl's dancing. One of her best dancers came in to announce that she was engaged and would soon be getting married. I told Elsa how sorry I was for her to lose the fruits of all the hard work she had put into the best dancer from her troupe. 'Nonsense'., she replied, 'Just another one gone from an overcrowded profession'.

Neither she nor her brother or sister Leila ever married. They were very close, as Hispanic families usually are. She used to walk around singing the song, 'Love and marriage, Love and marriage, Go together like a horse and carriage'. She said the words were very apt. She also loved 'Hernando's Hideaway' and would sing it with accompanying gestures, walking round the studio, hiding behind a curtain and jumping out from behind a pillar at the end to say, '*Olé!*'; 'Awe-lay', not 'Oh-lay'. In the bullring the accent falls on the '*ó*', '*Óle*' dragged out to 'AAwe-lay'! She loved the South African squashes called 'little gem'. On my return to South Africa I had to send her boxes of them, as you could not get them in London. She was a wonderful character.

Years later I made friends with Pilar Llorens who came from Barcelona and who had gone to London for three years to study with Phyllis Bedells. She too had taken Spanish dance classes with Elsa, so we could share our delight in this charming character. Her stage name Pastora Martos came about when she had to take over a part in a company of a dancer named Pastora, and the programmes and posters advertising the company were already out. Pilar once told me a fascinating story. She had been asked to be on a panel of five critics, dance writers and teachers, to judge a choreographic competition. Mariemma's prize pupil had the leading role in a ballet entered for the competition by Antonio Gades. All five judges chose the regional ballet by an unknown entrant. Pilar said it was so sensitive and low key and very moving. What an upset when it was announced. During the mixed reaction of the surprised audience, the judges filed offstage. A distraught young Swiss dancer rushed up to them saying, 'You have to leave at once to avoid being lynched. Mariemma is beside herself with anger and is gathering her 'troops' who will attack you as you leave. I shall take you to a back exit, but hurry'.

Pilar laughed and said, 'We did not know this kind Samaritan but were very grateful for his quick action. The waiting Mariemma was utterly dumbfounded when we never appeared'. Pilar was the editor of the beautiful arts magazine *Monsalvat* and also one of the authors of the history of dance and ballet in Catalonia. Her lovely daughter Gala danced in the *Ballet Nacional*.

I went back to Elsa three times but she could not forgive me for continuing to study in Spain as well. She said to me one day, 'Never deny your mother'. I think she felt that she trained people and then they went off to Spain and did not give her any credit. I certainly do. Her way of teaching castanet playing is with me to this day. José de Udaeta, Emma Maleras, Carola Goya and Matteo, all professionals, all play with minimum movement, for speed and strength. Today there is a tendency to lift the fingers high in the air off the castanet, which can be distracting. The dances I learned from her have stood me in good stead. She taught variety and not just flamenco, and I got to understand the rich treasures that lay waiting for me in Spain. They were put to use in 1956 in a recital in Stellenbosch.

6

Early Days in Spain, 1955

In 1955 I went to study dancing in Spain. Later I returned there to teach and examine the Spanish Dance Society syllabus, a teaching method I helped to form in South Africa. Memories of my early visits to Spain flood over me, a very different Spain from today's. Then, sleep was punctuated with *palmas*. One clapped one's hands for the *serenos*, or night watchmen. They walked the streets of Madrid with huge bunches of keys, to open the portals of whatever your habitation was. Then, the men walked behind you saying wonderful things to you as they passed, such as, 'Blessed be the mother that bore you', and after a while you started to believe them. The sound of the studios' old pianos in Madrid still tinkle in my ears. It is a sound used in the zarzuela (light opera) *La Boda de Luis Alonso*, to bring back the taste of an earlier era. I can still see little old ladies bent forward over ancient pianos, thumping out with earnest, dedicated concentration, flamenco tunes meant for guitars.

Teachers could not quite get over the fact that foreigners could also dance. Then, there were the great teachers – *La Quica* and an ancient Gypsy lady whom I found in Madrid; *El Cojo* (Enrique Jiménez) and Realito in beautiful Seville; and Emma Maleras of castanet fame in Barcelona, who was also Brunelleschi's great friend. I was able to learn rare regional dances from that fountain of knowledge, Marta Padilla in Madrid, whom Luisillo found for me. I walked into his studio in Calle de las Huertas and said, 'I would like to learn *corri-corri* from Asturias, or a Galician *Muiñeira,* or *Damas y Galanes*'. And he would rush to the phone, and phone around until he found someone who knew those dances. Marta often knew them all.

Spain was isolated by Franco. After Franco died, it was as though a cork popped out of a bottle and everything became like everywhere else, and mothers tore out their hair trying to control their teenagers. Yet the magic remains. The one thing Franco funded was folklore, which he encouraged through the *Coros y Danzas* folk groups. The later governments placed that responsibility on the various regional councils.

Today the streets are still washed down in Madrid early each morning at 1:30 or 2am, and the people are still so kind to me, and I always want to go back. I left the Spain of the fifties walking on a cloud and thinking that I had found heaven.

I had been told by Elsa Brunelleschi in London not to return without a recording of the pianist Soriano's rendering of de Falla's 'Nights in the Gardens of Spain'. I dutifully sat waiting for hours in a record shop in Barcelona for it to be fetched from some warehouse. Awed that Soriano could breed such dedication in a fan, they fed me with delicious grapes as I waited. It is still the best rendition of the *Zambra,* which still sends a thrill through me when the first note is struck, bringing the exact emotion to it, as no one else does. I met Soriano in Washington DC years later and I was able to tell him the story. The ambassador had invited us to a party to meet him after his performance. Everyone was crowded round the front entrance to the room, awaiting his arrival. We moved back to another part of the room. Suddenly a door beside us opened and there he stood. We had him all to ourselves for a while and I had a wonderful time telling him the story. Suddenly someone discovered us and took him in to meet the other guests.

At a similar occasion at the embassy we met the vibrant Catalan pianist Alicia de Larrocha. I had met her in Cape Town thirty years before. In Washington she had played exciting renditions at her performance, and the dinner at the embassy went on till the early hours of the morning. She and Mikael happened to be on the same flight early the next morning from Washington to Tokyo. After the long flight

Mikael was exhausted but Alicia was still full of energy. I remember studying her hands. She had the short stocky fingers that my Polish piano teacher had said to me are needed for strength. My teacher had looked critically at my long fingers, saying they were quite wrong.

In Madrid I had a man's suit made for me to dance in – a *traje corto* made by a famous tailor. I forgot his name and years later when I took a pupil from America to have one made, I thought I recognised the place and they were tremendously excited and looked up my card with my name and measurements. However, in the 1950s a woman could not be seen in Spain wearing trousers, and Brunelleschi had thrown all mine out of my suitcase before I left London. When I was being fitted, a bullfighter came for his fitting and I was bundled into a cupboard-sized room to wait. I peeped through the doorway, which I opened a crack, and saw him strutting in those lavishly embroidered clothes, which I subsequently saw torn to shreds and covered in blood in the bullring. For the moment they were all lost in admiration of the glittering figure in the mirror.

I bought sheet music everywhere. Some were later stolen in Nairobi while the plane refuelled and we were told to leave our belongings on board. Others were looted in Rome many years later. There were fascinating books but I had no money. I could only afford a few and today they are out of print and difficult or impossible to get hold of. Such is the human state. I bought castanets from Parramon in Barcelona and from Galiano in Madrid, where Gallardo fashioned my boots. In Seville I searched for a hand-embroidered shirt, white with lace down the front, to go with the suit. The salesmen of each shop I entered followed me to the next to give advice. We became a crowd, laughing excitedly as we wandered through that fascinating city's narrow streets. They also followed me to buy saffron for Elsa. Spain is metric and I knew only pounds and ounces. When asked how much I wished to buy, I said 'One kilo', and everyone collapsed laughing at the thought of one kilo of stamens costing the price of gold. We were hysterical.

In Madrid I ate dinner early. I was so hungry. My trip was prepaid but my money was running short. The money I sent to await me in the bank could not be found. I could only afford to eat once a day. If I ate in the day, I could not sleep at night as hunger gnawed at me. So I ate at night and slept. As I walked into the hotel's restaurant on the first night everyone was amazed. First, a woman alone, and second, eating at this early hour of 9:30pm. The orchestra leader hurried over and asked me to choose a piece of music for them to play. He fanned out the music across his arm, showing an assortment of various national melodies. I chose a *tanguillo*. They were delighted that I had chosen the Spanish one. After that, each night as I ravenously fell through the doors, the orchestra would strike up MY *tanguillo*. I would be escorted to my table by the headwaiter to that melody, and knowing glances were exchanged by the staff and everyone was happy. I sat in a solitary state throughout my meal, served by a battalion of waiters. Each course was severely studied by the headwaiter after his minions had fetched it. It was then dissected by one, groomed by another, put on a plate by a third, and a fourth stood ready to place it in front of me. All were wearing white gloves, all waiting in suspense as I ate. I had to exclaim at the excellence or I was sure the waiters would have been led to a dungeon and the cook hanged, or worse. The night was still young and it was not yet time for the Spaniards to dine. As I left, the orchestra would again strike up the *tanguillo*. My exit was equally grand, escorted again by the headwaiter between the empty tables. I was twenty-one but really green, and I was in my seventh heaven. Spain still goes to my head today and I am deliriously happy during each stay.

7

Paris and Preobrajenskaya, 1955

On the journey to Paris in 1955, where I was going to take classes with Olga Preobrajenskaya, I still had no money. My travel and hotels with bed and breakfast were all pre-paid, otherwise I do not know what I would have done. I had money in the bank in London, but again the money sent ahead had not arrived at the bank. On arriving home after my trip in Europe, and after a lot of correspondence about it, my money did come to light and it was sent back to me in South Africa.

I sat on the train with the equivalent of about £2 in my pocket and sick with worry. I knew no one in Paris who could help me. At lunchtime everyone in the carriage got up and went to eat lunch. I sat. At teatime everyone again left to have tea or coffee. I sat. A portly Dutch businessman sitting opposite me asked whether I was not going out. I said no. He came back with a bun for me. I wanted to cry at his kindness. It was hard to swallow it with nothing to drink but it did relieve the emptiness in my stomach.

Arriving in Paris, the Dutchman asked me where I was going. I told him and asked whether my £2 would get me there. He said that he was going in my direction and would I share his taxi. Arriving at the hotel, I proffered my money and he smiled and said, 'Just enjoy your stay', and drove away. I do not think that it was on his way; he was just looking after a stray young girl whom he was worried about.

After the warmth and friendliness of the people of Spain, Parisians came as a terrible shock. I asked for directions to the bank and was grumpily told a direction but nothing specific. I asked my way there from people on the street, most of whom rudely sloughed me off. No money. My asking to see the bank manager was dismissed as impossible and they practically threw me out onto the street. I made my way back to the hotel and cried on the doorman's shoulder. He was very sympathetic. He sent me to his bank around the corner and said, 'They MUST help you'. He gave me the name of a teller at the bank who found someone who spoke English. I was taken to an office upstairs. I begged to be allowed to phone my bank in London. In those days phoning was expensive and shocked glances passed between them. The possibility of not getting their money back was obviously in their thoughts. At last a call was put through to Lloyds Bank only to be told that they could not help me. I was aghast. At last the manager allowed me to phone my friend Susan Collins, who by a miracle was at home, and she was given the mission to get money transferred to me at that bank. Whether she advanced me the money or whether she persuaded my remiss bank to cough up the money I do not know, but the next day my troubles were over. I was forever grateful for Susan's effort on my behalf and that she happened to be at home when I phoned her. A small miracle from a very staunch friend.

This was my first trip abroad and I was so inexperienced. Not knowing foreign languages was a great drawback. I have never gone back to Paris and have not missed it. I have been blessed to see French ballet in America. What dancers, what productions! The kindness of the Dutchman and the doorman remains with me forever.

I did the 'tourist' thing of museums and sightseeing, plus going to the theatre and music concerts, and a magnificent world exhibition of the Impressionists. Seeing them on the original canvases one was enchanted by the vibrancy of the colours, especially those of Dégas. These paintings are engraved on my mind forever. It was worth the whole trip for this experience.

There were no ballet performances except in operas. I was led to my seat in the darkened auditorium by the usherette. My seat was behind a pillar. I asked to move but got nowhere. The usherette held out her hand. I looked down at it but it was empty. I asked what the matter was and she started screaming at me. I was rigid with shock and everyone was staring at me. I was at a loss. Finally someone said in English, 'She expects a tip'. I scrambled around in my purse, found what was probably much too much, and she departed, leaving me shattered.

By peering round the pillar, I could see an enormous tenor chasing an equally enormous soprano round tiny rosebushes. However, the dancing was very good. After two music concerts, I was standing in the foyer at the intermission, looking out over Paris, when a young man came up to me and introduced himself. He said that he was a student at the conservatorium and had been sitting near me at the opera and had seen the fuss. He was pleased to see that we obviously were going to the same performances. We chatted and he explained that the ushers were paid very little and depended on the tips given to them. I told him my sad story and he said, 'Let me drive you home afterwards and on the way show you my Paris that I love so much. Perhaps you may then feel differently about it'. He took me to Montmartre and Sacré Coeur and we looked out over Paris from the highest point. He showed me photographs of his grandmother, which he said he did to reassure me that he was a nice person. It was a truly magical experience. He spoke faultless English. Despite his grandmother's photos, as we arrived at the hotel I suddenly had misgivings about how the night might end. But my fears were groundless and he helped me out of his car, kissed my hand, said that he hoped I now saw a different Paris, wished me well and drove off into the night. My doorman friend opened the door to the hotel with a broad smile and I went happily off to bed.

I also went to classes with Preobrajenskaya in Salle Wacker. A man, to whom I took an instant dislike, took my money. I arrived very early to my first class. A minute woman in a black tunic that reached almost to the ground was watering the wooden floor of the studio with a small green watering can to make it non-slippery for the dancers – this was before the use of resin. Outside the sky was grey, and she walked to the window and fed the pigeons. It was Olga Preobrajenskaya, the teacher of my teacher in Cape Town, Cecily Robinson. I felt I was touching history. Cecily also watered the studio floor in Cape Town, better than resin for my allergy. I thought of all the historic things that bind together; the teachers who played small violins when they taught, like Bournonville and Legat – the latter had inherited the small violin his teacher had used to play for the classes that he taught. Preobrajenskaya spoke some English, telling me of her time in London. 'So hard, so hard'. Preobrajenskaya said that in Russia she danced one or two performances a week, with time in between to prepare and to rest. In London she danced every night and sometimes twice daily when matinées were scheduled. 'I became so very tired. It was a very hard time'.

Other dancers began arriving, treating her with great respect, the men kissing her hand, the girls curtseying. The class began. She paid a lot of attention to me, immediately focusing on all my weaknesses but with praise here and there for encouragement. Halfway through the exercises her mind began to stray. She started sketching an *adage*. A male student went up to her and whispered that we had now reached the *allegro*. She listened and nodded, starting new choreography. When the class ended she took my hand. 'Are you tired?' she asked, talking about my overarched back. 'Did you enjoy the class? Will you come back?' I assured her on all counts, thanked her and wanted to cry. She kissed me on my cheeks. There she was at ninety-two, struggling to bring bread to her mouth, the French students obviously there to kindly help to support her.

Some years later, back in South Africa, I read in the *Dancing Times* a request from Irina Baronova, one of the Diaghilev era's 'baby ballerinas', who asked for financial contributions for Preobrajenskaya, who was destitute. I sent my meagre contribution and later received such a charming handwritten letter of thanks from Baronova. I was so impressed. Such a gracious personal touch added to her really generous gesture of help.

8

Christmas with Karen in Hanover, 1955

Karen was the first of us to join a non-British company. She was visiting the British ambassador's daughter in Germany, went to look at Frau Georgi's company in Hanover, and decided to join them. I spent several delightful Christmases with her.

She had a room under the eaves of a house, with an iron stove in the middle of the room. This was fired to boiling point because she felt that she was never ever going to be warm again. In the mornings she went downstairs for freshly baked rolls from the bakery next door. There was another South African dancer there as well, Eleanore Laubscher, also ex-UCT, from the 'Botty Bellairs' era. Once we decided to bake a goose for Christmas dinner and it took forever. The other residents of the building, who had booked the kitchen on rotation, had to wait for hours. It just never seemed to get done and eventually Karen went off to perform and we had our Christmas dinner late that night. To Karen's surprise, I had peeled the potatoes in my white gloves, not wanting to spoil my hands. Those were the days – as I look at my hands now!

The Germans decorate their streets most artistically with green boughs and red bows all so tastefully done. Their Christmas trees are also beautifully decorated. Three times I was to experience this with Karen, taking home handmade Christmas tree decorations.

Karen Langerman. Photo: Kurt Julius, Hanover.

9

New Year with the Gruts in Copenhagen, 1956: The Royal Danish Ballet, Vera Volkova

Leaving Karen after that first Christmas, I continued on the last leg of my journey, going from Germany to Denmark. Before leaving South Africa for this overseas journey in 1955 I had contracted measles and was desperately ill. A friend came to visit me and brought along his friend Mikael Grut who said, 'I hear that you are going to Europe on a visit, and should you go to Copenhagen I am sure that you can stay with my family, whether I am there or not'. He gave me his address. I was going to Copenhagen to see the ballets of the Romantic era choreographer August Bournonville. How glad I am today to have seen all the famous dancers performing the original ballets, with original décor and costumes.

On New Year 1956 my trip was ending in Denmark. When my letter reached Mikael in Copenhagen to say that I was taking up his offer, he had forgotten all about it! However, his family were good sports and they put me up. I was in high spirits as I was at last going to see the Danish ballet.

In my suitcase was the elegant male dancer's *Traje Corto* made for me in Madrid. I had been longing to wear it. I asked if they minded if I put it on and danced in it in the living-room. What could they say?

I think his father was very amused by my antics. Mikael told me later that his father was delighted and that he had liked me very much and marvelled at my energy. I was so glad to have met him because he died, very young, before our marriage.

Copenhagen is such a beautiful city, on a human scale with no towering skyscrapers, and the old buildings lovingly preserved. Mikael took me around and showed me 'Wonderful Copenhagen' and we really did have a wonderful time together. We laughed so much that I remember holding on to a tree for support at one stage, with tears of laughter pouring down my cheeks.

It had snowed and it was crisp and bright. We went to his aunt and uncle Bente and Børge Moltke-Leth for New Year's dinner. It was a very 'family' occasion, with Torben and Kjeld, his cousins, letting off fireworks in the garden and his uncle teaching me how to 'skål' (toast) correctly. Thus: raise your glass, look deeply into the eyes of the person you are 'skåling', drink a sip of wine, raise the glass again looking deeply again into the eyes of your partner, or around to the other guests if it is a general toast, and replace your glass on the table in front of you. Mikael's Aunt Margit told me that when she was young a woman could only drink if someone raised their glass to her. If a guest was forgotten, the hostess would take pity and lift her glass to the sufferer.

I was glad to be present because I was able to meet Mikael's grandmother, Mary. Everyone was very lovingly solicitous towards her. Years later I was to get to know all about the family through reading her diaries. She had started writing them when she was fourteen years old.

Royal Danish Ballet

It was due to a friend of Mikael's parents, Henning Brøndstedt, that I was able to see the ballet at all. He was the director general of the Royal Danish Theatre, the home of the Royal Danish Ballet, in the King's New Square – Kongens Nytorv. Otherwise my trip would have been useless from a ballet point of view, as all the seats for all the performances during my stay were sold out. Director Brøndstedt found tickets for me – theatres always keep tickets for emergencies, or give up the two house seats usually held on standby.

It was fortuitous that I saw the Bournonville ballets closest to the originals and before successive artistic directors tampered with them, trying to modernise. I was able to see the ballets with the older generation of dancers, such as Niels Bjørn Larsen, Gerda Larsen, Gerda Karstens, Mona Vangsaa, Henning Kronstam, Frank Schaufuss, Margrethe Schanne, Kirsten Ralov, Fredbjørn Bjørnsson, Toni Lander, Erik Bruhn, Svend Erik Jensen, Inge Sand and Børge Ralov. This was to be a great bond between *Dancing Times* editor Mary Clarke and me in her later years. She was enamoured of the Danish dancers and their August Bournonville, and was given the highest Order of the *Dannebrog* (the Danish flag) for her writings about the Danish Ballet, their ballets and dancers – a rare honour. People forgot to put that after her name when using it in a programme or list of benefactors. I think it was little known, and not understood like the British honours are, plus the fact that she was a very modest person. I own a small book about the old school Danish dancers written by the critic Sven Kragh-Jacobsen, which she produced for their first visit to London. It is invaluable.

The company changed when it opened up to foreigners. That is because its previous relative isolation had preserved the Bournonville French style from the 18th and 19th centuries. This is also the period in Spanish classical dance of the *Escuela Bolera* that is like the Bournonville style threatened with extinction. His ballets are tampered with at home and abroad by successive ballet masters. I am not appeased when I am told that taking away the daily Bournonville classes does not matter. The ballets are filmed and notated but the essence of the dancing can still be lost. A style is ephemeral and if the dancers do not study it daily in class, it is not in the body's memory. To my relief, Bournonville classes have now been reinstated in the Royal Danish Ballet School, while the older generation still know the style.

An example of this is Flemming Ryberg who has saved the last dances from Bournonville's ballet *Toreadoren,* the Spanish *Escuela Bolera*-style dances *Zapateado* and *Jaleo de Jerez,* by learning them from Hans Brenaa and Gustav Uhlendorff. They found it easy to remember the dances from their childhood because they had been included in their daily classes. They were in their bodies. David Poole told a story about an homage to the choreographer Andrée Howard. Dancers had been invited to take part in the ballets she had choreographed and they had performed. Everything went well until the finale of the ballet *Sea Change*. No one could remember it. They quickly choreographed something, as the performance was imminent. Then, at the performance, when there was an orchestra, lighting and costumes, to a man they all danced it – their bodies had remembered.

Queen Margrethe II of Denmark is very interested in ballet, often attends performances and has designed ballet costumes. Many years later, in connection with the Bournonville Festival in June 2005, I attended a performance of *Napoli* at the Royal Danish Ballet, after which I had been invited to a party by Frank Andersen, the artistic director. It was for a 40th anniversary of the dancer Anne Marie Schlüter, and as she knew the queen she had invited her to the party. Frank Andersen, Flemming Ryberg, Thomas Lund, Henning Albrechtsen and Niels Balle did an improvised version of the *pas de quatre* from Act II of Swan Lake, turning it into a riotous *pas de cinq*. The queen laughed until the tears poured down her cheeks.

Vera Volkova

From the book on Harald Lander by the ballet critic, writer and university teacher Erik Aschengren one learns that an article appeared in the July 1951 issue of *Dancing Times* in London by Joan Lawson who 'writes that the world knows entirely too little about the Royal Danish Ballet, which has a character all of its own. Every dancer in the West can learn something'. The article said that the men in the company were very strong but the women less so. Harald Lander, the artistic director and brilliant choreographer of the Danish Ballet, read the article while he was on a train from London to Copenhagen with his wife, the technically strong and charismatic Toni Lander. They had been invited by de Valois to a summer school for teachers. It had been decided before he left Copenhagen that the Royal Danish Ballet should invite either Lawson or the Russian-born London-based Vera Volkova as guest teacher. Lander had written to Director Brøndstedt to say that it was necessary for the artistic development of the company, and Brøndstedt asked Lander to approach Volkova.

In 1951 Volkova was appointed to the Royal Danish Ballet, with which she was then associated for twenty-five years. The dancers adored her. I first met her when I lived in Stockholm in 1959-60, through my mother-in-law's friend Henning Brøndstedt and his wife. Volkova and I became friends during my frequent visits there and I carried messages between her in Copenhagen and Mary Skeaping in Stockholm. She took me backstage to show me the wonderful old theatre in Copenhagen and to meet some of the dancers she was training. On one visit in particular, when I was covering a Danish festival for *Ballet Today*, she was very excited about Kirsten Petersen and Flemming Flindt dancing in Ashton's *Romeo and Juliet,* and she rushed me backstage to meet them. It was charming to witness the interaction between them. They were flushed with the applause that they had received, especially as there were critics from all over Europe and the USA attending. She was so proud of having taught them. They had an intense discussion about the details of their dancing. There was a humorous side to that evening as I was seated beside an American critic in the auditorium and he kept saying how sexy Kirsten Petersen was. I murmured that I would not accent that part of her performance. He said vehemently, 'What do YOU know about sexy?' I was very amused as I knew that he was gay.

Volkova's flat was in Dronningens Tværgade (the Queen's Cross-street) near the Royal Theatre. There on one occasion she was particularly keen that I meet her husband, the architect Hugh Williams. They had a complex relationship and the Danes wickedly gave him the ironically meant nickname *slideren,* 'the workaholic' or 'the striver'. They felt that he was living off her earnings and not making an effort to earn a living. To be fair, he had rescued her from a hard life in China where she had landed after leaving Russia. He took her to London, a new life, and fame.

She was particularly keen for him to show me his works of art. On another occasion she wanted me to see his designs for furniture that he was working on. That was easier to comment on. He was hoping to earn some money from them. With the Danes being so clever at design I wondered whether he could compete with the established Danish designers. Perhaps she knew of his nickname and thought, rightly so, that I would hear of it. She wanted to prove them wrong. I felt ill at ease because of her eagerness to convince me about his skill. His art did not appeal to me but the sketches for furniture looked highly professional. They were folding chairs for use on board ships. I wonder what became of the furniture and whether it was ever manufactured, or whether he ever sold any of his artwork.

Once my mother-in-law and I were sitting having lunch on the veranda at the Hotel d'Angleterre on the Kongens Nytorv square. Volkova rushed past from the theatre, all of a flutter, registered us sitting there, backtracked, sat on the edge of the balustrade beside us and asked, 'How do I look? I'm going to have lunch with Freddie (Ashton) and I specially bought this hat, just for him. He's here on a visit'. We admired the hat and said that she looked very smart. 'Will he like it?' We assured her that she looked adorable and how could he not like it. She rushed off, looking back and waving.

She worried that not enough attention was given to the costumes when the Bournonville ballets were restaged. She felt that the cut and the cloth should be copied slavishly. She described how those things could affect the way a dancer moves in any given role and all that should be considered when costumes are designed; it really disturbed her. Mikael remembers how one night during an intermission at the theatre she was commenting on a performance that we had just seen. She was pulling at his clothes, bunching the cloth in her hands to illustrate her point of the unsuitability of the designs. He is six foot three and she was tiny as a bird.

After leaving Russia Volkova had no contact with that country, but when she took courage to go back on a visit she received a heartwarming reception and she met up with her colleague Vaganova. She told me that she felt that because she had worked internationally she had advanced in her teaching method, whereas the Vaganova method had not developed.

The last time we met was in South Africa in the mid-1970s when she was teaching in Cape Town for the Royal Academy of Dance. Mikael and I took her to lunch. The menu gave a choice between a buffet and *à la carte.* My husband said, 'Why should we help ourselves when we can sit here and be served?' She perked up, looked at me and said, 'Where does he get such delightful ideas from?' Later during her teaching course, I fetched her to come for her day off to my home in Stellenbosch. She welcomed the air-conditioning in the car, which gave respite from the summer heat. She said that she felt tired all the time. 'Here it seems worse and I find it hard to get through my heavy schedule. Maybe it's the heat'. I let her lie down and rest. I worried about her. She did not look well and I suggested that she tell the organiser that she could not cope with the schedule. She said, 'My dear, I could not. They have brought me all this way and will want to get what they can from my visit'. She was very ill with cancer of the liver. We did not know, and certainly that day she never expected that it was so serious. She died in 1975, shortly before her 70th birthday.

10

Return to London, and then South Africa, 1956

In London there was Susan Collins. We went to the ballet together and once queued for almost a day to get tickets for Margot Fonteyn. We were frozen solid and went home to Susan's room in Chelsea, filled hot-water bottles and thawed out under blankets, before going to watch the performance. Susan was to go on holiday, during which she took the place of an injured acrobat at a moment's notice to help a small group – they convinced her that she had to do it as otherwise they would have to cancel the show and starve. She stayed on with them, and fell in love with one of them, José Piñar. They married and spent the rest of their career happily creating magically imaginative performances together, while touring the world.

Susan Collins.

Home Again

Richard Glasstone had been teaching my Stellenbosch pupils while I was away. He and some other students were at the quayside in Cape Town to greet me on my return with the words, 'Dulcie wants you to come and perform tomorrow night'. I had hardly stepped off the boat and had not danced for many months. I was to dance in Dulcie Howes' *La Famille*, a clever version of Ninette de Valois' ballet *Façade* to the music of William Walton. It was a good idea from her very supportive husband Guy Cronwright. I knew the ballet and was being asked to help out in this emergency. Was this to be another *Swan Lake* fiasco all over again? The next night, after a sketchy rehearsal, I stood waiting in the wings for the music to start. My knees turned to water. How I got up on pointe and through the dance I do not know.

It was then that I decided that my ballet-dancing days were over. I continued doing recitals of Spanish dance in and around Cape Town and outlying towns. At that time the Afrikaners, like the Spaniards, were very disapproving of women wearing trousers. In an outlying town, I stamped my way through a *Zapateado* in my *traje corto* black suit, cordobés hat and boots. At the final dramatic flourish, I heard a woman in the front row say in Afrikaans, 'Now what was that all about?' It's called pioneering.

At some stage I was suddenly left with all the Spanish dance teaching in Cape Town. I was teaching at the university, in the city and at Stellenbosch. Jasmine Honoré had left to live in Ireland and Elizabeth Coombes had left Cape Town to get married and move to Bloemfontein. She had asked me to take over her school in the city, situated in an Anglican church hall on a hill. Karen Langerman's brother Rupert was a reporter at the *Cape Times* morning newspaper and he often popped in and we went off to lunch together to catch up on news.

One day some months after my return there was the noise of a scooter and a knock on the door, and there stood Mikael. It was a wonderful surprise. Did I want to go to Strand for a swim? Yes I did. I was actually terrified out of my wits to ride pillion but I was not going to say no. My mother was even more terrified for me. At the seaside were some of Mikael's university colleagues, and among them Paul Lange, my childhood friend from De Aar. They were all studying forestry at Stellenbosch University. I had often met Paul at the student dances but did not realise that he and Mikael were in the same class.

After this the scooter came to my door more and more frequently. Then Mikael became a regular guest at Sunday lunch. He went with his classmates to Knysna for work for a couple of months and our correspondence grew. He was to come back to Stellenbosch for the weekend. I sat up waiting for him. Late in the night I said to my mother, 'I don't think he is going to turn up. I'm going to bed'. My mother looked at me and said that it would be a terrible thing if I did not wait and he then arrived after such a long journey. Eventually he came, soaked through from a terrible journey in a storm, utterly worn out. My mother had expected this, and produced a hot meal for him.

After Knysna we went to cinemas, concerts and plays. Mikael was very interested in what I was doing and he suggested that I should do a recital. We had both become captivated by the rich Spanish culture already in our teens, he in Sweden in the poetry and prose, and I in South Africa in the dance and music. He thought that I could show my dancing in a recital where music, dance and poetry would be joined together. So he organised such a recital for me in the Botha Hall in Stellenbosch in 1956. Piano accompaniment for my dances was by my friend Enrique Breytenbach, the cellist was Bernice Easton who was accompanied by Esme Steenkamp on the piano, and the poems were recited by the great Afrikaans actors Pietro Nolte and Lydia Lindeque, the wife of the Afrikaans writer Uys Krige.

Then, in November 1956, it was suddenly time for Mikael to leave for Stockholm where he was going to do his master's degree in forest economics. This was a two-year stint. We were both devastated. We had come to rely on each other's company so much. It was to be a very stressing time. We corresponded for a year and then I was due to go on an overseas study trip again. We had a wonderful reunion in Denmark and I went to Sweden as well. It was hard to part again.

Once I had decided to leave my teaching at the University of Cape Town (UCT) to finish writing my book on the history of South African ballet – it took more than twenty years to complete – David Poole asked me to teach him the Spanish Dance Society syllabus so that he could take over the Spanish dance teaching at the school. He also asked me to teach him some dances that we could perform together in a recital. This was a very successful venture at UCT's Little Theatre on 26 May 1958. The critic Denis Hatfield wrote in the *Cape Times*: 'The last three items brought part of Friday's audience to a pitch of shrill enthusiasm such as I have never heard here before. I wanted to see all three again'.

Two years later Mikael received his master's degree and was offered his first job, as economist in the Stockholm office of Mo och Domsjö forestry company. He then proposed by letter, and I went to get married and live in Stockholm. He always says it is the woman who proposes, but I say that 'I have it in writing'.

11

Sweden, 1959-60: Marriage, Mary Skeaping, Rolf de Maré, Jenny Hasselquist, Björn Holmgren and the Royal Swedish Ballet

Mikael and I were married in the historic Swedish church in Copenhagen in 1959. The priest was far more beautifully garbed than the bride, in a magnificent robe of gold and subtle colours, a gift from a Swedish queen some centuries earlier. We trembled our way through the ceremony, and after a wonderful celebratory family lunch at my mother-in-law's home, we went next day by plane to Sweden and a new life in this beautiful country, with which I fell in love. Today, fifty-seven years later, I still get a thrill from the country and the people. Our now large family has chosen the idyllic and historic little town of Sigtuna near Stockholm as our annual family holiday destination. We all love its quiet beauty. I hope this tranquillity will last.

After three months of sightseeing in Stockholm, and setting up house and learning Swedish, I suddenly yearned to be in the theatre again. Dulcie Howes had given me an introduction to Mary Skeaping. I sent it off. She asked me to come and see her at the Royal Opera House, where she had been the artistic director of the ballet since 1953. I literally threw myself at her feet and begged her to allow me to do anything, anything in the theatre. She said that (at that time) the Swedes were very protective of their own. She could only employ a foreigner if she could prove that there was no Swede who could do the job. She suggested that I research Swedish dance history, and she started me off in the Royal Library, where I had Mikael's librarian aunt Margit Wijk to help me.

Skeaping came from a fascinating family. She and her brothers had no formal schooling. Their parents believed they could educate them themselves, and three remarkable artists emerged. One brother was famous for his animal paintings and sketches, especially of horses. Her other brother became a violinist, and she herself was to be awarded Sweden's highest honour for her work with their ballet company. She lifted the company and the dancers to a very high international standard in eight years.

Mikael's office overlooked the Royal Dramatic Theatre, a stretch of water, and the erstwhile home of Rolf de Maré (1888-1964), founder of *Les Ballets Suédois* in Paris in 1920. Today it is the Hallwylska – his grandparents' surname – Museum. It encapsulates life at that time, while at the same time celebrating his family. De Maré used to climb out of the back window at night in order to have some fun away from his grandmother's strict gaze.

The Royal Swedish Ballet was in poor shape in the 1920s, at the time when Rolf de Maré founded *Les Ballets Suédois*. The first woman to lead the Royal Swedish Ballet, Gunhild Rosén, had resigned her post with the company to concentrate on the school, which had produced dancers such as Jenny Hasselquist, Jean Börlin and the much younger Carina Ari. They studied privately with Fokine in Denmark, where he had settled after fleeing from the turmoil of the Russian Revolution. Because of the circumstances there, he had arrived too late in 1918 to take up a contract at the Stockholm Opera. The Swedish Ballet missed the great opportunity of appointing him to head their ballet. He was given some touring of the Swedish provinces, and later teaching at the Royal Danish Ballet. Fokine was eking out his living by teaching in his home on the outskirts of Helsingør (Elsinore) in Denmark, the home of Shakespeare's Hamlet, just across the water from Hälsingborg in Sweden.

The morale in the Royal Swedish company was low when Fokine

arrived in Stockholm and was invited to de Maré's estate in 1918. Fokine's advice to de Maré, who was wealthy, was for him to start a company to tour abroad. This fell on receptive ears. Fokine needed a job. The idea was for him to lead the company. However, circumstances were to prevent that happening and he went to the USA. The dancers were paid 400 kronor per month in Stockholm and would be tempted away with 1,000 kronor per month. Jean Börlin was to become the only choreographer of the newly formed *Les Ballets Suédois* in 1920. It survived only five eventful years and almost bankrupted de Maré. I wanted to hear about all this from the man himself.

When I heard that he was in Stockholm, I invited de Maré to dinner in our new home at Bergsringen 13, poised on a hill above the suburb of Alvik, looking out over Lake Mälaren. The train crossed to one of the islands of which Stockholm is composed. The view as one crosses the lake is breathtaking and we had a forest behind us filled with flowers in the spring and summer.

De Maré arrived by metro. He was elegantly dressed in a light-brown suit, the very epitome of an old-style gentleman. I had cooked a special meal and Mikael had bought three bottles of a reputedly good French wine. He opened one after the other and they were all equally bad. De Maré, being a gentleman of the old school, took it very well. Mikael was mortified. We began talking. He had a captive eager audience.

De Maré was fascinating. He talked about himself in the third person. 'De Maré had no qualms about taking away the dancers from the Royal Swedish Ballet company. It was to give them a chance to do more exciting performances and to travel abroad. They were not treated well at the opera as regards pay. So it was not difficult to get them to join his venture to take Swedish ballet to the outside world'. It was exciting to hear all about those troubled times. He was very bitter about the poor reception he had received from the press, especially the Swedish press, who resented his removal of the talent from the ballet at home.

'The attacks extended to Jean Börlin and eventually hounded him into poor health and court cases which bankrupted him and led to his death. Fokine was off to America and suggested that he (Börlin) should lead the company because he was the one who resembled him (Fokine) the most'. Still in de Maré's own words, 'De Maré wanted the Swedish company to be led by a Swede, and Börlin was the obvious choice'. 24 March 1920 in the *Théâtre des Champs Elysées* was the opening night of a company presenting Swedish ideas, in ballets with music by many French composers but with intellectual ideas which irritated the critics. I had a complete collection of their beautiful programmes. Regrettably I put up an exhibition of them at the UCT Ballet School, only to return next day to find them all gone. Naive of me not to expect that to happen.

Listening to de Maré tell of his many meetings and discussions with Fokine made me realise that it was perhaps Fokine's bitterness about his own treatment by Diaghilev that had led to the idea of another company to rival the latter's *Ballets Russes*. The First World War had ended and interest in ballet was booming because of Diaghilev. Before him sat a rich Swede who could realise this dream. However, Diaghilev's success was to be a stumbling block, which the company had to take on without Fokine.

It was a rare moment for us to hear of all de Maré's trials and tribulations. He died four years later. Like Diaghilev, he died in bitterness because of the power of the press. Dance is ephemeral, the written word remains. Does the press deserve this power if there is no discernment attached to it? Today choreographers try to resurrect the creations of *Les Ballets Suédois*.

The beautiful, delicate Prima Ballerina Jenny Hasselquist had also joined the *Ballets Suédois,* and she told me some of this when I interviewed her in 1960. She was living in a small, charming flat centrally situated in the elegant Östermalm area of Stockholm. She felt forgotten and left out of the ballet scene that she so loved. According to her, none of the dancers could have imagined the effect Fokine was to have on them. When they were introduced to him and his wife Fokina, they were placed in order of rank. Fokine asked to have the school's pupils as well as the company. He proceeded to ignore the hierarchy, choosing the dancers he wanted and placing them directly into roles. This was also his way of casting in St Petersburg. He found that the small Stockholm company worked enthusiastically and with temperament; the latter he had not expected. They had good training from Gunhild Rosén, and talent. He felt that what they lacked was a good choreographer. He singled out Hasselquist, whom he put into leading roles in the *bacchanale* in *Cleopatra* and the *Mazurka* in *Les Sylphides*. He told them to keep the styles of these two ballets strictly apart. Hasselquist said Fokine was very demanding, not only of the company but also of his wife, who was very soon bored by the constant repetition. When Hasselquist went to study with him in Denmark, he created a version of his *Dying Swan* solo tailored specially for her. All this was a good introduction to joining *Les Ballets Suédois.*

Directly from the Opera Ballet School he took sixteen-year-old Carina Ari who was later to show his influence in her own choreography (see Chapter 43). When Bengt Häger of the Carina Ari Foundation went to visit Hasselquist many years later, she was living in one room in an old people's home surrounded by boxes containing all her possessions – a repeat of Olga Preobrajenskaya's last years. Bengt said sadly that although Hasselquist had had an illustrious career in film as well as dance, she was at the end of her life surrounded by elderly women who had nothing in common with her.

Valborg Franchi was the next teacher after Gunhild Rosén who was to produce talented dancers like the brilliant principal male dancer of the company, Björn Holmgren. In the school he was taught by her through the Cecchetti method, so dear to Skeaping. She was the next person to be of great influence to the Royal Swedish Ballet. When I interviewed Björn, he said that he and Skeaping were made for each other: they spoke the same language – Cecchetti. I have much more to say about her in the next chapter.

12

Stockholm 1959-60, continued: Mary Skeaping and Balanchine's Vida Brown

Mikael's Aunt Margit lived in the Östermalm area of inner Stockholm and she crossed the beautiful Humlegården park to go to work at the Royal Library where she was a senior librarian. Saying 'I know exactly who should teach you to speak Swedish', she introduced me to a remarkable, tall, elderly Swedish woman – Estrid Linder, part of Östermalm's social history. She and her siblings were known as 'the Linder Sisters' – 'Systrarna Linder'. While doing research, I kept coming across cuttings about them. Someone else who lives there is Björn Holmgren, and that is where I visited him for interviews. He had just retired from his valuable work of teaching in the Royal Swedish Ballet School.

Estrid in turn introduced me to Barbro Thiel Cramér who taught Spanish dancing, and later I was to teach in her studio. She had been the pupil of Kurt Jooss, the choreographer of that amazingly prophetic ballet *The Green Table*, which won him the first choreographic prize in Europe in 1934. It is still so relevant today, tracing all the stages of war brilliantly in dance. It should be shown repeatedly throughout the world as a warning of the consequences of war. This is the most significant and meaningful ballet that I have seen, together with *The Moor's Pavane* about an incident between Othello and Desdemona, choreographed by

José Limón. It intrigues me that both are contemporary and not classical ballets, and yet I was a classical ballet dancer. Choreography fascinates me, and the inventiveness of Bronislava Nijinska's profound *Les Noces* affects me as deeply as some of the Spanish folk choreographies created in villages by untrained dancers. The latter are likely to be lost to the world because they are never seen outside of Spain, and are disappearing there too; each region shows such historic folk costumes, diverse steps and styles, music and musical instruments.

Also studying with Jooss at that time were Birgit Cullberg and Ivo Cramér, whose brother Casten Barbro married. Barbro and I used to meet in Spain through the years. We would go to different teachers and then hire a studio and teach each other the dances we had learned, doubling our knowledge for less cost.

Estrid was to comfort me when I arrived at class having burned Mikael's meals day after day, poor man. I could not cook because my mother would not allow me in the kitchen, saying, 'I'll save you that drudgery while you are with me'. So Estrid took me by the hand, led me across the road to a shop, saying in her deep voice to the shopkeeper, pointing at the shelves stocked with food, 'We will have two of those and two of those ..'., and turning to me as we left with our bags she said, 'Mikael must learn to eat tinned food'. Years later in South Africa, a parcel arrived from her containing beautiful huge silk-embroidered Spanish shawls, a magnificent black lace mantilla and fan. She had bequeathed them to me in her will.

Mikael's Aunt Margit led me to fascinating research through her knowledge of the material available at the Royal Library. Together with Mary Skeaping I visited places such as the famous library at Skokloster, which was privately owned. Skeaping had arranged our visit but the count could not see us because he was out cutting the enormous hedge surrounding his palace. We were told to please go ahead. Such amazing trust in us, all alone surrounded by priceless volumes.

I learned about Swedish history and ballet from the ground up. Skeaping asked me to write for the magazine *Ballet Today* and I went to the Danish and Swedish festivals as a critic. She was also most generous and allowed me to sit in her box for performances of opera and ballet in Stockholm. I love Swedish opera because the artists can not only sing but act as well.

Skeaping had been brought to Stockholm by the intelligent and so sympathetic director of the Royal Swedish Opera, Joel Berglund. He had seen examples of her work and asked her to take over the ballet company and wake it from its sleep, as in *Sleeping Beauty*. She performed that miracle. I have written extensively about this period in my book *Royal Swedish Ballet, History from 1692 to 1962,* which she encouraged me to start researching, and which Bengt Häger of the Carina Ari Library and Foundations later asked me to complete. It was gruelling work, and my encouraging husband helped me so much with the old Swedish language, and with the computer, the formatting, the proofreading, the checking of the innumerable facts, and more. I sat staring at rolls of film with white writing on black, which was hard to look at. Many times my courage flagged and Mikael encouraged me to keep going.

Skeaping kept me from meeting Häger, considering him 'a dangerous man', which was not at all true. He was a dance critic, writer, impresario and chairman of *Dansfrämjandet,* an organisation for dance promotion which provided a means for the Swedish dancers to earn a living through performances during the holiday periods when the Opera House was dark. He augmented the local dancers with visiting guest artists from England, Russia and elsewhere. For example, it was he who provided the first international exposure for Merce Cunningham, when he brought him to perform in Sweden.

Skeaping considered Bengt a rival for the dancers' time. In a way she had to be merciless if she was to train them up to an international standard. Of course he did not see it like that. He felt that they could have complemented one another. However, seeing the standard of the technique then, which she felt she had to hide under long skirts for the *corps de ballet* in *Swan Lake* – her first hugely successful 'trial' production for them – one has to feel sympathy for her. Over the years Bengt had admired Skeaping when he visited London and saw her teaching and rehearsing the Sadler's Wells company. He felt she was never given her due there, and that the company profited from her selfless dedication without her ever receiving proper acknowledgement for her contribution.

Director Berglund had also recognised Skeaping's calibre when he appointed her after watching her working. It was a mammoth task which confronted Skeaping in Stockholm. Bertil Hagman, another person she feared unnecessarily, praised Berglund on his retirement as Opera director for the renewal he had brought about in the ballet. The eyes of the world had been opened to the Royal Swedish Ballet by the fact that it now had a repertoire into which guest artists could step to excite the public, and the fact that the local dancers had achieved a standard to showcase them. Through touring they had also raised the interest in ballet.

Being a discerning and kind man with a feel for artistry, Berglund had a charming relationship with Skeaping. Each trusted the other completely. However, this was to bring some anguish too. She signed a three-year contract which they never discussed again, and as her stay progressed into eight years and she knew that his tenure would come to an end, she felt insecure and at risk. Especially touching was the dancers' show of affection, love and respect when they went to her funeral in London years later, despite having complained of being overworked by her!

Before Skeaping's arrival in Sweden the great Swedish theatre historian Professor Agne Beier had discovered the lost 18th-century theatre in the grounds of Drottningholm Palace near Stockholm, with complete décor from that era intact. This glorious gift from the past created a perfect foil for her interest in historic dance, enabling her to create delightful period ballets. Skeaping and Beier found forgotten music manuscripts and stories for the ballets performed there. It was the last functioning 18th-century theatre in the world. Copies of the décor were made, and the delicate ancient ones preserved for posterity. Stringent fire regulations are imposed because of the age of the theatre as well the contents. Even the delicate floorboards are guarded from misuse.

Queen Elizabeth II and Prince Philip came on a state visit in 1956. Beier suggested that Skeaping create a special ballet for the Drottningholm Theatre on 14 June for that occasion. Skeaping chose designs from the 18th century by Bérain and also decided that she would use as many as possible of the tricks the theatre had, such as trapdoors, waves, thunder and the quick scene changes of the décor, sometimes taking only seconds, in front of the audience's eyes. The Queen and Prince Philip sat on the chairs made for Sweden's 'Theatre King'

Gustav III (1746-1792) who had the Drottningholm Theatre designed by Carl Fredrik Adelcrantz. Special electric light bulbs that flickered like candles were in the ceiling candelabras. Beier found a suitable story and they titled it *Cupid Out of His Humour*. Mary decided that the music should be by an English composer, in honour of the Queen. She chose Purcell. The music needed a lot of preparation and the finished product only arrived on the day, just before the performance. Mary had no idea as to what was going to happen. Before the performance she was introduced to the Queen who asked, 'Please tell me what we are about to see', and Mary replied honestly, 'I really don't know, Your Majesty'. She was almost fainting from nervous strain by the time the curtain descended, as she had watched the ballet unfold from the back of the theatre, under-rehearsed with the orchestra. In the final scene, as the principal dancers, seated on a cloud, were swept up into the sky, Prince Philip shouted from the audience, 'Fasten your seatbelts'!

Beier told the Swedish King, while discussing his find, that what surprised him was that the only things missing were the ropes that pulled the décor up and down for scene changes. A very apologetic, embarrassed but honest King Gustav IV Adolf confessed to being the guilty party. When he and his brother were children, they used to go and cut bits off them to use for their sailing boats. So the ropes were replaced.

This is a good place to discuss the superstition that it is unlucky to whistle in the dressing room. It stems from the time of sailing ships. Because pulling the décor up and down needed strong men's muscle power, stevedores were employed for performances to do that, and they were accustomed to communicating by ringing bells or whistling. So it was forbidden in the theatre because performers could cause confusion if they joined in and a scene change took place mistakenly at the wrong time.

I arrived in the midst of all this activity in the opera and the historic Drottningholm Theatre. The dancers were delighted to add the latter to their venues, although they became overstretched by Skeaping's zeal and said that they ended up with no family time. They often had to return to the opera in the evenings because the rehearsal room was also shared by the school's afternoon children's classes taught by Albert Kozslovsky. Mary had invited Kozslovsky's wife, Nina Dombrovska, to join her husband, as she considered her to be an exceptionally good teacher. The dancers in the company also did not like to share leading roles between several casts but she was adamant about that in order to do away with the cancelling of a performance if a dancer was indisposed. The problem of titles and payment was cleverly solved by paying the dancers a principal's salary while dancing the roles, but they were not given the title, even temporarily. They soon settled down to all that when more studio space was later provided for the company.

Many years later, in 1998, Mary Clarke, Clement Crisp, my husband and I attended a charming performance in the Drottningholm Theatre in connection with the 225th anniversary of the Royal Swedish Ballet, to which I had been invited by the then Artistic Director Frank Andersen. After the performance we were treated to dinner on a boat which took us back to Stockholm on the beautiful Lake Mälaren in the lingering twilight of the Nordic summer evening.

Another precious little theatre in Stockholm is *Confidencen* which is situated in Ulriksdal Palace, owned by the royal family. It was converted into a theatre in 1753 and it is Sweden's oldest rococo theatre. Gustav III himself performed on that stage. It was there, accompanied by Mary Clarke and Clement Crisp, that we attended a memorable concert as part of the above-mentioned anniversary. After the concert I had an appointment to meet the opera singer Kerstin Dellert, who was director of the theatre, to ask if they could not sometime perform Spanish classical dance there, but she said that the stage was so old that it was too delicate for dance.

During that visit to Stockholm I also met Horst Koegler, the author of *The Concise Oxford Dictionary of Ballet,* 1977, which is still the definitive dictionary of ballet. He told me that he had prepared a new edition and was bitterly disappointed when the Oxford University Press gave that job to someone else. His manuscript is now in Germany.

Back to the Stockholm of 1959/60. Suddenly Skeaping became very possessive and needed sympathetic attention at all times of the night and day. The unrenewed three-year contract left her feeling vulnerable. She needed reassurance and she phoned me incessantly. Luckily Mikael was away travelling, otherwise it would have disturbed our marriage. She developed a persecution complex, believing that everyone was plotting against her. And then suddenly she was gone, without having phoned to say goodbye. The Opera said stiffly that she was in London but refused to supply an address where I could contact her.

Her return was to happen equally as suddenly when sometime later I received a phone call asking me to come and watch the rehearsals of two Balanchine ballets to be staged by Vida Brown. And that is how I met Vida. We were later to be reunited in Washington DC, through our dentist! Also watching in the box with me was a young English musician, a violinist. She told me that she was recovering from a nervous breakdown and had met Skeaping at the hospital where she also was recovering. They had become friends and Skeaping had invited her to come with her and experience the teaching of these ballets. Skeaping never said a word to me about this. She just resumed our relationship as though she had never been away.

It was fascinating to watch Brown teach and rehearse *The Four Temperaments* and *Symphony in C*, especially because the young visiting musician explained to me what was happening musically, making Balanchine's work even clearer. 'That is a broken cadence', she would exclaim, as a dancer was lifted offstage and suddenly dropped her head back. Brown and Skeaping came to our flat and met Mikael and we became friends. She said that Balanchine saved her life when she had a child. She had to stop dancing, yet that was how she earned her living. Aware of her predicament, he asked her whether she would be prepared to become his rehearsal assistant because she knew his ballets so well and he could rely on her. When I last contacted her she was living happily in Edgewater, across from New York.

Mary Skeaping told me how, when she was in Cape Town in 1939 for the Cecchetti examinations, she was about to return to London via Southampton, when the war broke out. She wanted to stay but Dulcie Howes practically carried her on board the ship. When I spoke to Howes about this afterwards, she said, 'But of course. I could never have coped with Mary for the duration of a war. She was much too intense'.

During the last week of December 1959 and the first week of January 1960 Mikael and I went to Leningrad, as it was then, and Moscow on a tour organised by a Swedish student organisation but attended mainly by American postgraduate students. That was when we saw Maximova,

Struchkova and Fadeyechev dance (Chapter 2). We were also some of the last people to see both Stalin and Lenin in the necropolis on the Red Square because soon afterwards Stalin's body was removed. In spite of the bitter cold there was a long queue, but as foreigners we were allowed to break it, to our embarrassment.

13

Back in South Africa, 1961

We returned to South Africa as a married couple, Mikael to lecture in Stellenbosch University's forestry faculty. He wrote the first book on forestry in South Africa. Dulcie Howes asked me to teach Spanish dance at the UCT Ballet School. Jasmine Honoré had left for Ireland so that her children could have a Catholic upbringing. She was to return after a twelve-year absence and then I taught her the syllabus of the Spanish Dance Society (SDS) each morning before my classes started, leaving my home in Stellenbosch at a very early hour.

Richard Glasstone left for London, where Len Martin suggested that he should attend an audition for the Scapino Ballet in Amsterdam. He was accepted and his subsequent fascinating career in Holland, Turkey and England can be followed in his autobiography *Congo to Covent Garden* (2015). I only learned on reading it that for his audition in London he performed a dance I had choreographed for him to music by Ibert during performances at the Little Theatre by our UCT choreographic group. We rarely or never saw ballet performances, so I was influenced by seeing a performance by the mime artist Marcel Marceau. Len Martin had joined the Sadler's Wells Royal Ballet after the company's return from its historic tour of South Africa. He and Sven van Zyl were chosen by Barbara Fewster to join a group from the company to tour and to perform in New York. It reflected the high standard of teaching at the UCT Ballet School.

On a later occasion when Richard again left Cape Town for Holland he was accompanied by his lovely wife Heather Magoon. She had studied at the UCT Michaelis School of Art and her sketches adorn my *Dancing Times* article on the Vestris gavotte and the Basques; see Chapter 15. He then asked me to take over the ballet history course at UCT, adding another string to my bow there. After teaching this subject for a while, I realised that they were learning about ballet everywhere except in their own country. As there was only John Worrall's slim but excellent volume on this subject, I set about doing some research. It took some twenty years for my project to be brought to completion and by then we had moved to Rome where I completed writing *The History of Ballet in South Africa,* which was published in time for my arrival in Washington DC in 1981.

Before I left to move to Rome, working together with Dulcie Howes we managed to get the university to approve a degree to add to the diploma course for the students. A great achievement by Dulcie. All the students had to do was to add an academic subject such as English, and they would be able to teach in schools, get a salary and eventually a pension. I was happy, but in the end it was not to be. We also worked together for dance at the EOAN Group, which promoted the performing arts in Cape Town's underprivileged areas. I arrived as usual half an hour early for a meeting. Dulcie joined me, smiling. 'The two of us…' she said, meaning that we always arrived early to meetings.

14

Working in the Theatres of Cape Town and Stellenbosch

The 1960s was a very rewarding period for me in Cape Town as I was asked to do choreography for theatre and opera as well as for CAPAB (Cape Performing Arts Board) Ballet. At the invitation of Rosalie van der Gucht of the UCT department of drama, Robert Mohr transferred there in 1960. He was extraordinarily multitalented as a director of plays, operas and musicals, a writer and translator, and an inspiring teacher whose pupils went on to succeed all over the English-speaking world. An actor who studied with him is Richard E Grant of *Withnail and I* fame. The following year, 1961, Robert Mohr was succeeded in his post at the Stellenbosch Drama Department by the Flemish director Fred Engelen, who was accompanied by his wife, the actress Tine Balder, and their children.

I thoroughly enjoyed being involved in Robert's light touch to the production of Julian Slade's musical *Salad Days* in 1962, with a charismatic young couple in the leading roles. Mikael still recalls them and the production, and sometimes quotes '...remind me to remind you' from it. And in 1964 I also very much enjoyed choreographing the dances for the ball scene in Norman Marshall's production of *Romeo and Juliet*, using the danceable compositions by Vaughan Williams which were very suitable for that period.

I was getting such valuable experience from the diverse use of dance in the various plays and later operas, working with directors in many different theatres. For a young person it was heavenly and challenging. You could not just sit back and choose from ballet steps, you had to be inventive each time. Working with non-dancers also meant being inventive in a different way.

Next came two plays in Afrikaans for KRUIK, the Afrikaans acronym for CAPAB. The first, for the Republic Festival in 1966, was *Die Laaste van die Takhare*, 'The Last of the Backvelders (hillbillies)' by the playwright and poet CJ Langenhoven. An ox wagon without the oxen decorated the programme cover. It was directed by the actor Johan Fourie, and the Dutchman Boudewijn Scholten arranged all the author's songs, sung by the exquisite handpicked voices of his select choir. The Cape was always alive with performances and characters in the arts world. The talented artist Stephen de Villiers, who designed the costumes for the play, was a teacher at UCT's Michaelis School of Art.

Boudewijn had been a child in war-torn Holland when food was scarce. He told of his mother berating his sister for taking too much cheese for her sandwich, saying, 'Who knows when we will be able to get more?' His sister said, 'That is why I am taking it now!' He also mentioned the family's fear when they had two English airmen hiding in the attic and there was a knock on their door one night and German soldiers entered to search for the airmen. Had they gone into the attic they would have found them and the family would have been punished. When the soldiers started to leave, they heaved a sigh of relief, but then one soldier turned back, took out his gun and fired shots into the ceiling. The family were stricken. Once the soldiers left they rushed up to find the shots had missed the men by a hair's breadth. It could have cost them their own and the airmen's lives. There was much hunger in Holland during the war and yet they shared the little food they had with these men.

Langenhoven's secretary Sarah Goldblatt was a real virago obsessed by his work. I came up against her. She interfered all the time with ridiculous ideas. I went to the director, Johan Fourie, and said that I would have to leave as she was stupid and rude. I was left in peace to do my work after that and I am pleased to say that it was very well received.

In April 1967 DJ Opperman's play *Voëlvry*, meaning 'Outlaws', was staged by Fred Engelen. He was to die unexpectedly after an appendix operation in that year. Engelen had also brought out the Flemish director Marc Leemans for Lorca's play *Yerma*, translated from the Spanish by Uys Krige. It was exciting to work with an overseas director with whom I was so much in tune. He used a lot of songs for which he needed group movement, and for that I became responsible. On his departure, Leemans presented me with a signed copy of his book, with a charming dedication.

In 1968 I was involved in the production of a light-hearted play by Sergeant titled *Cape Charades*, based on the characters of early Capetonians.

15

Studying with the Basques

Many Basque dances seen on the internet are not carefully executed. They have agility, energy and enthusiasm, but lack the precision of dedication. To explain my concern, I have to go back to my studies with the great Basque teacher Juan Urbeltz, director of the company *Argia* ('light') in San Sebastian.

In the 1960s I was producing performances in three theatres in Cape Town, where the municipal orchestra had a Basque guest conductor for a while, Enrique Jordá. He conducted for performances of the University of Cape Town Ballet Company. His wife attended my shows and in one of them saw some Basque dances which I had produced. Jordá came up to me and said that his wife had been thrilled with what she had seen. He suggested that if I was interested in studying further, I should go to Maestro Juan Urbeltz, to whom he would give me an introduction.

Later, on one sunny day in San Sebastian, I looked out from a regal white hotel that has since been demolished, over an incredibly beautiful bay with a rolling white beach, fishing boats at one side and a cliff reaching in a semi-circle as if to embrace it from the other. Each day after I woke up and before I went to bed, I looked out and marvelled at such beauty. I was also taken around by car by Juan and Mariana Urbeltz to see the marvels of the surrounding countryside and to eat the delicious Basque food. It was one of the highlights of my career to study with such a knowledgeable and generous teacher as Urbeltz, together with his company. I was accustomed to very good ballet and other dance teaching, so I knew immediately that I was with a master.

The classes took place in the old and imposing former monastery of Santelmo. We danced where the altar used to be, in front of a vast, imposing mural in shades of brown, depicting Basque fishermen valiantly battling with the cruel, heaving sea. The atmosphere was magical. The lessons were serious and precise, accompanied by live musicians and the company dancers. Most Basque dances are for groups. Juan Urbeltz, his wife Mariana, the leader of the orchestra and his company *Argia* were all gathered to meet me on the first night. When Juan opened the door to the former monastery church, a very large group of dancers and musicians were waiting for me.

Every step that I was taught was carefully explained and every dance that I had requested was taught to me, even though some were not in their repertoire and they had gone to old manuscripts to learn them. This was told to me by a young American dancer from Boise, Idaho, where the *Argia* company went regularly to perform. He too was there to study the dances and, in his case, the language as well. The dancers and musicians gave me generously and unstintingly of their time.

Much detail in the steps had been lost because of the civil war when they were only able to dance and play their music in small towns in the hills and mountains. Refinements such as the *rond de jambes,* the subtleties of how and where to make the circles of the leg, were lost and became small kicks. These matters Urbeltz had researched in the invaluable book on the dances of Guipúzcoa by Juan Ignacio de Iztueta, and the old steps had been replaced. Such dedication. In Guipúzcoa they do what Americans call a 'hitch kick', and they change their legs in front in the air before placing the foot across to turn. In another region, the legs swing round during the turn, one after the other as they turn. There are variations in what the French Basques and Spanish Basques perform. For example, the *Vestris Gavotte* originated from a French Basque dance. Many years later I wrote an article for the *Dancing Times* about this connection. Illustration 15-1 below shows the first page of this article.

More than a coincidence?

Marina Grut looks at the connections between the *Vestris Gavotte* and Basque *gabota/gavota*.

Drawings by **Heather Magoon**

Some years ago, when I was teaching and lecturing on Spanish dance at a Society of Dance History Scholars conference in Maryland, I heard emanating from a nearby studio music that sounded familiar. On entering the studio, I watched and listened with fascination to an erudite, carefully researched and beautifully danced presentation by Sandra Noll Hammond on the *Vestris Gavotte*.

Before my eyes she presented something that had strong echoes of a French Basque dance I had learnt in London in 1955 from Elsa Brunelleschi, the well-known teacher of Spanish dance. It was titled the *Gabota* (*Gavota*) – the Spanish "b" and "v" are similarly pronounced. Had I not seen Sandra performing the *Vestris Gavotte*, I would never have been aware of the fact that the music, construction and steps are very similar. In my book *The Bolero School* (2002) I mentioned this similarity; in this article I suggest how it may have come about.

The gavotte seems to have originated as a peasant "kissing" dance of the Gavots, the natives of Gap in the south-eastern French province of Dauphiné. The kissing later became an exchange of flowers. The dance became fashionable at the courts of France and England in the 17th and 18th centuries, including in the *galanteries*. The dance had a stately 4/4 time, but was later danced in a "lustier" 2/2 time. The latter tempo is more akin to the French Basque version, but easier to count in fours as originally danced. The Basque version is accompanied by the *txistu*, a three-holed flute played with the left hand while the right beats the rhythm on a tabor or drum slung over the left shoulder.

Basque dancing is famous. In the 1960s I studied with the great scholar and doyen of Basque dancing, Juan Urbeltz, and his company Argia (Light). He told me that the distinguished French dancer and author of *Letters on Dancing*, Jean-Georges Noverre (1727–1810), had studied with the French Basques in the province then known as Soule (Basque: Zuberoa, Zuberus or Xiberoa), renowned for its traditions of dancing and singing, situated in the French Basque Country. I think it highly likely that during his visit to Soule Noverre learnt the Basque *gabota*, and that he later passed it on to the choreographer of the *Vestris Gavotte* in Paris. I shall come back to that.

Noverre's attraction to Basque dancing was noted in France by the dramatist Etienne Juoy. He wrote how Noverre and the French dancer and choreographer Jean Dauberval (1742–1806) were intrigued by an energetic Basque dance called *mouchico* performed to perfection by a large group of people dancing in an enormous circle while singing emotionally and movingly. The two men wanted to present this at the Opéra in Paris, but they did not know how to portray the national character of the Basques. It was not only the movement of the arms, legs or the body that achieved the character they wished to capture, but also the "soul" of the Basques.

The *Vestris Gavotte* first appeared in Grétry's opera *Panurge dans l'île des lanternes* with choreography by Maximillien Gardel among a series of dances that brought Act II to a close. The tune of the *Gavotte* was titled *Les Morlaques*, and was first performed by the French dancer Auguste Vestris (1760–1842, son of Gaetano Vestris), on January 25, 1785. It was said to be due to Auguste's interpretation of the dance that it subsequently became known as the *Vestris Gavotte*. My suggestion is that the *gabota* was passed from the Basques to Noverre, from him to Gaetano Vestris, and then to Auguste. The *Vestris Gavotte* and the *gabota* have such similar steps, floor patterns and choreographic composition that they can be danced to either score. The dance became immensely popular, especially in England, and it created a stir amongst dancers and teachers alike. It even became a requirement of the French military for the title Prévôt de danse.

The dance teacher, writer and notator Friedrich Albert Zorn could not praise the artistry of the movements of the dance highly enough. He stated: "The entire dance may be divided into various *enchaînements*, which can be used as exercises, and he who masters them will have received a thorough course in dancing." The dance was so revered that it was titled *La danse classique*.

Gaetano Vestris was greatly respected as a dancer by Noverre, and they collaborated often. In both the Basque *gabota* and the *Vestris Gavotte* the music is quite straightforward. The rhythm is the same, the melodies in each comparable. ➤

From top: the *Enseñaría*, the *Kantiniersa*, and the *Zamalzaina*. All drawings courtesy of the Spanish Dance Society.

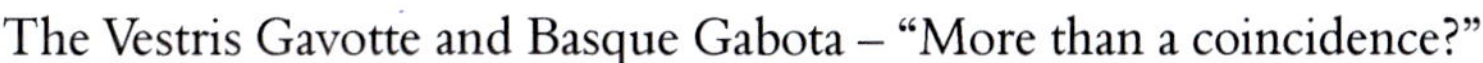

The Vestris Gavotte and Basque Gabota – "More than a coincidence?"

On my departure from San Sebastian, among the many gifts given to me was a copy of Iztueta's masterpiece of preservation of a dance style. It is printed on one page in Basque and on the opposite page in Spanish. The musicians allowed me to record the music so that I could be well prepared when we performed their dances. They played and danced every dance with me, fitting me into the group so that I could understand the configurations. They would not accept any remuneration for all the lessons and recordings. I discussed this with the young American Basque who said that I must not protest as it would upset them. It was their gift to me.

On the last night of my visit they gathered in costume and performed for me. I was sitting alone in that vast space, with the atmospheric mural as a backdrop. They performed every single dance that I had learned, 'so that you will have a visual picture and not forget them'. They had a ceremony afterwards and Juan made a farewell speech and gave me a treasured gift, among many others. All this bounty is forever indelibly impressed on my mind. I belong to them forever and it was an unforgettable experience.

They were a large company with many men and women, all dancing superbly. The men were practising ceaselessly and told me that they wanted to do nothing else, but had to work at other careers to earn a living. I went home laden with gifts, books on the dancing and music, notes and sketches that Juan had made for me to explain the dialects and dance props, as well as sketches that I had made of all the costumes which they had brought out for me to see.

On my return to Cape Town, a surprised customs official surveyed my baggage of a *txistu* or Basque flute, a drum, a tambourine and eight large wooden hoops which I carried slung round my neck. The hoops had been especially fashioned for me from chestnut wood. 'You cannot replicate the sound with other wood', I had been told. The customs official scratched his head and surveyed the scene. Suddenly his face brightened. 'You are from a circus', he announced, happy to have solved the puzzle.

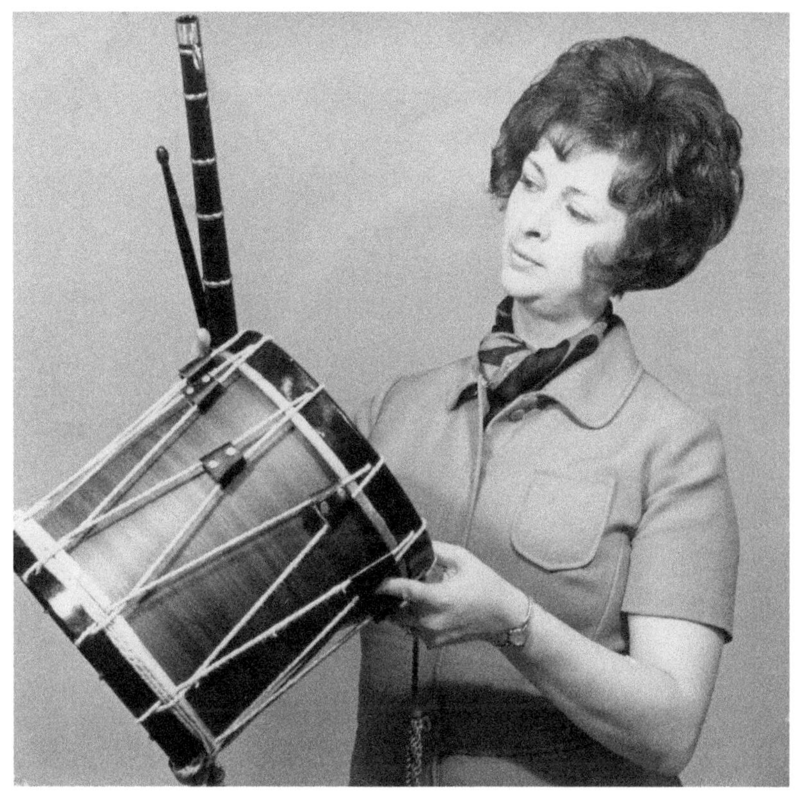

Marina with Basque drum and txistu (flute).

Years later I was able to welcome the *Argia* company on a stop-over in Washington DC to give a much appreciated lunch-hour performance at George Washington University's large Lisner Auditorium. On another occasion, as I mentioned in the Introduction, I was also able to welcome the Basque President who had come to meet the local Basques in Washington DC. As he stepped out of his car, to his surprise the Spanish Dance Society's Spanish Dance Theatre, accompanied by the Basque flute and drum, performed in Basque costumes the *Erreverentzia*, a dancer's welcome, and several other dances that I had learned from Juan Urbeltz and his company. What treasures they had given me. I thank them here for enriching my life.

16

South African Ballet Becomes Professional, 1964

Dulcie Howes worked diligently to get the government to subsidise the UCT Ballet Company, the oldest in South Africa. It led to all the provinces getting subsidies for their ballet, opera and theatre companies. In August 1965 the lives of artists in South Africa changed. For the first time funding was given to existing companies in the four provinces, with each company taking a typical bureaucratic title.

The Johannesburg company, Ballet Transvaal, became the PACT (Performing Arts Council of the Transvaal) Ballet Company. The Durban company in Natal became NAPAC Ballet Company. In the Orange Free State, where Frank Staff was eventually to stage such brilliant choreographies when he took on the artistic directorship, the company was called PACOFS. CAPAB Ballet, under Dulcie's directorship with David Poole as ballet master, had its acronym derived from the Cape Performing Arts Board, and was the former University of Cape Town Ballet Company, a name known all over Southern Africa and in Britain. South Africa being a bilingual country, all the names of course had Afrikaans equivalents. Visitors from abroad had no idea what these letters represented or how to pronounce them. The theatre and music companies had corresponding names.

For the first time I was well paid for the choreographies I created for the ballet, opera and theatre companies. My first commission for the CAPAB company was a trio, *España,* to music by Chabrier, on 8 March 1965. I choreographed a trio for two pretty girls, Ingrid Sebba and Joyce Paterson, charmingly costumed by Stephen de Villiers, together with Owen Murray. Owen was a pupil of Joy Shearer in Durban and they had studied together in Spain.

España (Chabrier), choreograhy Marina Keet. Ingrid Sebba, Owen Murray, Joyce Paterson.

In 1966 David asked me to choreograph *The Three-Cornered Hat,* one of Massine's ballets from the Diaghilev era, for Phyllis Spira and Gary Burne. I knew de Falla's music well and felt that it needed cutting if I was to do the choreography. Massine was a master choreographer, and mime was his forte. The moment I was able to cut the music it came into its own and was very popular. Keith Anderson designed a really inspired full set with overhead borders framing the stage. When we performed it with Maxine Denys, and at Maynardville with Hazel Acosta, both partnered by Owen Murray, this shortened version thrived. The first performance was on 9 December 1966.

Mercedes Molina undertook to choreograph this ballet for her Johannesburg company, and she phoned me to discuss her problems. I suggested that she cut the music. I recently read an article by Barbara Newman who found the same problem when watching a production of that ballet in Spain, and found it not succeeding.

I watched David Poole turn a brash, young, unbelievably talented Phyllis Spira into a dramatically moving and graceful ballerina, resembling Alicia Markova. Despite the adulation of the audiences, Phyllis told me that she felt very lonely when she returned to her empty flat. However, she later entered a happy marriage with Philip Boyd. He was also a dancer, but later in life he became a radio journalist and then a dance entrepreneur. While working for a Cape Town radio station he gave me my best interview ever – as a former dancer he knew which questions to ask.

David Poole also improved the company's mime. A queen mother in *Swan Lake*, a Drosselmeyer or Dr Coppélius and the characters in de Valois' *The Rake's Progress* were always works of understatement. Seeing other versions came as a shock after this. I really admired him in the theatre. We worked well together – when my work was not too interfered with.

Like Phyllis Spira, Gary Burne was also hugely talented. There is a biographical article about him in my book on ballet in South Africa. His physical beauty was matched by his charisma. He also had a great sense of humour, which came to the fore in his adored curtain calls. When recalled over and over, he would tease the audience and let the clamour grow. Then his hand would appear around the front of the curtain and slowly he would emerge to receive the delighted shouts and stamps – a great showman. Periodically he would take leave from the company to dance abroad for a while in order to, as he said, 'polish my halo'. When he visited us in Stellenbosch the locals would gape as he drove by in his open convertible car with his black Toulouse-Lautrec hat, and his black cape billowing behind him.

This was such an exciting time for the arts in South Africa. The Cape Province was far larger than the other provinces, which made touring more expensive, and yet it was originally given less funding than the others. However, Dulcie Howes drove a hard bargain. At first that was what the grant covered – touring losses. However, the Cape

Province also had the Dulcie Howes Trust Fund, and the company retained the right to perform as the UCT Ballet when they performed to mixed audiences, which was often. The company itself also remained multiracial. She was adamant about this and her elegant, good-looking husband, Guy Cronwright, was placed on the board.

Someone said, after reading the blurb on one of my books, 'Well, *my* family always came first'. 'So did mine', I replied. Once I discussed with the children whether I should stop working, and Vicky replied, 'Please don't, you always bring the theatre back with you and it is such fun'. It was possible because of the help, first from my indulgent parents, then from my very wonderful, caring husband Mikael, who babysat for my night rehearsals. Once the extraordinarily clever housekeeper Susie Adams came into our lives, there was not a worry in the world. She became part of the family and my best friend.

Susie had come in answer to an advertisement in the local paper. I was desperate and had just hired someone, about whom I was very dubious. When I opened the door and saw Susie there with her broad smile, I just knew that she was a delight. I had to tell her that I could not take her on because I was committed to someone already. I said, 'I want you to work for me', and she said, 'I want to work for you'. It was so amazing and so sad. Susie left and I had stupidly not asked for her address. When the other woman did not turn up to work, my search started and I eventually found her on a farm nearby and my life changed. She wanted to be a housekeeper and she was brilliant at it. I was free to work untrammelled at last. Susie lived in an apartment we had built for Mikael's mother when she came on a visit from Copenhagen. Our lives were idyllic in Stellenbosch.

With my morning university hours corresponding to the children's school hours it worked like clockwork. The children never suffered from my work, and my selfless mother was there to oversee things when I had to be away. Nicolai became an animator and has worked on my books, creating covers and the artwork and editing my Bolero School DVD. His amazingly loving and dedicated wife, Lorraine, cared for him during a life-threatening illness, in faraway Canada. The oldest of our three children, Vicky, is a several-times-over award-winning short story writer and teacher of creative writing at a London university. She is the contented, happy mother of two, married to a good-looking, supportive Welshman, Bill. Our oldest son Edmund is also very artistic and wanted to do architecture but was led into the related field of civil engineering. He now has a senior position in a Danish firm – and six children with his beautiful Danish wife, Pernille. I am very happy to say that my eight grandchildren are doing exceptionally well.

17

Spain Again, 1965

When Vicky was about four years old and Edmund about two-and-a-half, Mikael said one day, 'How would you like to go to Spain for three months?' 'How can you be so cruel to taunt me' I replied, 'Of course I want to go'. Mikael said that he had been asked by his former Swedish forestry firm to do a survey for them of eucalyptus resources in Spain. He would take leave of absence without pay from the university to accept this offer. Perhaps my mother could look after the children and I could join him? And that was what I did.

We had a wonderful time, starting in Madrid, then Seville during Holy Week and the Feria – and on to Lisbon and back to Madrid, while Mikael went to Galicia. I attended a lot of classes, and as usual Luisillo helped me to find people who knew the dances I was searching for (Chapters 18 and 19). Then he too went away and his wife, the beautiful singer María Vivo, and I had a lot of fun going out together.

When both our husbands were in Madrid, the four of us went out together and it was wonderful to have Luisillo discussing the dances at the tablaos which we went to. Mostly he would be recognised and they would dedicate a song or guitar piece to him. Luisillo was very highly strung and restless, like me. We went to the *Zarzuela* one night. He could not sit through it and spent most of the night pacing up and down in the passage outside our box. He told me a story about his absentmindedness. He had his six-year-old son Luisito with him when they parked in an enormous parking garage. On their return he could not find the car, it was getting dark and Luisito was exhausted. So he parked Luisito on the pavement and went on his own to look for the car. He was so thrilled to find it eventually that he leapt in and drove off. Suddenly, when he was almost home, he thought, *There is something missing. What have I forgotten*? Then it dawned on him and he tore back to the garage, and there on the pavement alone in the dark was little Luisito.

Luisillo and his manager Roberto Zafra were such great friends, more like brothers, and when one was with them, they provided many laughs. Roberto and the stage staff often went ahead of the company to set up the stage and unpack the costumes. In Brussels once he went to the theatre and was met by an effusive theatre manager who said, 'I have set up the curtains for you and I found a bottle for you'. There on the stage were curtains in red, green and gold hanging all round the stage, and in the centre on the table was an enormous bottle of papier mâché. Roberto, puzzled, had it all torn down and set up black curtains. Backstage they unpacked and hung out the ironed costumes. Seven o'clock and no Luisillo or company; 7:30, still no one, and the audience started to file in. Suddenly there was an irate Luisillo on the phone. 'Where are you?' he said. 'The audience is in already.' Roberto was at the wrong theatre. He tore down all the curtains, stuffed costumes in skips and was running out of the theatre, when the manager ran after him with the huge bottle. 'Your bottle, your bottle!' he shouted. Later Roberto found out that he had blundered into a temperance meeting.

The fun about them was that they had very quick brains and as you talked lightning repartee and humour flowed, and often we 'laughed till we dropped'. It is something Mercedes Molina and Rhoda Rivkind knew well, but others, like Bernice Lloyd, found Luisillo cold and heartless like when she was robbed of her pay cheque while on tour and he refused to lend her money; he was really careful about money and touring was expensive.

Rhoda Rivkind told me about an incident while she was in his company. They were always trying to economise. One economy which was forbidden was to cook their supper in the dressing room during the performance. That night it was a stew, stirred by anyone who did not happen to be performing in a ballet at that moment. However, during the finale, everyone was onstage in this ancient theatre. Suddenly there was the most tremendous crash in the wings. The stove, which was heavy with the stew pot, had crashed through the rotten beams of the upstage floor, which was also the ceiling of the stage, but it luckily fell in the wings. The delicious smell of stew wafted over the stage into the audience. All the dancers had one thought – *There goes our supper*. Anguished glances were cast towards the disaster. Luisillo, of course, saw matters differently.

Geoffrey Neiman tells how the company was about to leave for a Paris engagement. He was with Luisillo on the staircase leading to the basement rehearsal rooms in *Calle de las Huertas*, arguing for a raise in salary as he could not live from it, especially in expensive Paris. He poked Luisillo in the chest for emphasis, Luisillo lost his footing, hurtled down the stairs and broke his ankle. Geoffrey said laconically, 'To succeed, it seems that one has to be pushy', because after that incident he was to perform all the leading roles in Paris, and the salary was commensurate.

18

The Founding of the Spanish Dance Society, 1965

In 1965, encouraged by the Royal Academy of Dance examiner in Johannesburg Ivy Conmee, a group of Spanish dance teachers in South Africa launched the Spanish Dance Society (SDS), which became the International Spanish Dance Society as our work spread. Luis Pérez Dávila, known as Luisillo, was to have a great effect on Spanish dancing, especially in South Africa, because of his many visits with his company *Teatro de Baile Español*. The word '*teatro*', theatre, was very descriptive of his work. During a period of ten years the great Antonio and Greco also toured South Africa, but Luisillo went many times, starting a frenzied interest in this dance form.

Mercedes Molina, a Cape Town dancer whom Luisillo swept up out of Elsa Brunelleschi's studio in London, and nearly everyone else among the founders of the Spanish Dance Society, had at some time or another danced in his company. His influence was far-reaching. With his company he brought to London and cities around the world every aspect of Spanish dance's rich folklore encompassed in his choreographies. Years later I asked him why his company and those of Antonio, Greco and Mariemma, which presented this variety, had stopped touring. His reply was that the cost had become prohibitive. I dare say that the major London critics like Clement Crisp, Mary Clarke and Freda Pitt who had experienced those exciting glory days, mourn being served only flamenco today. The Maestro Antonio preceded those companies, setting the trend with his brilliant dancing and choreography. Geoffrey Neiman (Enrique Segovia) and Irena Campbell (Irina Monter) were soloists in his company.

Years later in London Mary Clarke phoned me from the *Dancing Times*: 'You have a fan – Michael Lipschitz. I received a letter saying that the 'flamenco only' seen in London should be rectified. He wrote, 'I was brought up in Cape Town on Marina Keet's programmes showing all of Spanish dance's variety'. She published his letter because she too wanted the variety.

The Spanish dance teachers Mercedes Molina (deceased) and Rhoda Rivkind, invited other teachers to join them in formatting the technique of all types of Spanish dancing into exercises and graded examinations, each culminating in one or more dances. These cleverly incorporated the steps taught for that examination. Gone was the old tradition of teaching a dance by rote. It was the cooperation of several knowledgeable Spanish dancers and teachers, unselfishly sharing ideas, which gave the Spanish Dance Society's method its great strength. It was a unique idea in the world of Spanish dance.

For me it started when the telephone rang in my Stellenbosch home. It was Mavis Becker, the Cape Town Spanish dancer. She had been asked by Mercedes Molina in Johannesburg to contact me to find out whether I was interested in joining them to develop a Spanish dance method of teaching, through an examination system like that of the RAD. I said that I was very interested because I knew from my university teaching that examinations set a time limit for the preparation of candidates, and that worked wonders. I explained that although I was very interested, I was about to leave to study in Spain, and gave her my address there.

The following story is known to many but here it is again for the uninitiated. A letter arrived for me in Madrid from Luisa Cortes in Johannesburg. It was written so precisely and pedantically that I imagined it written by a grey-haired old lady with her hair in a bun. We arranged that I would stop over in Johannesburg to stay with her and catch up with what had been done while I had been away. Imagine my surprise when an attractive young girl with red hair, wearing a bright floral dress and high-heeled shoes, bounced up to me – and it was Rhoda Rivkind; Cortes was her stage name. It was the start of a fifty-year working relationship, a lot of laughter, steaks and chocolate.

I stayed many times in her home to work on the syllabi, theory and history, paying my own way from the Cape by air. She would march up to the dining table where we worked, carrying a two-pound box of chocolates, and we munched our way through it as we worked. She would fall asleep over it, and Geoffrey (Neiman) and I would pull out the papers and continue working. When she woke up, she would retrieve them and we would continue till we dropped. Geoffrey, a pupil of Mercedes (Molina) who had been dancing in Spain under his professional name of Enrique Segovia in companies such as that of the great Antonio, had joined us after his return to South Africa. It was hard work but great fun. Geoffrey did not stand a chance with the chocolates. We had no money, but as my father used to say, 'We don't have money, but we do see life'.

I am amazed at our confidence. We just knew it was something wonderful that we had started. Once we were laughing so much while dancing *Sevillanas* together during a recording session using Rhoda's tape recorder, that the pianist walked out. Little did she know how hard we were working. There we were, utterly exhausted and reacting to that. Rhoda was hiccupping and I could not control my laughter long enough to say *Tanguillo* for the recording. The pianist's departure finished us off; we just collapsed laughing. We had reached the end of our strength for that day. She must have lost her patience at our antics. Many years later, when we were older and should have been wiser, I had just taught a tricky Mallorcan dance. Frustrated that people just could not understand its subtleties I said, 'Come on Rhoda, let's show them', and to the surprise of everyone watching we leapt around the studio waving our arms and 'sent it up', laughing all the way, Rhoda sometimes careering off in the wrong direction – she claims. A much better reaction than crying.

Many of us worked together on the practical dances and exercises, joined by the Cape Town Spanish dancers Deanna Blacher and Cynthia Rowe, and Mavis Becker when she returned from Luisillo's company. We went over what we had done before. Rhoda used to come and look over my shoulder and check the steps in my notes. I always notated every step in my notebook. Intrigued, Geoffrey also came to look over my shoulder and said, 'I also want a book like that'. And so the notated syllabus was born; it did away with arguments. I had to work hard at the notation because first I had to record the syllabus in my own shorthand and then

I had to rewrite it to make it intelligible for everyone to understand. I remember one day, lying in my passage at home in Stellenbosch, notebook in front of me, phone in my hand, going through Geoffrey's choreography of *Sacromonte* for him, which he wanted to check before teaching it. The telephone is the best invention in the world.

From a later date I have a photo of Rhoda standing next to me holding the first printed syllabus. We look like cats that had not only swallowed the cream but digested it. How we dared to go ahead with no finance is beyond me. We just never stopped to think. We paid our own air fares between Cape Town and Johannesburg and we stayed with each other. Perhaps the examiners also did so in the beginning. Once the examinations started they brought in a small income which we could use for travel. Through my teaching position at the Cape Town University Ballet School, and because of the interest and kindness of Dulcie Howes, who thoroughly approved of what we were doing, I managed to get the syllabi and theory printed at UCT. After all, they were important for the UCT dance students as well.

Marina and Rhoda with the first SDS syllabus.

João dos Santos was my Spanish/Portuguese pianist. He was recommended to me as a remarkably talented student at the university's College of Music, next door to the ballet school. He was later to transcribe, notate and record the music on cassette, and the Society printed it. He was a wonderful pianist and became an international concert pianist. Sadly, his recorded music is no longer used for examinations. On one occasion Mavis and I were examining together and as the music started Mavis shot up in her chair asking, 'Who is that playing?' I answered, 'João of course'. It was from an old recording still left over on that tape. His playing of the dances is sheer artistry. He had grown up hearing Spanish music played and sung by his mother, and he understood the ethos of the music and interpreted it correctly. Mavis said that her pupils had a hard time learning the dances he played because she never looked at them to give corrections; she just could not resist dancing to his beautiful playing. I have been told that it is a mono-recording but I have also been told that with modern technology that type of recording can be changed. João was very temperamental. When the students played their castanets badly timed to the music, he would leap to his feet, slam down the piano lid, sit on it, fold his arms and say severely, 'LISTEN to what Miss Keet says. Dance to the MUSIC!' Lack of musicality really hurt him – and me.

Marina's pianist João dos Santos.

I was the only one who had examined before. Ivy Conmee, however, who became president of the society, trained us in timing each examination,

UCT students in lecture-demonstration by Marina about the new syllabus.

how to examine and how to write a report. She also spent time doing mock examinations with each examiner and writing reports on their progress. Because of this we were utterly professional from the start. As we had all been professional dancers with experience of performing, the syllabus was geared to reaching a professional standard, led by Mercedes with her energy and determination. Geoffrey was a godsend, coming from the great Antonio's company, in refining the work for the male dancers. What a high standard was set at that time. Dancing has to be inspiring and exciting. We all examined each other's pupils. Soon we and our pupils went abroad and gradually the syllabus was spread beyond South Africa. The greatest satisfaction came from the Spaniards themselves, who valued the structured method instead of a haphazard approach.

During examination sessions, I watched pupils improve as they went from one examination to the next. I made my university students start with the primary examination to polish their basic technique and get feedback of value from someone else, the examiner, who was an experienced dancer and teacher. Once the correct basics are with the dancer, they are there forever, and they need have no worries when performing. On the other hand, retaining just one incorrect movement means that it too remains with them forever and is difficult to overcome. That is why a candidate should never be entered for more than one examination, only progressing to the next when the former has been correctly absorbed, otherwise the errors are carried forward to the next examination and the future of the student is on a shaky foundation. This can let a dancer down during a performance.

This means that the teacher has to set the class work inventively in order not to bore a candidate with grinding over the same work, but when necessary adding something different. Once a pupil understands the exercise correctly, it can be elaborated. For example, the candidate can do four stamps while turning, then stamping once across the other foot by not changing the weight. Thus: two stamps on place, then the third without changing weight, and the fourth putting the foot across the other one with a stamp. This releases the correct foot to repeat it alternately. So they have done four steps but with something new added for interest, etc. Every so often the teacher should return to running through the examination to remind them of the basic steps and sequence for the forthcoming examination session. My most experienced students found the primary examination the most difficult to do because it is so static and they were used to a greater challenge and movement. But it is of benefit to go back to basics.

The written feedback on reports from examiners is crucial. It supports what the teacher says or points out a weakness which may not have been noticed in a large class. The more senior the student, the more valuable even small nuances become. Vicki Kurland Ramos, now an examiner herself, was the first person to do the teachers' examination in Europe. 'What did you learn from this experience?' I asked her. She said, 'I learnt how important the reports were to me as a dancer as well as a teacher because I apply to my own dancing and teaching what the examiners wrote and I have improved immeasurably as a result'.

An encouraging word works wonders. After an examination session in Europe, the teacher asked me to conduct a class for her students. The pupils were very enthusiastic. She said, 'I see that you teach through encouragement'. I said, 'Of course'. She said darkly, 'Well, I don't'. So I replied, 'I feel sorry for your pupils'.

First teacher's examination in London, 1989: Perete Ramos, Shelley O'Donnell, Vicki Kurland, Virginia Brown, Louise Jeffcoate, Naomi Kurland, El Osito; seated: Marina, Mavis Becker, examiners.

El Garrotín, Nancy Heller, Nancy Sedgwick and Lourdes Elias. Photo Vic Cohen.

The association with Mavis Becker grew into a great friendship. For me her dancing was *real* dancing, with sensuous movements within the body, through the arms with great style, strength and charisma. Through the years I was able to refine these talents during rehearsals, having learnt from how David Poole moulded Phyllis Spira. Mavis is the main contributor to the flamenco section of the examination syllabus.

Rhoda Rivkind is a charming dancer and an excellent teacher. She and Geoffrey in their wisdom of maturity are giving the candidates such special attention, sharing their experience and knowledge. The candidates are being prepared carefully and lovingly through the written reports that the students take home with them – every nuance, every follow-through from one movement to another. The students and teachers alike understand how privileged they are to be given this gift of years of experience. Would that everyone could be that intelligently understanding.

These people are the backbone of the society and the hope for the future of our dancing skills. The teaching of whatever subject, from junior school forward, is the shaping of the future generations. It is an exciting act to shape the candidates into moulds that will set them on the right track for success. It is an honour to be a good teacher. It is the most difficult and underestimated profession in the world.

In 2015 the Spanish Dance Society celebrated its 50th anniversary worldwide, most spectacularly in Spain, where the organizer María Jesús García de Bayarri hosted a lavish celebration in the magnificent opera house, the *Palau de la Música*, in the beautiful city of Valencia, to which members came from all over the world. Teachers such as María Jesús and Mercedes Fernandez said that the syllabus had changed their lives. It is the most significant contribution to dance teaching to have come out of South Africa: a unique method and syllabus for the teaching of Spanish dancing in all its rich facets of classical *Escuela Bolera*, regional and flamenco dancing, with the addition of what is known as Stylised Spanish Dance, *Danza Estilizada.* This originated when *La Argentina*, Antonia Mercé, started performing Spanish dance steps to classical music, with great effect. Her parents, both dancers, had moved to Argentina, where she was born and grew up.

During the last fifty years the SDS method has spread from South

Africa to other countries and it is now also used in Spain, Britain, Greece, Italy, Malta, America, Australia, Thailand, Canada and Mexico.

Caracoles, Conchita del Campo in a Danza Estilizada, choreography by Pericet, music by Soler

Comments on the Spanish Dance Society by Irena Campbell (Irina Monter, former soloist with Antonio)

When I first learned about the Spanish Dance Society and its very valuable teaching syllabus and graded examinations to measure a student's progress and accomplishments, I was very impressed with the value of this teaching method. I felt very lucky that Dame Marina Grut had moved to Washington DC, and was established on the teaching faculty of the George Washington University Dance Department. The scope of the syllabus, with the many flamenco, bolero and regional dances taught, the graded exercises for castanet playing, the knowledge imparted on the theory, Spanish terms for the names of the steps, and choreographic construction of the dances, are all extremely valuable. The meticulous recorded music for each of the exercises and dances to be taught is also an extremely valuable contribution.

The music is available printed and recorded on CDs, both with piano music and excellent guitar and sung renditions, which is extremely helpful both for teacher and student. Also the possibility of having 'visiting examiners' to evaluate the students' progress and to provide examinations with Certificates awarded for each level from beginning through advanced technique and dances, is a wonderful opportunity for both students and teachers to receive advanced Spanish dance education. I have found that the syllabus and examinations are a wonderful tool for advancing the understanding and performance of all types of Spanish dance, through the written feedback for candidates and teachers to study the progress made by the candidate.

The Spanish Dance Society has teaching centres located in many countries of the world, including Spain where it has received enthusiastic acceptance.

Irena Campbell

50th anniversary celebration of the SDS in Valencia, hosted by Maria Jesus García. From left: Rhoda Rivkind, Geoffrey Neiman, Marina Keet de Grut, María Jesús García de Bayarri; flanked by her students. December 2015.

19

Luis Pérez Dávila (Luisillo)

I have already mentioned Luisillo, so important to Spanish dance in South Africa. He was born in Mexico in 1927 (some sources give 1925 and 1928) of Spanish parents. In the building where the family lived was a dance studio where he studied ballet and Spanish dance. We are told that he also did boxing when he was young, and he was certainly besotted with bullfighting. Juan María Bourio, in his book *Archivo de Baile Español,* tells that when Luisillo's teacher went to Mexico City to choreograph dances in the operas, the fourteen-year-old precocious boy accompanied him. He then returned home to repeat the dances in the area where he lived. His presentations came to the attention of an impresario. He was taken to New York where he joined the company of the beautiful Teresa Viera Morales, daughter of a Manchegan mother and a Canary Island father. They became famous in America as *Teresa y Luisillo*, performing in festivals in *Chateau de Madrid* in New York and *El Patio* in Mexico City. From there they joined the company of Carmen Amaya in 1946. He told me that Carmen had taught him 'everything he knew' about dance. He revered her. She took them to the *Champs Elysées* Theatre in Paris and the *Teatro Fontalba* in Madrid. In 1950 they toured Europe as *Teresa y Luisillo*, and in 1953 and 1954 they toured the world.

He enlarged his choreographies when he and Teresa split up their partnership and marriage. She remained in New York and he formed his *Luisillo y su Teatro de Danza Española.* Luisillo choreographed ballets such as *Luna de Sangre* (Blood Moon) which had a great effect on my own choreography. It was as riveting as Roland Petit's *Le Jeune Homme et la Mort.* But being set in Spain it was different, with a man entering holding a lantern to tell the tale. This was riveting theatre and was followed by his many other marvels of theatricality. His suites of regional dances were light, entertaining and showed the breadth and diversity of regional dances. He claimed that other choreographers copied his ideas, for example using shells rubbed together as an instrument in Galician dances, which was copied by Antonio. The use of shears to produce a clicking sound while the men danced, he claimed became thought of as part of the regional dance, but was his invention. Being innovative, he wished to extend his work theatrically.

He never totally managed to throw off the lure of the bullring. He insisted I go and see for myself. It took a lot of persuading until I at last accompanied him there. It was the first time in my life that I needed a drink. I was in total shock and felt really ill after a young bullfighter was gored and thrown by the bull. What had preceded this was also horrifying. I got up and ran out and Luis followed me and took me back to the hotel. He was mystified. I once was almost crucified when I argued about the cruelty of bullfighting with a famous musician who said that I shouldn't discuss it because I knew nothing of the historic aspect or the mystery – and then it was he who got up and left.

Years later Luisillo invited me to see the film he had made about death and a bullfighter who returns to the empty bullring to take his farewell. He had a ballet dancer, the lovely Aurora Pons, in the role of Death. It was filmed in a bullring in the heat of the day and the dancer was walking slowly down the spectators' steps towards the bullring and the lone bullfighter, dramatically fetching him to his fate.

Luisillo in South Africa

I met Luisillo the first time he came to South Africa in 1957. The next time he came I was invited to a party held for him but did not think that he would remember me. To my surprise he walked up and took my hand saying, 'Marina, how nice to see you'. I was so taken aback that

I poured the sherry all over his hand. He put his hand to his mouth, tasted the sherry and said, 'A very good vintage'.

On his visit to Cape Town in 1968 Luisillo asked me to stand next to him at the back of the Alhambra Theatre and we surveyed the scene of the orchestra overflowing the edges of the small orchestra pit to sit at the audience level on either side. He turned to me, 'Ontidy, no?' I said that nothing could be done about it. But Luisillo could. Saying, 'We see', he walked purposefully down towards the stage with his coat draped over his shoulders and flapping behind him. That night the musicians were all neatly tucked into the orchestra pit, with violinists perilously striking their bows past colleagues' noses and trombonists leaning back and playing their instruments to the skies. But they were all neatly and tidily inside the orchestra pit!

One year his impresario went bankrupt during his Southern African tour. Luisillo was in a terrible situation and had to make a decision, whether to pack up and go home or honour his contract in Cape Town. He phoned me from Mozambique to ask whether I would fly up to East London over the weekend, learn parts in his ballet *Bolero,* to Ravel's music, and teach them to my students. They could then be integrated into the company temporarily, rehearse the ballet with the other dancers, and perform it at the Alhambra. He could then send half his company home and reduce the cost. What could I say but yes; he was always so kind and helpful when I needed dances. I flew to East London, watched the matinée and turned pale when I saw what I had to learn. It was a series of very complex duets, of which I had to learn four, the men's roles and the finale. He started directly after the performance and taught me three of the duets. I learn quickly, and afterwards spent late Saturday night notating them, and then at 6am I went to the stage and rehearsed. By 10am I knew them thoroughly. 'Good morning Marina', he said. 'I don't want to use those sections. I will teach you new ones'. I nearly fainted.

I was to fly home after the Sunday matinée, when he called me into his dressing room. There were some boys and girls of the company waiting. 'Now', he said, 'we teach you part of *Rapsodia Español*'. But this time I said no. I only had two weeks to teach the *Bolero* to students, not professionals, and then rehearse it with no company to fit into.

We joined the company when they arrived. Dulcie Howes had given her permission for them to rehearse in the large studio at UCT. We were waiting when Luisillo swept in, late. He introduced us to the company and said, 'Mrs Grut knows, and will take the rehearsal'. He swept out again accompanied by Mr Clarke, the Alhambra Theatre manager, and his young beautiful dancer wife. There stood the Spanish men leaning against the UCT ballet barre with folded arms, daring me to start. Hazel Acosta saw that the situation was drastic, and she said, 'I'll help you'. We leapt into action. We had that rehearsal and a stage rehearsal before the show. They were all good troupers and the performances were a great success.

Marina's UCT ballet students join Luisillo in his ballet Bolero.

However, the problems were not over yet. One of the male students came up to me after a performance to say goodbye. I said, 'But we still have the last performance to do and you undertook to do it'. He said, 'Yes, and it was a lot of fun, but I have my plane ticket booked for home'. So much for Dulcie's motto, 'Only death is an excuse'. Of course Luisillo was in flames. I phoned my friend, pianist and ballroom dance partner Enrique Breytenbach in Stellenbosch. There was one day to get to Cape Town, learn the part and then perform. It took some pleading. He would not let me down. We fitted him into a costume and we started to teach him. Instead of being grateful Luis was upbraiding him, until I said, 'There is no one else, the other students have all left for the holidays. Let's get on with it; he has never danced Spanish in his life and he does not want to. He is doing you a favour'. Poor Enrique, but he and the company were marvellous. However, there was more to come. During our theatre rehearsal someone ran in to tell Luisillo that one of his company's girls was very ill and could not dance. Joy Shearer, who was on a visit from Durban, had been watching the rehearsals, so she understood how the ballet was constructed. She offered to dance the part and the company had to rehearse practically till the curtain went up. They adjusted a costume to fit her and the performance took place. All is well that ends well, as they say, but Enrique was close to a nervous breakdown. To help Luisillo I had filled two buses with audience members from Stellenbosch.

Mikael invited Luisillo and his principal dancer to join Dulcie Howes and Joy Shearer for lunch at a lovely restaurant up in the mountains near Constantia. We were to go in our and Dulcie's cars. I thought they could get to know one another. Mikael and I froze as we heard Luisillo walk around the hotel knocking on bedroom doors saying, 'Mikael and Marina are asking everyone to come for lunch'. In those days there were no credit cards. We had brought along enough money for the six of us but not enough for a company, nor was there any transport for the others. Luckily they all mumbled sleepily that they wanted to sleep late. He came back and apologised, and we breathed again.

Luisillo once said to me that he had two great wishes. One was to own two jaguars (the animal, not the car) and the other was to have an ostrich egg. The next time he came I decided to fulfil the latter rather than the former because jaguars were beyond me. It was the most difficult job to find the egg but finally I did and met him at the airport and gave it to him. The *Burger* newspaper's photographer was there and loved it, delightedly snapping us. Luis took the egg home to Madrid and said that he had made an omelette and fed twelve people from it.

Marina presenting an ostrich egg to Luisillo at the airport in Cape Town in 1966. Photo: Jasper Kruse, Die Burger.

20

Misa Flamenca, 1971

Our Stellenbosch neighbour Elaine Aucamp designed my beautiful Goya costumes for dances of that era, the turn of the 18th and 19th centuries, which I had brought back from Spain. I had learned those dances from the knowledgeable Carmen Gordo at the *Coros y Danzas* group in Madrid. They were part of a series of such groups set up by Franco as a clever way to keep folk dancing in Spain foremost in people's minds. Art is very political. Sometimes it works the other way and dictators forbid some dances and music which create separatist feelings, as with the Catalan *Sardana*.

Elaine brought a new dimension to dance costuming, and those costumes are still used in America. On the 50th anniversary of the *Coros y Danzas* in 1999, I was invited to their remarkable celebratory concert in Madrid, where there were members of the Spanish dance elite in the audience, such as Mariemma. At the end, to my great surprise, I heard them thank me from the stage for my presentations of Spanish dance. I was deeply moved by the totally unexpected honour.

In Stellenbosch Elaine had her three children at the same time as each of our three were born – all at the same hospital. She blamed me for her pregnancies! She said, 'I shall just ignore it and it will go away'. Nevertheless, they are all adored, and my son Nicolai and her son Armand grew up together like brothers. My friends worked hard for me. How lucky I was to be surrounded by such talented, supportive and generous artists. My mornings usually started with taking Nicolai and Armand to school before I left for the university in Cape Town. They were considered too young to go on the school bus. Sleepy little Armand always stood waiting for us on the pavement, clutching his small suitcase, looking like a tired businessman going to his doom.

Elaine and Emile Aucamp were both at the HB Thom Theatre which was part of Stellenbosch University drama department. Elaine was in charge of the costume department and Emile was in charge of décor, lighting and management of the theatre. He designed the most dramatic and inspired lighting for my ballet *Misa Flamenca* (Flamenco Mass). I was excited to accept the contract when David Poole asked for a new Spanish ballet for the CAPAB Ballet Company with the words, 'Thrill me, Marina'. I knew exactly what I wanted to do: a flamenco mass. Also for the first time in my life I was being paid well for the work I did for CAPAB. David Poole was very good about that.

Not long after that, Mikael came home one day and said, 'I have been offered a very good job overseas during the university holidays but if I take it I won't be able to help you at home during that time. Can you still cancel your programme for CAPAB?' 'I can't possibly do that', I replied. Our wonderful housekeeper Susie then appeared in the doorway. 'I heard all that', she said. 'You need not cancel your show. I will stay here day and night when you need me.' And she was true to her word. A friend indeed.

I wanted to portray the evocative feeling of each part of the mass in dance, not tell a banal story about churchgoers etc. I always have lighting in my mind as I choreograph each ballet, and Emile was able to bring this to theatrical fruition. I am not religious and I am not a Catholic, but the instructions to each part of the mass given to me by a Jesuit priest from the local Stellenbosch monastery led me into the mystery of the Catholic mass. That and the costume designs and drama of the three crosses suspended over the stage, designed by Stephen de Villiers from the Michaelis School of Art at UCT, fused together to produce dramatic results. It contributed greatly to the amazing success that this ballet was to have. Like our other productions it attracted audiences and produced sold-out performances. An extra matinée was offered and although tickets to only the lower part of the house were for sale the rest of the house had to be opened – unheard of at a lunch-hour performance.

Ritual grandeur of the Mass in ballet

THE FIRE of Anadalusia and the ritual grandeur of the Roman Catholic Mass were combined by Marina Keet in Misa Flamenca, a moving ballet of great beauty, which had its premiere at the opening of CAPAB Ballet's new season at the Nico Malan Opera House last night. Cape Town S. Africa September 1971

"I never thought I would see Spanish dance so well presented at the other end of the world."

García Asensio, Conductor

Marina's Spanish ballet Misa Flamenca in Cape Town in 1971, and excerpt from review.

While I was still planning the ballet, Stephen de Villiers asked me whether I had ideas for the *Sanctus* section of the mass. I said that I wanted to bring in the folk element of peasant women drawing up from the back the top skirt of their dress forward over their heads like a shawl. He said, 'You must also use a child, and I know which child'. He was referring to my daughter Vicky, who was then ten years old. Thus she arrived from backstage, walking through the large trellis gates, slowly across the raised section of the stage, down onto the diamond-shaped dais which he had designed, extending forward from the raised stage. Stephen de Villiers told me that he had taken instruction to become a Catholic. The theatricality of the rituals had appealed to him but eventually the dogma turned him away. However, his knowledge made him able to bring theatrical symbolism to the costumes. He was drawn, as I was, to the ballet's mysticism through the music. He was the perfect choice as designer. The Jesuit monk who taught me the gestures we used for the priest was also perfect in fitting it all together. We worked so well together, lost in this experience of something beyond the norm. The role of the priest was performed by John Simons, who joined Vicky on the dais. From the wings came the sound of finger cymbals that I had added for effect, and the women came from either side to dance on the front section of the stage. I used Mallorcan steps and low rolling arm and wrist gestures for their limping dance and it juxtaposed the flamenco dancing. It was a theatrical and moving moment. Audiences were as drawn into it as we all were. This was followed by a rousing regional *Verdiales* with castanets and flying ribbons, and the ballet ended on a happy flamenco.

Vicky told me when she was an adult that she had been terrified while waiting for her entrance. She was not supposed to be alone but the people who were meant to be with her never appeared. There she was in the dark, with the vast backstage area in stygian darkness behind her. And she never complained.

One great advantage of the Nico Malan Opera House, where CAPAB performances were held, was its amazing facilities. The stage could be raised to several levels and it could also be tilted. The sound could be projected from several vantage points. I used this with great effect to surprise. Suddenly a singer's voice – because this was flamenco – could be heard from the back of the theatre behind the audience.

Occasionally it was projected from the corners instead of from everywhere in the auditorium. I decided to raise the back level for a dramatic entrance by Hazel Acosta traversing it, pulled with a shawl by two men dancing backward towards a single spotlight, changing hands to face forward for an exciting exit offstage and appearing suddenly lower downstage. There the darkened stage was then lit to show all the men kneeling, waiting to join in her dance. She danced alone among them a slow refrain, while they responded with a stamped percussive one. Mavis Becker's solo was a *Zapateado* in a white dress with a long train.

One performance of *Misa* terrified me. David Poole and I were watching it from the back row of the auditorium. We saw the three huge crosses that were suspended over the stage slowly start to sag in the middle over the dancers. I was so shocked that I shook and the whole row shook with me. Leaping to my feet, I picked up the skirts of my long dress and started to run to the backstage area. I had to leave that part of the building, go outside and cross the road to reach the backstage. As I ran I heard them announce over the Tannoy: 'All theatre staff from all the theatres to go at once to an emergency on the Opera House stage'. I reached the stage and David joined me in the wings. We watched the three heavy, enormous crosses slowly realign themselves in the original slanted position, levitating across the stage. David put his arm around me and felt me trembling. 'Don't worry', he said, 'they are fixed so that they cannot fall on the dancers. I thought you knew'.

The first performance of *Misa Flamenca* was on 1 December 1971 at the Nico Malan Opera House in Cape Town. The *Cape Times'* ballet critic Eve Borland wrote about it:

> 'The new work, *Misa Flamenca,* choreographed by Marina Keet, is a profoundly spiritual ballet of great beauty. In a traditional yet theatrical manner, through the glorious music of Andalusian folk tunes, arranged for guitars, solo voice and choir, five sections of the mass celebration is depicted. Miss Keet, using as guest artistes the fine Spanish dancers Deanna Blacher, Cynthia Rowe, Mavis Becker and Hazel Acosta, together with an excellent corps of twenty-six expertly led by Owen Murray, Michael Wright, Eugene Christensen, Basil

> Poole, Elizabeth Triegaardt and Roberta McKenzie, has created a work of excitement and artistry unlike anything in Spanish dance ever seen in Cape Town before…
>
> Using a child, the gentle and musical Vibeke Grut, as the symbol of purity, innocence, peace and serenity for the Sanctus, was a perfect touch after the dramatic tension created by the Credo… The lighting, devised by Emile Aucamp, is so beautiful as to leave one in wonderment, and the glowing richness of the costumes and magnificent simplicity yet grandeur of Stephen de Villiers' décor combined with artistic staging, makes this work one of the finest that the CAPAB company has ever presented.'

A congratulatory letter arrived from a Welsh critic who had happened to be visiting South Africa. She wrote how moved and impressed she had been by *Misa Flamenca* and she regretted that such an artistic event would not get a wider public. She had submitted an article about it to a British ballet publication but the editor could not publish it because of the apartheid boycott.

The UCT Ballet School and the CAPAB Ballet Company did not practise discrimination, and my ballet had dancers of mixed race. In fact, several members of the ballet school staff were of mixed race, as was David Poole himself. However, CAPAB did receive funding from the government, and the South African government at the time did practise a policy of apartheid. In the end it was the boycott that brought down apartheid, and without bloodshed, with the wise Afrikaner politician FW de Klerk as prime minister negotiating with another man of wisdom, Nelson Mandela. They were jointly awarded the Nobel Peace Prize.

On a later occasion my ballet *Fiesta Manchega* (19 December 1972) was on the programme with *Misa*. I had used the music of a Spanish *zarzuela,* or light opera, for that ballet, cutting the music to suit my choreography. At our final dress rehearsal I was called aside by the Cape Town music enthusiast Hans Kramer. He said, 'This is our visiting conductor from Spain, García Asensio, and he would like to say a few words to you'. I felt my knees go weak. I had to sit down on one of the seats as I thought he was going to heavily criticise my efforts. Some

Spaniards can't believe that non-Spaniards can perform their dances, although many of the greatest exponents of Spanish dancers have been foreigners – you don't have to be German to play Beethoven. However, Asensio took my hand in both of his and said, 'I want to thank you for what you have done. I never thought that I would have to come to the other end of the world to see Spanish dance so beautifully presented'. I felt faint but managed to get to my feet and have a brief conversation with him. The rest of the rehearsal passed as though in a dream.

In March 1972 I produced a Spanish dance programme at the Little Theatre in Cape Town. Three years later, to celebrate the 10th anniversary of the Spanish Dance Society, I presented a lecture demonstration at the Little Theatre. Participants were eleven SDS teachers including Mavis Becker, Hazel Acosta, Sherrill Wexler and their pupils.

21

UCT Ballet School Performs in Lausanne, 1972. Other foreign interludes: Madagascar, Burundi, New Zealand

Meanwhile at the UCT Ballet School preparations were going ahead for our visit to the Fourth International Festival of Youth Orchestras in Lausanne, Switzerland. The performance was scheduled for Friday 5 August 1972. There was no theatre large enough available in Cape Town to accommodate the large company that was going to tour the ballets, so it was rehearsed in the HB Thom Theatre in Stellenbosch. There Emile Aucamp from the theatre's staff did the lighting and assisted with the décor and staging, Pip Marshall acted as administrator to assist Dulcie Howes, and Dudley Tomlinson taught the daily ballet classes. I was to stage my Spanish ballet *Fiesta Manchega*, and David Poole was to stage his and Frank Staff's ballets.

David's thirty-minute ballet for the occasion, *Le Cirque* to JS Bach's Suite No. 3 in D Major, was set in a circus ring to a contemporary theme about three groups of clowns and a bureaucratic ringmaster. It had a definite political message that struck a chord with the audience. Staff's *Peter and the Wolf* was great fun. My contribution was a Spanish dance ballet with castanets, set to enjoyable regional music from a light opera. This was one of my Spanish ballets which had delighted the visiting Spanish conductor García Asensio in Cape Town. The ballet told two stories: a romance and an amusing lovers' quarrel. The mixed race dancers also struck a chord; blond Izak Coetzee was later to dance in the Birgit Cullberg Swedish company, and Abdullah Patten won the first Cecchetti medal in Johannesburg.

UCT students in Marina Keet's Fiesta Manchega in Lausanne.

The thirty specially selected students shared a chartered aircraft with a junior orchestra of the South African Broadcasting Corporation, travelling from Johannesburg on 17 July to Zurich and returning home on 7 August. Dulcie Howes, in a frank newspaper interview, voiced her disappointment that it was not the professional company performing abroad. That had always been her dream, she said. David Poole could not pluck up the courage to take the professional company outside South Africa. He made several attempts but always backed down. It takes a lot of bravery to step out of the cocoon you build for yourself, and be counted. They could have had great success with Frank Staff's brilliant and diverse ballets.

Dulcie Howes was very nervous about not knowing French, and David had his work cut out to try to keep her calm. He said to me, 'Let this be a lesson to us Marina, never to become like this'. But Dulcie Howes' bravery won the day, and the whole trip and performance were a triumph. As she said in an interview, it was an unforgettable chance for our students to meet 1,500 other students from Holland, France, Japan, Canada, Australia, the USA and Yugoslavia, to exchange ideas and watch them perform. They became particularly attached to the dancers from Boston and cheered each other's performances. The aim of the festival was to foster international understanding and in this it succeeded. Many donations in the Cape made this huge undertaking possible. Neither Dudley nor I could sleep during the flight. Dulcie Howes wrote thank-you letters all night.

We arrived home with praise from the ballet critic of Lausanne's largest newspaper *24 heures:* 'It would be a miracle to describe in just a few lines the freshness and youth which this South African ballet company has brought – this performance which comes from the other end of the world surprised me with the qualities of gentility and charm. The quality of this evening is that it maintained its youthfulness and enriched the festival as a whole. Last night I watched dancers, and it warmed my heart.' (Translated by *The Sunday Times*, 6 August 1972.)

I was able to visit one of Mikael's charming relations, the Reverend Nicolas de Haller, in his beautiful chalet up in the mountains. I have a photo, standing in front of it, holding Dulcie Howes' huge bouquet of the longest-stemmed red roses I have ever seen. With her usual generosity she gave them to me after the performance, to give to him. Those are the moments one remembers.

Frank Staff's *Peter and the Wolf* set to Prokofiev's music is a delightful ballet with humorous moments. I have already told (Chapter 2) the story of how Prokofiev had given Staff the right to do a ballet to this music in London during the Second World War. Staff was given special leave from the Argyle and Sutherland Highlanders regiment in which he was then serving. We often wonder whether he met Mikael's father who was also a member of that regiment during the war. There was an amusing incident when he and another Danish member of the regiment, both wearing Scottish kilts, were in a restaurant in England talking Danish together. The waitress said, 'Please excuse me for eavesdropping but I have never heard Gaelic spoken before'. The poor woman had to be disillusioned. Later in the war my father-in-law attained the rank of major but that was on Mountbatten's staff in the Far East.

Marina holding Dulcie Howes's bouquet at Mikael's family's chalet outside Lausanne, 1972. Photo: Hermione de Haller.

Other foreign interludes: Madagascar, Burundi, New Zealand

As this chapter is about foreign travel, perhaps this is as good a place as any to mention my visits to Madagascar, Burundi and New Zealand, spread over many years. My husband Mikael was senior lecturer in forest economics at the University of Stellenbosch. I took my role as a forester's wife seriously, and kept a notebook on the subject. In 1969 Mikael was a consultant in Madagascar for the Food and Agriculture Organisation (FAO) of the United Nations in Rome. I and our two older children who were then eight and six years old (I was pregnant with the third) joined him there for six months. Before we left our home in Stellenbosch their teachers told me what school work they would be missing, so that I could teach it to them. It was a fascinating visit – charming people and a very interesting country. The music is so melodious and the customs fascinating. People are buried in mausoleums above ground, and every few years the bones are removed, swathed in white cloth and carried around in a ceremony called 'the airing of the bones'.

Later, when Mikael worked for the World Bank in Washington, I accompanied him on two of his work-related trips, one to Burundi and the other to New Zealand. Mikael said that I would be a good forester: I advised the Burundians not to plough up and down the steep slopes but to do contour-ploughing so as to reduce soil erosion, and I told the New Zealanders that they could improve the efficiency of forest fire extinction by helicopter if they used two water scoops instead of one, so that one could be filled while the other was being emptied onto the fire. That was my short but, according to my husband, glorious career as a forester. Many years later a waitress said admiringly to Mikael, after I had justifiably rejected a whole series of tables where she wanted us to sit, until we finally found the right one, 'Your wife is just like a general'!

22

Dulcie Howes Retires, 1972

One day Mikael dropped me off at the ballet school and I suggested that he 'pop in and say hello to Dulcie'. We reached her office, where the door was always open to welcome anyone who needed her attention. I knocked and cautiously entered, to see her prostrate over her desk, her head cradled on her arms. She looked up, tears pouring down her cheeks, and said, 'God has sent you; please come in and shut the door'. She said that David Poole had just left, after delivering an ultimatum when she asked him to take over the company as artistic director. She felt that only in his hands would the company survive after her, in the way she wished it to. She had intended staying on as principal of the school but he insisted that he would only take over if he had both posts, at the school and the company. She knew she was trapped and could not say no. In one fell swoop he had destroyed her. I remembered Mary Skeaping warning me when I was to return to Cape Town from Stockholm. She said, 'You are no longer a student and Poole will treat you very differently now. You may be seen as a threat'. But that took some years to materialise.

Dulcie and David seemed to have come to some compromise and she remained for three more years as head of the school, retiring in 1972. The university gave her a glorious ceremony at the Little Theatre, attended by people from far and wide who had been associated with the school, including past and present pupils, showing the high esteem in which she was held. Pamela Chrimes arranged with great taste a *défilé* with all the pupils from the youngest to the oldest filing before Howes, dancing and making their obeisances. Sir Richard Luyt, the principal of the university, thanked her on behalf of staff and students. A farewell gift, a portrait with an excellent likeness of her, painted by Richard Broadby, was presented to her by Carol Shapiro. In my book *The History of Ballet in South Africa* I say that the atmosphere at the champagne party afterwards was more like a reunion than a farewell. However, at the launch of my book in 1981, the photograph of David Poole and Dulcie Howes looking at my book shows a sprightly David Poole and a strained Dulcie Howes.

When Poole became principal of the school, I had to put the ballet history course – which Howes said the university had been so pleased with – on a back-burner and go back to a simpler course with question-answer examination papers. Only when Elizabeth Triegaardt took over was it brought to fruition and developed for the students' great benefit as a degree course, including also an academic subject like English, presented together with the existing ballet diploma course, as a choice. The syllabus of the Spanish Dance Society was also included.

Poole and Triegaardt were later made professors.

23

Presenting South Africa's Best Spanish Dancers

'*Standing ovation*, loud whistles and calls for *more* by Capetonians on Wednesday night was a fitting tribute to an evening of high entertainment and skilful dancing of the Spanish Dance Programme by Marina Keet at the Nico Malan' (my italics). Thus wrote the *Cape Times* critic Michelle Maree in her review of my show *Fiesta Española*, on 12 February 1974 – many of my productions had their first performances during the summer months from December to February because that was the main tourist season at the Cape. Maree's review was reflected in the other newspapers. And she continued:

> 'The very accomplished Mercedes Molina is an exuberant and very vital dancer, and her strong talent for mime made her a firm favourite with the audience. Throughout the evening her partnership with Enrique Segovia displayed a marvellous blend of grace and taut control, and readiness to incorporate further interpretation to their dancing.
>
> *Patio Andaluz*, the flamenco section, contained some superb dancing. Antonio Salas, a polished dancer of great style, had a hypnotic effect on the audience in executing wonderfully rippling *zapateado*, and I enjoyed tremendously his *Seguiriyas*

> with Mavis Becker, a more self-contained dancer, impressive technically and projecting a very pleasing charm. Hazel Acosta was greeted with gasps and cheers but her *Mirabras* did not give her the possibility to show off her expertise. Emilio Acosta, in a *Farruca*, admirably sustained a lengthy *zapateado* which exerted a tremendous amount of discipline and energy from the dancer.'

This *Fiesta Española* was another big production of Spanish dance that David Poole asked me to create for the CAPAB Ballet. I had divided the programme into two sections. In the first half, titled *Plaza España,* I used the Nico Malan theatre stage on three levels, building a town around the edges, with a church centre back on the top level from where Deanna Blacher opened the scene, entering through the church door to perform a stately Galician dance. Michelle Maree wrote:

> 'The variety of colourful traditional dances were very well performed by CAPAB dancers and others, the sheer buoyancy of their dancing added to an infective *joie de vivre,* making the whole spectacle of the *Plaza España* of the programme a delight. Joined by Dudley Tomlinson, a Cecchetti-trained dancer and teacher from UCT, who added his professional bravura, and Lorna Levy's vivacity dancing with him added joy and charm. Another former Luisillo company member, Sherrill Wexler, added her Spanish dance expertise.'

All the regional dancers in the groups could be seen on the three levels. There was no 'back row' where they were hidden. It delighted dancers and the audience, and it was 'good theatre'. The Andalusian regional *Verdiales,* with long ribbons waving overhead and around, with crackling castanet rhythms and skirts flying as the girls jumped, turned and passed partners, made a rousing finale for the whole company. This was a contribution from Deanna Blacher and Sherrill Wexler who had learned the dance from Juanjo Linares, from whom Sherrill took her stage name Charo Linares.

After the intermission came the *Patio Andaluz* flamenco section. The front curtain remained closed. In front of the curtain were archways and the flamenco performances took place on the front apron, which was usually lowered to form the orchestra pit. This time the dancers were brought up on this semi-circular area, seated at tables playing cards, chatting and knitting in excitingly close proximity to the audience, who clapped and shouted their surprised appreciation as the stage was raised before them – guitarists, singers and dancers leaping into action.

Together with Mercedes Molina and Enrique Segovia (Geoffrey Neiman), the guest artists from Johannesburg, we had invited another guest artist as well, a handsome Spaniard from Seville, Antonio Salas. He was to partner Marina Lorca (Mavis Becker). Also performing were Capetonians Hazel Acosta and her husband, the Gypsy dancer Emilio Acosta, who had settled in Cape Town after a Luisillo company tour. This made a formidable group of top flamenco dancers. When the first announcement appeared in the press and the season was sold out by the second day, a friend phoned me to say, 'Do you realise that you are a very brave girl to put your head in the lion's mouth?', referring to possible professional jealousies.

Some years earlier I had persuaded the Cape Town Spanish dancers who taught in Cape Town to join with me and present a really high standard of Spanish dancing. This was before *Misa Flamenca*. They were, in alphabetical order by surname: Hazel Acosta who had also stopped over from Luisillo's company with her husband Emilio; Mavis Becker, stage name Marina Lorca; Deanna Blacher; and Cynthia Rowe. They drew such enthusiastic audiences that they could see the advantage of joining forces instead of 'going it alone'. I was working in several theatres and could offer them this chance of displaying their artistry. David Poole provided CAPAB's backing for this venture, and without his encouragement and enthusiasm it could not have been achieved. We also had Owen Murray from CAPAB Ballet joining the guests with his Spanish dance experience. Night after night, the audiences and dancers had a whale of a time, and I took three months to recover from the whole experience.

In conjunction with these very successful performances, and using all the principal dancers from the show, I also presented a lecture demonstration at the UCT's Beattie Theatre to an ecstatic audience of 3,200 people.

Geoffrey Neiman and Mercedes Molina. Photo: Gyenes.

What came before *Fiesta Española*, at our last dress rehearsal of the *Plaza España* section, needs telling. The finale started with one of the soloists, and when a second one entered and joined in, the first one stopped and said, 'Off, off', with a dismissive gesture of her hand. The second one said, 'Nobody except Marina says "Off, off" to me!' Dudley Tomlinson was standing beside me and I said, 'What do I do now?' He said, 'Call a tea break'. I shouted 'Tea break' and the delighted dancers trooped off, after just having trooped on. We sorted out the problem, caused by a missed rehearsal where sequences had been changed. My husband said that my job was like that of a lion tamer.

In the flamenco section I thought that, with Emilio able to ride, I could bring him on riding a horse with a pretty girl seated behind him and the company entering doing *palmas* (hand clapping), with singer and guitarist walking on playing. But David said, 'No horse'. So I had a think and came up with a solution that 'wowed' the audience, namely using the orchestra pit as described above. At the audience's reaction on opening night, David Poole, who was standing beside me at the back of the auditorium said, 'Aren't you glad that I said no to your wretched horse?'

The first hurdle was to allocate dressing rooms, as there was only one star green-room. In order not to have to choose, I said that the oldest could have it. Nobody stepped forward. So I said, 'Then I suggest we give it to our guest from Johannesburg, Mercedes Molina'. Nobody wanted to be difficult about that.

Hurdle number two was the *sevillano* Antonio Salas. He went to David and said, 'I want to recite a Spanish poem'. David said severely, 'The audience is English-speaking and won't understand a word. No poetry. This is a dance programme'. At the dress rehearsal we came on to the stage to check that all was well, to find a rostrum centre stage between the arches placed there for the flamenco scene. Puzzled, David called the stage manager to remove it. We went and took our seats in the auditorium. As the lights came on, the podium was back in the centre and on it was Salas, spouting forth in Spanish. David shouted, 'LIGHTS!', and podium and Salas were removed without so much as a murmur.

Next, Emilio wanted to dance the last solo. I granted his wish but said, 'I know you Emilio, you will want to change costume and you will delay the show, and the excitement which has built up will die down and drop. If you agree to stay in your costume, you can dance last'. At the dress rehearsal, after Emilio had finished dancing and after his exit, there came a long pause. David Poole muttered, 'I know what he is doing'. For rehearsals there were steps to give access from the auditorium onto the stage. On the stage were the guitarist and the singer. They fled as David gave a roar and plunged up the stairs to murder Emilio, who appeared ashen, in a new costume. David said in a low voice, far more frightening than his roar, 'You heard Miss Keet say 'No costume change'. So get back in your other costume and we will continue, and don't you dare disobey an order again'.

The lighting changes were all timed automatically once the show started. So each solo's first change was carefully signalled to the electrician. In his solo, Emilio said that he would give a *llamada,* a call using a loud stamp or clap. But how was the electronics engineer to know when at one of the performances Emilio changed his stamp to finger clicks? I realised that all the lighting would be wrong from there on – so once again I had to 'up skirts and fly', this time to the lighting box.

When it became such a success, my friend phoned once again: 'Congratulations. But you do know what this means, don't you? That it will be the last large Spanish dance programme you produce for them. There is such a thing as too much success. Bye.' And he was right, as we shall see in the next chapter.

24

Cape Performing Arts Board (CAPAB) Music, and *Danza Lorca*

In 1975 I was asked to direct a touring programme for Mavis Becker, Hazel and Emilio Acosta, and the two guitarists Pablo Navarro and Santiago Luna. The show, *Olé,* was presented at the Hofmeyr Theatre in Cape Town, and then on tour by CAPAB Music's manager Tom Veldhuis, a charming man. I decided to have variety because an entire flamenco programme would have been heavy for the country towns. The two women did not want to jump in the regional dances so I decided to add some dances from Latin America instead.

I was going to Spain, where I asked Mercedes y Albano in Madrid to teach me some Argentinian dances to intersperse between the flamenco during costume changes. They directed me to a newly arrived Argentinian, Nestor Epifanio, who was a great dancer, gorgeous to look at and very amusing. So we laughed our way through the lessons, and the programme was really successful. Emilio choreographed the opening item to Gimenes's *La Boda de Luis Alonso* for the three dancers. The usual flamenco items were interspersed with the Argentinian *Zamba* and *Gato* for Mavis and Hazel, and Emilio did an Argentinian *zapateado* called *Malambo*, wearing spurs and a huge silver belt with buckle. A delightful interlude – and neither of the ladies needed to jump. The opening night of *Olé* was on 6 June 1975.

Programme for CAPAB Music's Olé with Emilio Acosta.

1976: *Festival in Spain* for CAPAB Music

Veldhuis was so thrilled that *Olé* had been such a success that he asked me to do a bigger production for them. I said that I would be delighted but there was one proviso. David was faced with problems from the guitarists and the singer each time we performed: a few days before opening night, they would turn up in his office demanding more money. They knew it was too late to do anything about it; I could no longer stand the strain of a walk-out at such short notice. If I could arrange for other guitarists and singers to take over from them at the last minute, if necessary, could the music department afford the airfares from Johannesburg plus their stay? He had never before encountered such behaviour, but he agreed.

The guitarists and the singer behaved exactly as before, issuing the ultimatum, only this time they were not facing a furious David but a very calm man who asked them seriously whether they could be persuaded not to carry out their threat. When they were adamant, he accepted their resignation, and they were stunned. There followed phone calls to the two stand-ins in Johannesburg and after some quick rehearsals the show could go on.

The programme was to consist of 'Bolero' (to music by Ravel), 'Escenas Vascas' (Guridi) and flamenco. The dancers were Dudley Tomlinson, Lorna Levy, Mavis Becker, Hazel and Emilio Acosta, Marilyn Sher, Sherrill Wexler, Sandra Pieterse, Glen Lawmon and Gerhard Prinsloo. I used the Basque composer Guridi's melodious music in a Basque scene with a theme to it, putting my studies with the Basque maestro Juan Urbeltz to good use.

Hazel Acosta in Marina's Bolero, with Gerhard Prinsloo and Glen Lawmon.

For this programme I choreographed a ballet for Hazel about a girl obsessed with finding her lover in a dream where she was repeatedly finding him and then losing him again. I used a silhouette of Emilio projected onto a white cloth behind a podium, where she kept reaching him, only for him to disappear as she approached. He would repeatedly appear and dance with her and disappear, only to be seen again as a silhouette.

It was Luisillo who had suggested I do my own choreography to Ravel's 'Bolero'. The structure of the music was fascinating to work with. Luisillo had also wanted to introduce me to the blind composer Joaquín Rodrigo, whose music I loved. I had stupidly not made use of the offer – with Rodrigo being blind and my poor Spanish, I could not imagine the encounter.

This proved to be another successful production for CAPAB Music which had taken us over when CAPAB Ballet stopped using us. The applause went on and on, until suddenly a CAPAB dancer appeared, took the curtain rope that raised and lowered the curtain from the hands of the technician – and held the curtain shut down! Then sometime later I was apologetically told by CAPAB Music that they had been told by CAPAB Ballet that the production of dance was *their* prerogative and the music department was not to stray into that domain. They were very upset because the performances had been such a success. Our poor Spanish dancers were the ones to suffer. I suppose one should be flattered to be considered a threat to such a large organisation. Mary Skeaping had warned me.

However, Mavis Becker was beyond their reach as a private entrepreneur, starting her very successful company Danza Lorca. They were able to use the Oude Libertas open-air amphitheatre at Stellenbosch, in an idyllic setting among the pines and the vines and the moonlight. The Stellenbosch Farmers' Winery, who financed my book on the history of ballet in South Africa, said that they were going to build it as a resident theatre for me. When I left South Africa in 1977, they said, 'How could you do this to us?' I pointed them in the direction of Danza Lorca.

So Mavis could pick up where I left off, and she invited me back twice to produce programmes at the Oude Libertas theatre. The first was in 1979 when I lived in Rome, and the second was in 1986 when I lived in Washington DC. The first one, *Rapsodia España*, was with the dancer José Antonio, the young artistic director of the National Ballet of Spain, and with the local dancer Emilio Acosta. I opened the show with Emilio riding through the pine forest towards the stage on a horse with a pretty girl seated behind him, and girls doing *palmas* (clapping) and men with live torches in a line following them. The burning torches were placed around the stage. On the stage was a fire burning in a cauldron, and the horse's tail almost caught fire. That scene would not be allowed by the Department of Health and Safety today but it *was* a magical delight for the audience.

In the second programme which I choreographed for Danza Lorca at the Oude Libertas theatre in 1984 was *Fiesta Olé* with the composer/guitarist Emilio de Diego, in which José Antonio and Emilio Acosta were joined by José's wife, the beautiful classical dancer Luisa Aranda. For Mavis and José I choreographed the *Magic Circle* to dramatic music by Surinach; and for Mavis and Emilio I choreographed *Percussion Bolero* to music which had been given to me by the American composer Richard Trythall in Rome. The third ballet I staged was *Gran Via*, a street scene set in 19th-century Madrid.

Marina Lorca and José Antonio in Marina's The Magic Circle.

One afternoon, during one of the first rehearsals for one of these shows in a second-floor studio in Cape Town, uninvited members of a Johannesburg Spanish dance company walked in and sat down to watch, looking grim. Our dancers collapsed in fright. I called José over to the window and whispered, 'What do we do now?' He opened the window, looked down at the ground, two floors down, gestured towards the open window, and said, 'Ladies firrrst'. But we survived to have an exciting performance.

High jinks by Emilio Acosta, Mavis Becker, Marina, and José Antonio Ruiz!

25

The Opera

I digress now from dance to opera. Hearing over the car radio Maria Callas singing the aria 'One Fine Day' from Puccini's *Madame Butterfly,* I was transported back to when I was sixteen. I had joined a visiting Italian opera company to dance with them at their season in Cape Town. Little did I realise that this was a potted introductory education into the realm of opera. It was also my first money earned from dancing. The drama and the music of Verdi and Puccini, with *La Bohème, Madame Butterfly, La Traviata,* and Leoncavallo's *I Pagliacci* taught me that there is more to stage art than just ballet. We were allowed to watch the operas in which we did not participate. It was a great gift to sit there for free, night after night, and watch the dramas unfold. I remember sitting in a box with the tears pouring down my innocent-of-life cheeks as *Madame Butterfly* was betrayed by Lieutenant Pinkerton. I sobbed at every performance, deep penetrating sobs, that left me exhausted. The same applied to *I Pagliacci*. I realise now that it was the storyline with which I could best identify.

Later it was Menotti's depiction of modern life that attracted me. His operas: *The Telephone* about the man who was in front of his girlfriend's high-rise building, could see her, but the only way to reach her was by phoning her from the street telephone when she stopped talking for a few minutes; *The Consul* and the suffering brought to the average citizen by bureaucracy; and his Christmas tale of the story of

Amahl and the Night Visitors was another – there a mother answers the questions of the Three Wise Men, searching for the baby Jesus with a heartbreakingly melodious song, 'Do you know a child the colour of wheat, the colour of thorn?' She replies that she does, repeating the same words, but is referring to her own lame son. Menotti died in 2007. History will define his worth.

It was between 1974 and 1976 that I was to arrange the dances for several CAPAB Opera productions under the dynamic direction of Angelo Gobbato. He was full of enthusiasm and excitement, which he instilled in the singers during Bizet's *Carmen.* I cast Hazel Acosta for the dances in this ballet, and in 1974 in Verdi's *Rigoletto,* and in 1975 and 1976 in my favourite, Mozart's *Marriage of Figaro.* This was a most fortuitous situation as I could give the company the actual *fandango* of that period. It is sometimes known as *Fandango antiguo*. Being a folk dance, the guests at the wedding could perform it themselves, making it more believable, instead of bringing in professional dancers.

Of the many types of *fandangos* that exist, Mozart based the construction of his on one of the dances of the Goya era in Madrid. The *Madrileños* used to dance in the meadow, or *prado*, outside Madrid on Sundays, and Goya portrayed them in all their shiny, elegant clothes. Today the museum of that name stands on the spot. Boccherini used the same construction for his exciting *fandango,* as did Joaquin Rodrigo in his *Fantasia para un Gentilhombre. Fandangos* are found mainly in the south of Spain but also in the Balearic Islands. They have a specific pattern of alternating verses and choruses but Mozart's does not.

Mozart's music is such a joy and all the singers were so happy. There was much fun during rehearsals and even performances. The *basso profundo* was Øystein Liltved, a Norwegian married to the South African lyric soprano Virginia Oosthuizen. She was singing the role of the Countess. Øystein was constantly playing pranks. At one performance, the character Susanna surreptitiously hands a note to the count, at that time the Welsh tenor Alan Charles. Turning aside he read it, whilst trying to retain his composure about the message. When he made his exit, he said hysterically to everyone in the wings, 'Who wrote that? Who did this to me?' Øystein had written something very wicked but funny in the note. Luckily Alan was a good sport and it ended in much hilarity.

I had studied all the dances of the Goya period with the *Coros y Danzas* of Madrid, where María Carmen del Gordo taught. I was able to follow the group of dancers and musicians to their performances around Madrid. She was a knowledgeable firebrand, and I was very lucky to be able to attend with her, not only the rehearsal but the performance at the Zarzuela Theatre in Madrid of all the companies representing the different regions of Spain. During the rehearsal she explained them to me.

I shall never understand why in Spain there is not a folk dance company that tours, like the company *Antologia de la Zarzuela,* an anthology of light Spanish operas. That company was founded by, and the performances were created and directed by, José Tamayo. They included popular extracts of singing and dancing from the *Zarzuelas*, a type of light opera or operetta. They presented the music played on authentic regional instruments such as bagpipes, lutes, guitars, different flutes and drums etc. The dances were theatrically presented and excitingly choreographed by Alberto Lorca in magnificent regional costumes. They showed the vast variety of Spain's rich cultural heritage, which no other country can rival. Yet today it lies buried by flamenco, a very sad state of affairs. The name of the theatre, *Zarzuela*, is derived from a castle in the countryside outside Madrid, which is now the holiday residence of the royal families. The *zarzas* are brambles surrounding the castle.

26

Foreign Guest Artists Invited by the South African Government

In 1974 PACOFS, the Performing Arts Council of the Orange Free State, brought out the New London Ballet under André Prokovsky and Galina Samsova, two brilliant Russian dancers. In 1975 the Royal Danish Ballet teacher and former dancer Hans Brenaa did a brilliant production of August Bournonville's *La Sylphide* in Cape Town for the Cape Performing Arts Board (CAPAB). He was highly entertaining. I baked some Danish delicacies for him which were appreciated very much.

Then in 1976 came a big adventurous influx. It was also a big, well-kept government secret, presumably because of boycott fears. No one in the South African ballet world knew about it but we were delighted when suddenly it was announced that we were to see performances by the New York City Ballet dancers Suzanne Farrell, Peter Martins (later to become artistic director of NYCB), Peter Schaufuss and Niels Kehlet. The men were all Royal Danish Ballet dancers who had moved to New York, sadly a great loss to the Royal Danish Ballet.

The South African government was trying to prove that not everyone was boycotting it because of apartheid. Thus it enticed international stars to tour Bloemfontein, Cape Town, Pietermaritzburg and Johannesburg. It was to be the first time that South Africans saw their own John Cranko's *Romeo and Juliet pas de deux* danced by Liliana Cosi and Marinel Stefanescu. Quoting from my *The History of Ballet in South Africa*, published in Cape Town in 1981 by Human & Rousseau:

> 'Choreographies by Robbins, Balanchine, Béjart, van Manen and van Dijk were seen for the first time in South Africa, and so were dancers such as Alexandra Radius and Hans Ebbelaar in van Manen's interesting modern *Twilight* (Cage), and the Japanese technicians Yoko Morishita and Tetsutaro Shimizu who caught the public's fancy, almost making them miss the sheer artistry of Suzanne Farrell and Peter Martins from New York City Ballet, who were brilliant in Robbins's *Afternoon of a Faun* (Débussy) and *In G Major* (Ravel) and Balanchine's sparkling Tchaikovsky *Diamond Pas de Deux* from his ballet *Jewels*.'

Mikael and I attended all the performances. One night Suzanne Farrell and Peter Martins danced Robbins's *In G Major* in a particularly unforgettable way. Peter said thoughtfully to me afterwards that it was indeed a very special performance. The memory remains indelibly with us. One Sunday I took Farrell, Martins, Schaufuss and Kehlet to our home in the beautiful nearby town of Stellenbosch to show them the lovely vineyards and majestic mountains of the Cape. I cooked Danish and Swedish food for lunch. They ate so much that they asked if they could 'swim it off', and we went to the home of a friend who had a swimming pool. I still have a photo of all of us there at the pool.

I saw Kehlet many years later with Elsa Marianne von Rosen, movingly dancing the old couple in a Flemming Flindt ballet in Copenhagen. I was amazed when I went backstage to see her, and Kehlet came up and said, 'Marina!', greeting me with a hug. I had not expected him to remember me, as so many years had passed. At that time Elsa Marianne was still full of vigour, running up the four flights of stairs to her flat, but sadly she later had a stroke. She passed away in September 2014 at the age of ninety.

27

Leaving South Africa and Arriving in Italy, 1977

Leaving South Africa was so traumatic but we had always intended that when the children were teenagers we would take them to experience Europe, and especially of course Sweden and Denmark where Mikael's family roots lay.

Mikael was offered a good post in the Food and Agriculture Organisation of the United Nations (FAO), situated in Rome. When we left for Rome, we cried the most when we said goodbye to our housekeeper Susie Adams. Mavis Becker and I also wept as we walked to the aeroplane. Those days, at least in Cape Town, you could take your friends or family right up to the plane before saying goodbye. Mavis sobbed, 'What am I going to do? There will be no one to look at my dancing and advise me'. She trusted me utterly. I knew that I would miss her dearly. We used to talk for hours on the phone. Those were the days when there was telephone tapping in South Africa, and Mikael said there would be one resignation after the other from exhausted policemen who were listening in to our endless talking. It was actually not so amusing at the time.

We thought our move to Rome was to be permanent but it lasted only four hard years. It was a bad period for Italy, known today as the Years of Lead. The Red Brigade was rampant, and Prime Minister Moro and many others were kidnapped and killed. We arrived in the middle of all that. However, our life was relieved by happy summer holidays in Sweden and Denmark.

Vicky was fifteen years old, Edmund thirteen, and Nicolai seven. It was hard for them to leave their safe, settled lives and dear friends in Stellenbosch and start anew in a strange culture; hard to move from a beautiful small town to a large metropolis. Luckily there was the English school for Nicolai, who became the first of us to speak Italian fluently – including Romagna, the Roman dialect which was used in the playground. For the older children there was the international but mainly American St Stephen's School in an old monastery at the foot of the Aventine Hill, right next to FAO. It had a wonderful faculty, teaching the International Baccalaureate. The music teacher was Richard Trythall, whose compositions included music for several French films; the art teacher was Peter Rockwell, a sculptor using the famous Italian marble. He is the son of the artist Norman Rockwell who created a series of covers for the famous *Saturday Evening Post* in America, drawing memorable scenes of ordinary America of that period. In St Stephen's the children were taken for their history lessons to actual historic sites, even as far as to Greece, which was unforgettable for them.

One of Nicolai's friends was a boy from one of the old Roman families, the Borghese, who had a dungeon under the family home. Nicolai visited it and was most impressed. Our older children had in their school a teenager from one of the other princely families. He had come from the English school. One day there he had walked down the staircase on the side which was designated 'Up', when a prefect stopped him halfway and told him to go back and come down on the 'Down' side. He is reported to have said, 'Do you know who I am? I am...... ; nobody tells ME on which staircase I may go down'. The prefect replied, 'I don't care WHO you are. Go back and come down on the 'Down' side'. He did so, and he also left his school for St Stephen's. The fact that the prefect was a girl no doubt contributed to his irritation.

The children had a wonderful time once they had settled down. Their friends were from many countries. One night they had a party by the fireside in our new home. All their friends were invited. Greger

Hatt with his flute and Teddy Jefferson with his guitar improvised the most glorious melodies. Everyone stayed over, sleeping all over the house, from the basement, the children's domain, turned into a room for them, to the upper second floor.

28

Oh Roma, Roma!

My life in Rome was going to be hard so I gave up teaching and gave away my shoes and castanets when I left South Africa, knowing that I would have to do all the housework, plus care for the family. After eight years with Susie looking after us, it was going to be more than hard – a complete readjustment.

We first rented a flat in EUR, a modern part of Rome, while we searched for a house to buy. Very few foreigners in Rome bought their homes, but we bought a lovely house called 'La Brisa' (Spanish for 'The Breeze'). We thought that this would be for the rest of our lives. How naive we were. We had been totally spoiled by Susie. I was having a hard time, so while we were still in the flat Mikael put up a roster in the kitchen of what we expected each child to do, and I added a note underneath: 'THERE IS NO SUSIE HERE'. Years later, Mikael met up with the owner of the flat. She said she was so pleased to meet him because something had bothered her on her return. She asked, 'What is a 'Susie'?' Mikael thought, *Susie? Susie?* He told her that he had no idea what it could be. Well, she said, behind the kitchen door was a notice saying, 'There is no Susie here', and she wondered what it was that was missing in her flat!

When I left South Africa, a Johannesburg newspaper carried an article about me. Working at the South African Embassy in Rome was Sandra Kietzman, a pupil of Mercedes Molina and Rhoda Rivkind in

Johannesburg, and she tried to trace me in Rome as she wanted me to teach the Spanish Dance Society (SDS) syllabus there. After three weeks of phoning around she found me. It was her sheer determination that won through. It was also a miracle because at FAO I was known as Grut, not Keet. I told her that we were very unsettled and I could not even think of teaching. When the local Rome teachers saw Sandra dance, they said that they too wanted to dance like her. I had to teach.

Each weekend Sandra Kietzman, Marie-Louise Ihre, Sara Tamasco and Susanna Moraleda-Dragotta came to beg me to start teaching them the SDS syllabus. By the third weekend I said to Mikael, 'What do I do?' He replied, 'Give in'. They returned with a petition stating why it was my duty to teach them. Before they could start reading it out, I said that I would teach them. Sandra did not turn up, and I sent Marie-Louise to find her. She had passed out in her room; she had advanced cancer. I arranged for the South African Embassy to send her back to South Africa. She recovered and returned to Rome, but sadly was to die from the disease.

They placed a floor of thick plywood on the tiles in our basement, and every Saturday they drove out to our house on the outskirts of Rome, in the Viale di Castel Porziano, the long pine avenue leading to the King's old hunting lodge, on the way from EUR to Ostia. Our lessons culminated in examination sessions. The first examiner to come was a very pregnant Sherrill Wexler from London. She had queued for days outside the Italian Embassy only to be sent away each time it closed at midday. The third day, as the doorman came to shut them out again, the man in front of her, who had also been there day after day in the snow, hit the doorman with his fist and as he sailed across the room the man entered the consulate and Sherrill hurried after him and managed to get her visa.

Today when I see these photos of my former Spanish dance pupils in Rome I feel so proud of them, and I admire Marie-Louise Ihre for having made such a success of the Italian branch as Organiser for nearly forty years.

In the fourth and last year of our stay in Rome Mavis Becker came to examine and we did a show at which I lectured – in Italian! Afterwards Mikael said, 'I do admire you for doing it in Italian'. I nearly collapsed because it had not occurred to me that it was a brave thing to do.

Top, from left: The three Rome teachers Susanna Moraleda-Dragotta, Marie-Louise (Maria Luisa) Ihre and Sara Tamasco demonstrating the SDS syllabus.
Below: Sara Tamasco and Micaela Belfiore dancing Panaderos de la Flamenca.

For weeks I called a man 'Mr Falegname', not realising that the word merely meant 'carpenter'. Well, 'Mr Falegname' walked through our living room pronouncing which pieces should live and which should not. He pointed to the cupboard and said loudly and clearly, *Bella* (beautiful). We were so relieved. His voice again rang out as the desk was also pronounced *Bella*. But then he looked at our bookshelves, put his hand dramatically to his forehead and shouted *Brutto* (ugly), damning it forever. With a significant look in my direction, he continued on his way upstairs to join the builder, architect (who appraised the house for us) and other workmen, to discuss cupboards to be built in the bedrooms. I had not asked for his appraisal of our furniture; it was given gratis, free and with great relish. Rome is one huge theatre and every Italian is a performer. They wanted their work praised and they wanted applause. Until we finally moved into our house I was expected to do this for every brick that was laid and every job that was completed – all with, at that early stage, very little knowledge of the language. Luckily, as a dancer, I recognised these needs and supplied them, but I was exhausted at the end of it all.

Upstairs a royal row developed over my cupboards. The builder knew how they should be, the architect thought differently and the carpenter had his opinions. I tried to say what I wanted but the carpenter turned to me to say severely, 'Signora', significant pause for gathering everyone's attention, '*I* made the President's cupboards'. And that was that. He turned back to the men and the voices were once again loud, each stridently arguing his case, echoing in the empty house. I fled to the garden.

I did not realise that, although it was funny, it was also significant. I was a woman in Italy and for many men that did not count. I once stood in front of the desk of an official of the electricity department, trying to get our bill corrected. I could have been invisible. He served the men who had arrived after me, and ignored me. After twenty minutes of such rebuff, I turned to walk out and his voice called me back. One had to protest, even silently, to be heard. He who shouts loudest gets served.

To the Italians we were crazy foreigners who wanted everything white. My husband and I looked in the shops for white cupboards. We found only heavy dark and ornate wooden ones. Once we found a shop where there were white cupboards with central panels of different colours. The lady in the shop pursed her lips when we asked to see the white cupboards. 'I do not have any', she said firmly and finally. We pointed to them and enquired, 'Can the panels be changed?' She nodded a 'Yes'. Could we put in white panels? She thundered 'NO', and she was adamant. If we were going to turn them into all-white cupboards it would be over her dead body. She said, 'I know that you foreigners like white furniture but we Italians associate it with hospitals'. That was why we had to have cupboards made. Also, one day in our house I arrived just in time to stop them putting up the white wallpaper with the beige back to the outside.

We installed burglar bars and a wrought-iron cover over a deep well in the front of our garden to prevent our children from falling into it. Earlier the builder, Mr Ciuccoli, had called his staff together to discuss the painting of the iron trellis cover over the well. It was like a low pergola. He said, 'This is to be painted white'. 'No, no', I said eagerly, 'black'. I did not wish to draw attention to it. He sighed deeply. 'Signora', he said, 'you want the walls white, you want the cupboards white, you want the burglar bars white, you want the fireplace white; you – want – this – white'. And he left. The toothless old painter sidled up to me, knowing that I was dismayed. 'Signora', he said, 'you don't want this white but you also don't want it black; you want it brown'. And that is what it became.

Mr Ciuccoli told me that he was a builder and not a destroyer. To take down the huge fireplace in the centre of the living room and reconstruct a smaller one nearly killed him; each brick was pleaded for. 'You really want me to take this away?' he would ask. When it came to the last bricks of the front pedestal, he just could not get himself to do it. 'Please say I can leave it Signora. Please say *si* and not *non*, Signora', he begged. I was worn down and said 'Si'. He said dramatically to his workmen, 'Did you hear that? A weak *si-i-i* and tomorrow when I return it will be a firm *NON*'. How right he was, poor man.

The Italian author Luigi Barzini, in his book *The Italians* pities the foreigners who come to settle in his country, full of enthusiasm but not understanding the country and just landing into one bout of trouble after another. I do not refer to trivial, amusing moments but to really painful ones – read on. This is a *cri de cœur.* However, if you don't like misery, then skip to the last paragraph of this chapter.

When we moved in, we needed to get our telephone connected; living in an isolated area, with three children, it was important for us to have a telephone. Our builder said that when the technicians came to do that, we had better have plenty of cash at home. Soon they declared that there was a problem and that they had to leave. I asked how much it would cost to fix the problem. They mentioned a sum and I handed it over. Soon there was another problem – and so on. When Mikael came home from work that evening I told him what it had cost to have our telephone connected. He asked me if they had given me a receipt. I said no. 'Then you have paid your first bribe', he said.

Because we lived outside Rome we had a septic tank. This had to be emptied regularly, or disaster happened. To do this, one had to drive to the town of Ostia, stand in a queue for a form, join another queue somewhere else to buy two stamps, and then another where a man affixed the stamps to the form and signed it, after which one then went to another building to pay for and register one's request. It often happened that one had joined the wrong queue and had to start all over again. Nothing was easy. I was expecting guests, decided that it had to be done before the weekend, and drove to Ostia. As I reached the final stage the official looked up from his desk and said, 'Where is your passport?' I gasped, 'My PASSPORT!?' 'Yes', he said calmly, 'your passport'. I said, 'I have been living here for four years and I have never needed my passport to have my septic tank emptied'. 'Well, now you do'. He was playing a little power game and I was powerless. I lived twenty minutes away, and the office closed at 11:30am; it had taken me from 8:30am when the office opened till 10am to get to this stage. I would have to drive home and back and, depending on the traffic, perhaps not make it. I was frantic at the thought of a house full of fourteen people all using the bathroom. It was also the end of my tether with Italy. I leaned forward, took all the papers on his desk and threw them up in the air. The rest of the people in the queue were delighted; they cheered and applauded this wonderfully theatrical event of the day. I rushed out and tore home, got my passport, rushed back and made it before 11am by the skin of my teeth. As I walked up to his desk he said, 'Oh Signora, were you angry this morning'.

One morning I was in my nightgown in the kitchen when I saw two men creeping past the gate to the electricity box in the wall. I rushed out, nightgown and all, and shouted, 'WHAT ARE YOU DOING?' I had lived in Rome for years and had become so aggressive that I hated myself. They told me, rather sheepishly, that I had not paid my bill for the October quarter and therefore they were turning off the electricity. I fetched my receipt to prove that I had paid it. They scratched their heads and mumbled that they could not understand this. Lo and behold, half an hour later they were back doing it again. To have it turned off would have been a disaster. It could take weeks to get it turned on again and we would have had no lights or water, which worked from an electric pump. When I went to the electricity company, I found out that the non-payment had been at a time when I was not even living there. From the butcher I found out that they had forgotten to send out accounts to the whole area some years ago, and that I had better pay it if I wanted electricity.

As a foreigner in Italy you are a sitting duck and everyone can hardly wait to take a pot shot at you. The beautiful tree-lined avenue where we lived had been turned into a racetrack by two youths, one on a motorbike and one in a car. On this narrow road they roared their way up and down all weekend long. I had warned the police that there would be an accident one day. One Sunday afternoon came the inevitable collision and the boy on the motorcycle broke his leg badly. Our neighbour and the farmer across the way and my husband all saw it. Everyone disappeared and only my husband went to help the boy who lay screaming in the road. He fetched something for him to lie on, called the ambulance and police, and comforted the boy. When the policeman came, our neighbour said to my husband, 'Don't say anything'. But my husband told the policeman everything that he had seen. Then my husband was sued for damages by the boy's family who claimed that my husband had burned leaves and that this was the cause. Our Danish insurance company handled it and it did not go to court, although it dragged on for seven long years after we left Italy.

On our arrival in Italy I had been warned never to stop at a scene of an accident. Being a foreigner, we would be drawn into it and everyone would try to get us to pay for it. That was exactly what had happened to us. Talking about court cases, my husband had a German colleague who bought a little farm high up in the Abruzzi mountains to the east of Rome, where he hoped to 'get away from it all', but within a year he had four court cases against him.

We paid for a night watchman. The watchmen were nice people, but it was really a protection racket. I was weeding the lawn one day when I looked up to see three men standing over me. It was like watching an American gangster movie. They wore raincoats, dark glasses and hats. I could not believe my eyes, as it was midsummer and too hot for a coat. My husband politely invited them in. They told him that they were from the night watchman company and that they were doubling their monthly fee. Mikael said that doubling it was a bit steep but that he would talk to our neighbour and if the latter paid double then he would also pay double. Bad move, because after that we had one burglary after another. That was at the time when the Hunt brothers in Texas had cornered the silver market and the price of the metal went through the roof, unleashing thefts of silver all over the world, including in our area.

One day I went by bus to fetch my car from the garage where it was being serviced. The bus broke down a short distance from our house and so I walked to the nearest bar/café and phoned the garage to say I would be late and why. Some youths were drinking there and heard my conversation. With them was one called 'the Egyptian'. When I returned home the house had been burgled. Huge dirty handprints were on the walls, the place had been ransacked, cupboards and beds were overturned, and everything was tossed out of drawers onto the floor. All my pillowcases were gone. They had been used to transport the loot. Everything of value that had been in the family for generations had been stolen. The silver, the jewellery, everything. There were still things piled at the door: crockery and glass waiting for transport. They had been disturbed by my neighbour's return home. They had sprayed the neighbour's dogs with anaesthetic to put them out of action. The poor dogs were sick and vomiting for days afterwards.

My husband was away and when he returned he mentioned to the police that perhaps the youths in the café might have been responsible. One day when I went to buy my milk there, 'the Egyptian' came up to me and said, 'You denounced me to the police and I now denounce you'. I rushed home to phone a pupil of mine who was married to an Italian lawyer. She said it was very serious and she would send her husband out to me. Together we went to the police. The lawyer asked how it was possible that something said in confidence could get back to the person who was suspected. There was much arguing and suddenly the policeman slammed his hands on the desk and said, 'Enough. The conversation is closed'. The lawyer rose to his feet and said, 'Very well, but I will hold you personally responsible if anything happens to Mrs Grut or her family'. We left and he said to me, 'We won. You are safe'.

Someone told my husband that there was a bar in the nearby suburb of Casalpalocco where the thieves congregated, and that one could buy back stolen goods from them. He went there and the manageress confirmed that this was indeed where the thieves congregated. She suggested that he should put up a notice with information about where and when the burglary had taken place, asking to be contacted and why, and giving our telephone number. He wrote out such a note, and she corrected his Italian and put the notice on the board. However, we never heard from the thieves.

At that time my guitarist said that he had heard that I been burgled, that he had a friend who was a thief, and that if I gave him the time and place of the burglary he would find out what had happened to our things. At the next class he said that the silver had been melted down and the jewellery disposed of. He told me that the thieves of Rome have divided the city and its suburbs into districts, and that there was one gang per district. Rome was surreal.

We left after three burglaries and almost three nervous breakdowns for me. While searching for Red Brigade members in an abandoned farmhouse near us, the police found four little boys between the ages of eight and ten bound and gagged and up for ransom. I had coped with three burglaries, once meeting the intruders face to face, and after the last one the thieves had left our house flooded. Because there was nothing left to steal, they punished us by opening every tap in the three bathrooms and we arrived home that night to find water rushing down the stairs through the living and dining rooms and the study, and into the basement. They had also set fire to our back garden. I had had enough. I wanted to leave.

A friend said severely, 'You must be doing something wrong. We have lived here for twenty-seven years and never been robbed'. Shortly afterwards all her jewellery and silver were stolen from her bedroom while she was having a tea party downstairs with some other ladies. A friend's daughter was threatened with having her face slashed if she told the police who the youths were who had robbed the home of mutual friends; a woman's car tyres were slashed at a stop light and the people who pretended to help her fled with her handbag.

One night I was returning from the Spoleto Festival with a visitor from Sweden, a very pale blond South African ex-student of mine, Izak Coetzee, and my small son Nicolai. I took the wrong turn onto the ring road and when I saw a break in the dividing hedge I crossed it to go in the opposite direction. Unbeknown to me the chief of the carabinieri had been shot by the Red Brigade and Rome's entire police force was out looking for the culprits. They thought I had seen them and was trying to make a getaway. They all came screaming after me with sirens blaring. I drew to the side and found three machineguns pointed at me. I explained that I had lost my way. They peered into the car and saw my son fast asleep on the back seat, and they said, 'Signora, Signora', wagging their fingers at me. Shaking their heads, they told me how to get to Rome. When I looked at Izak he was so pale that he had turned white. After frantic searching, we reached home at 5:30am. I was sick with worry, and apologised to Mikael who replied, 'Oh, I thought you would be late. You were meeting afterwards with the National Ballet of Spain, José Antonio and Gades'.

In Italy you buy your house in front of a *notaio* (notary), a highly paid government legal official who is there to ensure that all is correct, and to collect the transfer fee. When we sold our house again, the buyer's lawyer found that one of the official receipts was missing. My husband repeatedly went to the notary's office after his work but she would not receive him. He then went to her head office in central Rome, where they gave him the missing receipt. He saw that the transfer fee which he had handed over to the notary four years earlier had been far higher than the correct amount. The notary, now scared, gave him a personal cheque for the amount which she had stolen. 'Is that the end of the story?' she asked worriedly, and it was.

In spite of all that, Rome itself is a wonderful city, so full of history and art. And most of the people we met were wonderful. They were the ones who slaved away working and keeping the country going, while others rode on their backs: Mr Ciuccoli, our builder, who drove for miles to us in winter to check our heating system because he said that he could not bear the thought of the children being cold; my neighbour who came to help me do the last frantic cleaning when we were leaving; the greengrocer who was so happy to see me return after an extended holiday that he fashioned a herb bouquet as a gift, adding a carrot for colour. In spite of all the problems during our four years in Rome, I shall always remember them and the many other wonderful and talented people I met there. My children loved Rome and get very upset when I tell my gruesome tales. They lived charmed lives. We were there at the worst time, the time which the Italians today call 'the days of lead (*piombo*)'. I believe it is very different today.

29

The History of Ballet in South Africa, 1981

When I taught ballet history at the University of Cape Town it occurred to me that the students were not learning anything about the history of ballet in their own country, South Africa, nor was there any literature on that subject. So I began to research it, and in 1981 I completed my book *The History of Ballet in South Africa* (Human & Rousseau, Cape Town, 1981, 492 pages, ISBN 0 7981 1089 9). I collected most of the data when I was in South Africa, I did most of the writing when I was in Rome, and the book was published when I had just arrived in America. Here, with the kind permission of the American author and dance critic Jack Anderson, is his review of my book for *The Dance Chronicle* in 1982. It describes the book better than I could do.

> 'A wonderful book for the balletically inquisitive to browse around in, Marina Grut's *The History of Ballet in South Africa* serves as a reminder that the ballet world can have many capitals and it sensibly warns us against assuming that only the ballet we are used to seeing or reading about can possibly be of interest.
>
> Most balletomanes probably know that South Africa has produced some important dancers and choreographers: such names as John Cranko, Maude Lloyd, Frank Staff, Nadia Nerina and Monica Mason come readily to mind. But what we may not know anything about is the sort of ballet culture from

which those artists developed or what sort of ballets continue to be produced in South Africa.

Answers to all one's questions about South African ballet can probably be found in this history, the publication of which was made possible by Stellenbosch Farmers' Wineries. Grut is a South African dancer and writer who, until her marriage to a Danish Doctor of Forest Science, choreographed under the name of Keet. Her account of ballet in her homeland includes 336 pages of narrative text, 233 illustrations, and a formidable set of appendices. Among them are a chronology of the activities of South African companies and visiting groups, a brief discussion of the RAD teaching method in South Africa, biographical sketches of prominent members of the South African dance community, and list upon list: a list of awards to South African dancers and choreographers, a season-by-season of the personnel of South African companies, a list of the personnel of South African companies, and a list of every known ballet produced in South Africa between 1802 and 1980.

'Despite the peculiarities of South African histories and politics, the story of South African ballet may sound very familiar to American readers. As in America, there were sporadic ballet performances in the 19th century. But again, as in America, ballet never really took hold until the 1930s. If some of the early South African groups seemed modelled on Marie Rambert's Ballet Club – and South African dancers naturally turned to England for guidance – the courageous women in charge of them are surprisingly akin to such pioneers of American regional ballet as Dorothy Alexander and Josephine Schwartz.

One of the most remarkable South African teachers and Directors appears to be Dulcie Howes, who in 1934 began teaching ballet and dance at the University of Cape Town, an institution that had long had an enlightened policy of encouraging the arts. With the support of the University and the Little Theatre, she and what must have been a band of Bohemians and arts-crazed academics founded the UCT (University of Cape Town) Ballet and she guided it for decades,

Cover of The History of Ballet in South Africa, 1981.

eventually making it into a professional company. Since South African racial policies are objectionable to many outsiders, it is intriguing to read in a book published in South Africa that, under Howes, the UCT Ballet was always "multi-racial... without making an issue of it", and that since her retirement as company director Howes has been working "to have ballet established as a subject in coloured schools"'.

David Poole, Marina, and Dulcie Howes at the book launch in Cape Town in 1981.

'A less controversial South African peculiarity becomes apparent when one learns that, with its professionalisation in 1964, the UCT Ballet became CAPAB Ballet. Later one follows the fortunes of companies such as PACT, PACOFS and NAPAC. South Africans are infatuated with acronyms and not simply as a convenient way of referring to organizations in a bilingual country, for at least one government body has totally different initials in English and Afrikaans. Rather, South Africans seem to love initials for their own sake. Even though the ballet acronyms derive from the initials of the regional arts boards

> that sponsor them, Grut deplores this form of nomenclature on the grounds that outsiders have no idea what the initials stand for and "foreigners do not know how to pronounce a word like CAPAB". (Come to think of it, how does one pronounce it? KAY-pab? kay-PAB? Kah-PAHB?)
>
> But if one starts wondering about a matter like that, one has obviously become vicariously involved in the saga of South African Ballet. And the fascination of Grut's book makes one long for similarly detailed accounts of activities in other places in which there is a lot of ballet which we in America may know very little about: in Yugoslavia, for instance, or in Hungary, Czechoslovakia, Poland, Argentina, and Brazil. Armchair balletic globetrotting can be enlightening and fun'.
>
> Jack Anderson, *Dance Chronicle*, 1982.

When the book had been published, Victor Holloway, the culture editor of the main Afrikaans newspaper in Cape Town, *Die Burger,* said to me: 'This will be the Bible of South African dance for the future'.

30

Washington DC and America, from 1981

In June 1981 we went from Rome to Washington, the United States capital, in the District of Columbia (DC), where Mikael was appointed forestry specialist at the World Bank. With us was our youngest son Nicolai, eleven at the time. Our two older children had left home and were studying in Europe.

'You never told me that Washington is so beautiful', I said to Mikael. The homes were elegant and the wide avenues were so majestic and easy to drive along. I never ceased to say my mantra, 'It is so beautiful', until the day I departed. It just captivated me during the whole of my stay. The city's beauty was largely due to the generosity of one woman, Lady Bird Johnson, wife of President Lyndon Johnson. She made an endowment that keeps Washington covered with beautiful flowers in great abundance. In spring came first forsythias and daffodils, their bright yellow heralding spring, and the prolifically flowering azaleas and rhododendrons echoed in people's gardens. Some of the streets were lined with white dogwoods, others with pink and white cherry blossoms. Those mirrored in the water of the tidal basin were a magnificent Japanese gift. It was a sight that visitors came from afar to see. I felt I was in heaven.

The Chinese 'fossil trees', *Gingko biloba*, brought more yellow to delight me in the autumn. They withstand urban pollution well and grow magnificently tall. Trees lined all the streets, squares and traffic circles and the always green avenues shaded one's way, very necessary in the humid heat of the summers. The many colours of maples and other leaves cheered up the autumn, while in winter, once the leaves had fallen and the snow had not yet blanketed everything, variously shaped icicles coated the bare branches, bringing about a magical glistening sight as they tinkled in the wind, preparing us for Christmas. Although Washington is on the same latitude as Lisbon, it is hotter in summer and much colder in winter.

However, we were missed by most of the hurricanes that hit the states to the south and the blizzards that hit the ones to the north. Only once did I witness a hurricane forge its very disciplined and leisured journey up Connecticut Avenue. The metal signs it had picked up along its route whirled around in the centre of its vortex. One woman said afterwards that she had clung to a lamp post, knowing that she could have been cut to ribbons by these signs if she had been swept up in the vortex. I stood in safety watching from the picture window of the hairdresser's salon. Had it not been a good little hurricane, there would have been devastation. On another much later occasion, after we had left Washington, a hurricane wiped out the 20th anniversary performance of the Spanish Dance Society which I had founded in Washington, leaving guitarists from Spain and the guest artist, charming Lola Greco, stranded, and the society with horrendously depleted finances.

We lived in a flat overlooking the Glover Archbold Park. Nicolai and I watched at night how deer, raccoons, foxes and other smaller animals roamed beneath our windows. Mikael was often away in Africa or Asia and I felt that he was never home for long enough to experience the good life in America. His life was hard.

Nicolai settled into an excellent international school offering a good education through the International Baccalaureate, the same curriculum that his brother and sister had followed in Rome. It gave him friends from all over the world. When he and his friends graduated, they went through Europe by Eurorail, staying with their families in Finland, Sweden, Denmark, Holland and Sardinia. These are still his friends today and they enrich his life.

Once our older son Edmund said that he felt hard done by because we had left South Africa. He felt rootless although he had Danish nationality, had studied at a university in Denmark, and had done his military service there. But on the other hand our youngest son Nicolai said, 'I feel that I am a citizen of the world'. Two different points of view. America made him happy. The Americans have this wonderful gift of making children believe in themselves and feel that they can achieve anything. That is why Americans are such achievers. I experienced this positivity at George Washington University. Whatever I wanted to do, my colleagues encouraged. In Europe there is reticence and often negativity. We can learn much from the American system of positive encouragement.

But I am racing ahead again. First I had to find work. Where to go? I enjoyed reading the ballet reviews by Alan Kriegsman, the ballet critic at the *Washington Post* – a real gentleman, elegant, intelligent and kind – and I decided to ask for his advice on how to proceed. It was an excellent way to start. He explained the dance scene to me and suggested I contact Mary Day of the Washington Ballet. She was most sympathetic and said that there was just no room to add another course because she already had to hire extra studios for the ballet rehearsals of the company. She spoke about how the Kennedy Center had decided to ask the American Ballet Theatre (ABT) to become the resident company, but that the dancers wanted to live in New York. Soon that company was only coming for a couple of seasons and then the whole idea fizzled out. Still they did not ask Mary's Washington Ballet Company, the obvious choice. She could not afford to hire the Kennedy Theater. After many years they started doing their Christmas *Nutcracker* season there, as it drew a large audience, and thus matters improved, leading to regular performances there.

Adding the choreographer Choo San Goh changed their fortunes. Mary was always entering international competitions. On one occasion the dancer she put her heart and soul into was the lovely Amanda McKerrow, blonde and beautifully trained. She was to dance the *Prélude* from Chopin's *Les Sylphides*. At the rehearsal before they departed for Moscow, it was thought that the dance was beautifully lyrically performed, but they wondered whether it was too lyrical, with most of the other dancers producing technical fireworks. However, Mary felt that that was exactly what would make it stand out. She was proved right because in the end Amanda McKerrow won the competition. Her ethereal quality and artistry had appealed to the international judges. It was a triumph for Mary Day and her judgement. As with some fairy tales, it had a sad ending: McKerrow only remained with the Washington Ballet for two years, before she was off to dance for the American Ballet Theatre (ABT) in New York, rising to principal dancer status in a very short time.

One night, after taking Mary home from a performance, we were sitting in my car outside the Washington Ballet School, where her parking place sign stated: 'Don't even think about it'. I told Mary that I was going to start a company. She said, 'Be careful who you invite on to your board and learn from what happened to Lucia Chase. She started ABT and when it was flourishing she was ousted by her own board'. Later, when I did set up the Spanish Dance Theatre in Washington, our chairman Joanne Petrie guided us through all these matters with great aplomb. Our structure of board, advisers and committees reads like a *Who's Who* of important and wise people who helped but did not interfere. In a political city like Washington DC these things mattered.

When I found that there were no jobs for me at the Washington Ballet, I considered the universities. I had a university on either side of where I lived on Cathedral Avenue, both with courses in dance: the American University and George Washington University (GWU). Both were a mere ten-minute drive away. We were so well situated, and Mikael took the bus from door to door to his office at the World Bank, a stone's throw from where I was to work. Of the two universities, I decided to approach GWU first because it had two theatres. Being almost fifty, I was aghast at having to start anew on a career in America, with my hat in my hand asking for work for the first time in my life – in Cape Town and Rome I did not have to ask, but had been asked.

When I enquired about job opportunities in the GWU Department of Theatre and Dance, I was first asked to give a masterclass to show my credentials as a teacher. I went well-prepared with all sorts of materials, sheet music, cassettes with recordings, and even records in case the guitarist failed to turn up, which was what happened. However, all my preparations were thwarted when the electricity also failed. There was a large class of students gathered before me, and I put on my castanets and began to teach, using their rhythms as accompaniment. At the end, when the applause from the students had died down, Professor Nancy Johnson said, 'You're in. I could never have done that. I would have been thwarted by the circumstances'. The guitarist did turn up – ten minutes before the class ended. I ended up as a professorial lecturer at the GWU, with right to the title of professor. In my Introduction I mentioned my incredibly supportive colleagues there.

In connection with my work of teaching the syllabus of the Spanish Dance Society at the GWU, I was invited to teach a class in New York to introduce it to interested teachers there. The doyens of Spanish dance in America, Carola Goya and Matteo, attended the class and were very impressed by the structured approach to teaching the technique and style. They invited me to accompany them to have supper.

Early on, Carola had made a name for herself in Europe and abroad. She was truly a pioneer and had toured as far afield as South Africa in 1939, with a pianist and her equally beautiful sister Beatrice Burford, a talented harpist. She could still make a little speech in Afrikaans, which she had learned when the audiences clamoured for encores. '*Dames en here, as u net so goed sal wees om vir my te wag, dan sal ek van kostuum verander en nog een keer vir julle dans*'. ('Ladies and gentlemen, if you will be so kind and wait for me to change costume, I shall dance for you again.') She said that she would never forget the kindness and hospitality she had received on her tour and she would do anything for South Africans in return. Years later, in someone's scrapbook, I found a newspaper cutting with a picture of her signing a little girl's autograph book in Cape Town. The child turned out to be Mary-Jane Harris (Mrs Duckworth), a friend of mine now living in England, and the retired chair of the Cecchetti Society. She was delighted when I gave her the scrapbook with those cuttings.

I had asked La Meri, an American dancer and teacher of Spanish dance, to be the patron of the Spanish Dance Society (SDS), and she had accepted. Matteo and Carola Goya became the honorary presidents. Later, when La Meri passed away, Carola Goya became the patron and Matteo remained as honorary president. They studied the syllabus so that they knew what they were representing as our patron and president. We were very impressed that they took their tasks so seriously; never before nor since have I found such dedication in office-bearers. Matteo was writing his opus *The Language of Spanish Dance*, and the three of us pored over his work, I helping where I could, in both Washington and New York.

Marina helping Matteo and Carola with Matteo's book *The Language of Spanish Dance.*

When I was approached by Maryland University to teach in their dance faculty, I was delighted to accept the offer. It was a joy to teach their beautifully trained dancers. However, when the demands of running a company and teaching at GWU became a full-time occupation, I sadly had to relinquish that post.

I did not realise that because of my recently published book on *The History of Ballet in South Africa*, my name was known in ballet circles. I was asked by the Italian editor of the New York *Dance Magazine* to help him with some research on the *Les Ballets Suédois* company. I knew that there was important information on that company's American visit in the Lincoln Center Library, and I phoned to ask them to send me photocopies of the material. After giving my name to the man who answered, he said, 'I know exactly who you are. I am holding your book on South African ballet in my hand and cataloguing it at this very moment'. Afterwards he wrote to me remarking on the coincidence.

From Cape Town I received the following letter about my South African book from Julie Mullard, author and friend of the author Mary Renault:

'8 Atholl Road, Camps Bay,
South Africa, 28–3–1981

Dear Marina,

I only got your book yesterday, but I spent the best part of the night reading it. I can't wait to finish it before I send you a word of congratulation.

You say in your foreword that you feel you have had a magical life. I believe that you have that very rare talent which is to write modern history in a way that is exciting to read and at the same time completely accurate. I never dreamed that a book of this nature would be written, to me it is like magic. I so admire your restraint, your faithfulness, I think that's the word nearest to what I mean. You diminish nothing.

Thank you for all the courage and determination you have shown in writing and producing such a splendid book. Mary Renault has not been allowed to set her eyes on it till I've read every word. She joins me in sending you our very best wishes.

Affectionately,

Your Julie'

Mary Renault was the author of the famous book *The King Must Die* and many others based on Greek mythology. She and Julie were fast friends and they were nurses during the Second World War. Their ship was torpedoed in the Mediterranean. Luckily they were able to swim to a nearby island and were rescued from there.

31

Starting with a Bang

I was determined to show Washington what *I* thought Spanish dancing was, and to show its vast range of styles and techniques, the richest in the world. All the local presentations were of flamenco, as the two Spanish ladies who taught Spanish dancing in the Washington area were themselves flamenco dancers. Both women turned down my offer to work together and enrich their repertoires. Had they done so, I would have remained in the background. They thus did me a favour, and I and the company that I formed, The Spanish Dance Theatre, gradually took over the local scene because of the diversity of our programmes.

The Spanish Dance Theatre was a rare company in dance history. The members were totally professional yet unpaid. Our Spanish guest artist at the Singer Sargent exhibition at the Museum of Art in Washington DC was astonished at the way they collaborated with a common purpose, and helped each other. He said that he had danced in many companies all over the world but never experienced anything like it. 'They are not only physically the most beautiful people – it was like dancing in a beauty contest – but they are also so nice.' It was their total commitment to their art that shone through, gripped the audiences and made them return to see our performances again and again.

I salute them and their really gruellingly hard work that made the company so special. The musicians, led by Ralph Pemberton, responded to them with equal dedication. My gratitude extends to my husband for believing in what we were doing and always offering his magnanimous support in so many ways. Since his youth, when he discovered Federico García Lorca's writings, he was overwhelmed, as I am, by Spain's rich cultural heritage.

I used the money which the insurance company had paid out on my jewellery that was stolen in Italy, to fund a show. The local guitarist Henry Jova told me about his sister Margarita, who was dancing in Madrid. I contacted her to join Mavis Becker and Emilio Acosta who I would be bringing from South Africa and Spain respectively. I flew to Spain to buy earrings, shawls, shoes, boots and fans.

Amazing Aguilar in Madrid

When I was in Madrid in 1982 I dropped in at a class given by the flamenco teacher Ciro, with whom I was having an interesting discussion after the class when suddenly from the back of the small studio a man hurtled towards me shouting excitedly, 'MarEEna KEET from CAPE Town'. It was Rafael Aguilar, an Ecuadorian who together with his dancer wife had a very successful company in Paris. He said that he had just returned from Cape Town where he had had a wonderful time producing a ballet for Marina Lorca's company *Danza Lorca*, and where he had heard all about me. His ballet was called *Llanto,* 'Lament', based on Lorca's *House of Bernarda Alba*.

He tucked his arm through mine and said, 'We must go somewhere and talk'. I told him that I was not good company as Mikael had just phoned me from Washington with bad news: I had been counting on borrowing costumes from the Cape Town Ballet Company for some of the items of regional dancing, but now the director David Poole did not wish them to leave the country. I would have to cancel the show. Rafael said, 'But you must not worry, there is no problem. I shall lend you mine. But of course you shall have them. Tell me which costumes you need. I have beautiful ones and I shall lend them to you. You will have your show'. I said, 'You don't understand: I do not have the money for the airfare to transport them, as Marina Lorca would have brought them with her from Cape Town'. He said, 'But I told you, you can have them. It is only right Marina; after all, they are my costumes, and as their 'parent' I should be responsible for paying for their travels to Washington DC and back to Paris'. What a wonderful human being. I feel so honoured to have met him. He also taught me several regional dances that I had been longing to learn, as a gift.

In the end I found a solution to my problem without his help, as we made our own costumes, but I shall never forget this remarkable, sensitive artist's generosity of spirit. Rafael took me around to all the shops where I could get the things I had come to buy and I was able to do it in record time with his help – a truly unforgettable man. He missed the greatest occasion of his lifetime when he was at last asked to choreograph a ballet for *Ballet Nacional de España*. As he started work with the company he died of a heart attack.

Margaret (Margarita) Jova had planned to arrive in Washington in good time for the performances. She was bringing materials for the company's flamenco costumes. This was not to be, as her plane crashed when it took off from the Malaga runway. She saved her life by moving across the tops of the seats to the nearest exit, because the aisle was jammed with people and black smoke was pouring in from the back of the plane. She then jumped off the wing of the plane. She said that she saved her life because she was a dancer and knew how to land from such a height. Some passengers broke ankles and legs, and others died from smoke inhalation.

When Emilio joined us from Spain, he had a magazine with pictures of the crash scene and in one of them was Margaret sitting dejectedly in the waiting room afterwards. She had lost all her precious costumes, shoes, castanets as well as her grandmother's jewellery which she was bringing to her mother in Washington. But at least she had saved her life and was not hurt. All the materials for our costumes for the show, which she was bringing for me, were also lost in the conflagration. She immediately boarded a plane to Madrid. There she borrowed costumes, shoes and castanets from her dancer friends. She then came to Washington DC to participate in the performance.

The Show

What a wonderful show it was. The three guest artists were just great. The audiences gave standing ovations every night of the three performances, and Emilio wanted it to go on forever, he was enjoying himself so much. We had started with a bang. In the audience was an elderly Spanish guitarist who lived in Washington. He held my hand and said, 'I thank you for making me so proud of my country's art'. It was very moving. He came each night, and each night he brought more and more people with him.

Following on after costumier Caroline Weinberg, Professor William 'Bill' Pucilowsky of the university's theatre department made our beautiful costumes for the Spanish Dance Theatre company. Bill and his partner Ashley visited us several times after we settled in London. Sadly, Bill passed away recently from a heart attack.

The encouragement from my American colleagues buoyed me up and I could be creative. Maida Withers' words for any suggested new project were, 'Go for it girl!' Nancy Johnson was always by my side. She and her husband Don adopted me, as it were. There is a famous actor also called Don Johnson. When Nancy once told her class she was bringing Don Johnson with her on an outing, they were very excited. She quickly said, 'No not HIM, my husband'. When Mikael was away on a mission, they would treat me to many an outing and meal. The main one was on the occasion of the Thanksgiving holiday.

George Washington University's two theatres are the large Lisner Center Auditorium and the perfect Dorothy Betts Marvin Center. The latter, with its amphitheatre seating, provided intimate contact between performers and audience – the audience at our feet, and the amphitheatre seats ascending, with the audience looking down on the stage. It was intimate theatre at its best. I revelled in it. It was especially suited to Spanish dancing. Would that Sadler's Wells had adopted that format for its new theatre in London. I am told that the dancers were consulted and chose the old format. They said that they were accustomed to looking up at the audiences in their boxes and in 'the gods'. With the space that had to be taken into consideration, there are sight-line problems for the audience in some areas.

PAGE 22 JALEO - JANUARY 1983

SPANISH DANCE SOCIETY OF WASHINGTON, D.C.

The following pictures were taken at the inaugural performances of the Spanish Dance Society last October. (See Jaleo, Aug/Sept 1982 "Marina Keet: South Africa's Loss -- America's Gain.") These and the cover photo were submitted by Society's director Joanne Petrie.

MARINA LORCA DANCING IN BATA DE COLA

(Photos by Ruth Bolduan)

Starting with a Bang

(photo by Sandra K. Nicht)

LEFT TO RIGHT: MANOLO LEIVA (CANTAOR), PACO DE MALAGA, MARINA LORCA, MARGARITA JOVA, AND EMILIO ACOSTA

Spanish Dance Society inaugural performance in Washington DC in October 1982. Guest artistes: Marina Lorca, Margarita Jova and Emilio Acosta.

Summer Workshops

Nancy Johnson and I presented three workshops. She planned the first one beautifully, and people came from as far afield as Germany and New Zealand. One of those who came was Chelo Jacobo from Florida. She was in her sixties and still as sprightly as the youngest in the class. She was thrilled to find a teaching *method*, as she had been to Spain many times in search of exactly that and had not found it.

JALEO

SUMMER 1986
Vol. IX No. 2

SUMMER COURSE:
SPANISH DANCE SOCIETY USA

[Submitted by: Matteo, The Foundation for Ethnic Dance, Inc., 17 West 71st St., New York, NY 10025, (212)877-9565, and Nancy Lee Ruyter, Dance Department/School of Fine Arts, University of California, Irvine, CA 92717, (714)856-7284]

Spanish dance instructors and students from the United States, Colombia, New Zealand, and West Germany spent June 16 to July 3 at George Washington University (Washington D.C.) in an intensive course on the first six levels of the Spanish Dance Society syllabus. This syllabus, similar in structure and intent to the Royal Academy of Dancing syllabus, was developed by the Spanish Dance Society of South Africa (founded 1965). It comprises six junior, three senior, and two teacher levels. Each level consists of exercises and dances from the area of regional, escuela bolera, and flamenco dance.

Primary instructor for this special course was Marina Keet, Lecturer in Dance at George Washington University since 1982, who presents her students in frequent productions in the Washington D.C. area. Assisting her was Visiting Examiner Luisa Cortez.

Ms. Keet was a founding member of the Spanish Dance Society and a major contributor to the syllabus during its formative years. She has studied extensively and intensively in Spain, and teaches a wealth of material -- from all Spanish dance genres -- in addition to the syllabus itself.

The Spanish Dance Society is the only international society dedicated entirely to the training of qualified Spanish dance instructors and performers and to the maintenance of high standards in the teaching of Spanish dance. The syllabus was compiled by a group of fourteen Spanish dance specialists including both performing artists and teachers. Since the beginning of the Society in 1965, autonomous branches have been founded in: Italy (1978), Great Britain (1979), the United States (1981), and subsequently in West Germany, Malta, Zimbabwe, Zambia, Australia, and Israel.

(LEFT TO RIGHT): VISITING EXAMINER LUISA CORTEZ, SANDRALABY, CHELA JACOBO, MATTEO, CAROLA GOYA, JANE LUSCOMBE, INSTRUCTOR MARINA KEET, NANCY LEE RUYTER.

George Washington University (GWU) summer school.

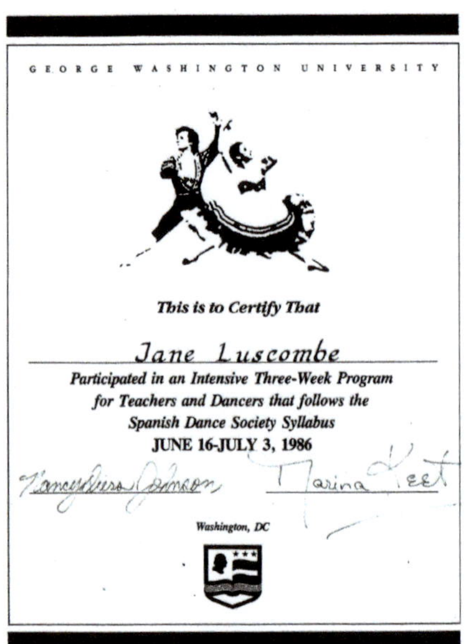

GEORGE WASHINGTON UNIVERSITY

This is to Certify That

Jane Luscombe

Participated in an Intensive Three-Week Program for Teachers and Dancers that follows the Spanish Dance Society Syllabus

JUNE 16-JULY 3, 1986

Nancy Diers Johnson Marina Keet

Washington, DC

GWU summer school certificate. Dancers Dudley Tomlinson and Lorna Levy. Photo: Keith Mackintosh.

From left: Chelo Jacobo (Colombia/Florida), Jane Luscombe (New Zealand), Sherrill Wexler (London), Professor Nancy Diers Johnson (hostess; GWU), Marina, and Ricardo Villa (Texas); summer school tea party by the Potomac River for foreign guests.

Jane Luscombe came all the way from New Zealand to all our summer schools, and she started the society in New Zealand. It was later run by Marilyn Swann Ebbs in Motutweka, South Island. I was able to go there for the first examination session because my husband attended a Commonwealth Forestry Conference in New Zealand and took me with him. I gave Jane Luscombe's pupils in Auckland a class and then went to the South Island to examine Marilyn Swann Ebbs' beautifully prepared students in Motutweka. New Zealand was a fascinating experience. I had no idea that it was so exotic, and I experienced the sulphurous geysers and the Maori dances and customs.

Back to the summer school in Washington. Before the end of the workshop, Chelo Jacobo, with twinkling eyes, excited at having found a syllabus, taught us a *Colombianas*, Colombia being her origin. The dance was as charming as she was, with sweeping fan movements and much grace. From New York came Carola Goya and Matteo to learn the syllabus. Sandy Laby came from California for our first summer workshop, liked it, worked very hard, and returned again and again. She and her husband Jordan, who had invented a machine to clean swimming pools, became patrons of our theatre company. She was a delight. She said, 'I am *nouveau riche*, and I love it'. She became our 'sugar mommy', bringing from California Roberto Amaral with whom she studied, as our guest artist, together with his guitarist. They were to perform with us at the Marvin Center. Sandy Laby thought he was such a wonderful artist and wanted him to be more widely seen. We also invited Marina Lorca to join us from South Africa, and had marvellous performances. He partnered her in our shows at the Marvin and then at the Kennedy Center with his guitarist Benito Palacios and the singer Chini de Triana.

Roberto Amaral is a many-faceted artist who can sing and dance and also has record sales as a well-known rock composer and singer. He was an international Spanish dance performer before he settled down in Los Angeles to teach and to run his own company. His innate musicality is such a joy to watch. José Antonio Ruiz, former artistic director of the *Ballet Nacional* in Madrid, has this same ability to just let the music flow through his body. Sandy and Jordan visited us and joined our board.

It was a rewarding association with Carola and Matteo. Our society in the USA worked at such a high level, surrounded by artists with great experience. Carola once phoned me to say, 'Marina, you know how you always say, 'Nothing in life is easy?' Well you are right, and I am going to have that engraved on my tombstone'. She was a consummate artist. She and her husband came to perform their castanet recital as guest artists with us in a performance in 1985 at the Marvin. They wrote to me afterwards that they had never before performed in such a wonderful atmosphere of mutual helpfulness and kindness from the company. This confirmed what the Spanish guest artist at the Singer Sargent exhibition had said. The 'niceness' and enjoyment of what they did came across the footlights too, and we became sought after and soon were dancing non-stop and scooping all the contracts in the area.

A group playing castanet concerts was formed by Carola Goya and Matteo. After Carola passed away in 1994, Matteo continued doing performances and danced a delightful item, to Joplin's music, which was a great success, and in which he was joined by Jerane Michel. In 1992, shortly after Matteo's and Carola's book *The Language of Spanish Dance* was published, we went to Madrid for the *Encuentro Escuela Bolera* symposium. What fun we had together. Carola was like a little bird, with bright eyes and a wicked sense of humour. I always enjoyed her sharp comments on what was going on around her. She missed nothing. Her bag containing her medication and reading glasses was snatched out of Matteo's hand at the Plaza Mayor. Matteo set off after the man and Carola was so afraid that he would be hurt or even be stabbed that she sank in a dead faint into my arms. She was so thin that she was no weight at all.

When talking of the Spanish dancer José Greco who wrote in his autobiography about all his infidelities, Matteo said, 'How lucky that you were a good little girl Carola', because she had performed with Greco's company. Once when she was in that company, in a pause during a rehearsal, they were looking out of the window over busy New York streets. Greco suddenly said, 'You see those crowds down there? Well, today they know you and not me. You are older than I am. One day they will know me – and will have forgotten you'. 'How right he was', she commented.

Carola Goya spoke of her time in Spain during the civil war. She and her father were living in Granada and she was inside the house, coming down a stairway with her hostess, who was heavily pregnant, and they looked through the large window facing them into the garden where her father was sitting under a tree, when a bomb fell. Luckily it fell behind the tree, which split in two, falling on either side of her father. The tree saved his life. The force of the blast shattered the window, showering the two of them on the stairs with glass. One of the shards split open the woman's abdomen. She was pregnant with twins. Carola sat on the stairs holding her until she died, with the little infants' feet in her other hand. In Granada, each morning at dawn, Carola Goya heard the lorries go past carrying the people who were to be shot. In one of them might well have been García Lorca, the poet.

It is an interesting thought that Carola's ballet teacher, when she was young, was Fokine. Her home was near his studio. I asked her where her Spanish name of Goya had originated and she said that it was a family name.

Performances

At some stage I needed to find money to pay our principal dancers. So Joanne Petrie wrote grant applications and we created a small group of five who could take time off from study or work to perform in schools. I look on the photo of them with pride. We had some delightful performers of varying capabilities and that gave us the chance to present the full range of Spanish dance to schoolchildren. Antonio Saldaña was the ***Asturian and Galician dancer, Jaime Coronado the flamenco buff,*** Joanne Erlebacher (Joanne del Rio) the classical, and Nancy Heller's regional was impeccable; ***but everyone could dance all*** the styles. Nancy Heller was also the consummate presenter and is today professor at the Philadelphia University of the Arts. Which child could ever forget her words as she entered onstage carrying a large, pink blow-up flamingo under her arm, 'It is flamenco, NOT flamingo!' To this day I still love the dancers in my company – their talent, enthusiasm, endless hard work. They charmed audiences everywhere. I hope they realise how good they were.

Spanish Dance Theatre's "Young Audiences" group. Back: Nancy Heller, Jaime Coronado. Front: Antonio Saldaña, Ziva Cohen, Joanne Erlebacher (del Rio).

I used to stand at the back of the auditorium to watch audience reaction to the items, for future programmes. There they were, straight from work, looking like the professionals that they were. The solidarity continued off-stage as well, and I shall never forget the love they gave me when Mikael returned after a car accident in Africa during a World Bank mission, and lay in intensive care in GWU Hospital. It was unbelievable. Ziva Cohen came to me and said, 'When you become too tired to sit with him, I shall take your place'. The bonds in the company were that strong and grew stronger. We never stopped performing.

Spanish dancing is mainly couple dancing and we needed to recruit men. I went down to the Israeli folk dance sessions and roped them in. Soon it became known by my dancers that 'no man is safe near Marina'. For the one Basque item I needed eight men to be able

Work in progress. TOP PHOTO, Committee, Facing: Mary Anne Shelton, Joanne Petrie, Ziva Cohen. SECOND PHOTO: Paul Bade and Steve Gerstein helping Jaime and Mary Anne. THIRD: Nancy Heller (on the floor). FOURTH: Nancy Sedgwick, Jaime Coronado.

to form the patterns required, while they beat hoops rhythmically and continually changed formation. The one Israeli dancer knew that I was looking for male dancers for this item. We met in a lift in the university and she asked, 'Do you still need a man?' I said, 'No, eight men, desperately!' and we became aware that there was a man in the lift behind us and that he suddenly cowered in the corner looking terrified at this woman who needed eight men, desperately. We got out as soon as we could and just stood laughing at his terror. It became a joke when we met and she would ask, 'Still in desperate need of men?'

Washington DC is a dancing city, and folk groups met in the evenings and weekends. One Sunday as Mikael and I explored the city we came across a group of men doing Morris dancing in Dupont Circle. They were ripe for the picking, so I approached their leader, an Englishman. I explained the similarities between Morris and Basque dancing and I told him how in both the dancers beat sticks, swords or hoops together while dancing; I then asked if they would learn a Basque sword dance to be performed in a theatre. The leader was game for it but he had to persuade three reluctant mates to join in. I had thought that it would be easy to teach it to them but how wrong I was. Morris dances are to 3/4 time, Basque dances to 5/8. I was told later that beer had flowed freely in the dressing room, supplied by their leader to keep them at their task, so as the rehearsals proceeded inebriation set in. The performance was a huge success but when I met one of the Morris dancers again later and asked if they would be willing to repeat it, he said absolutely not because in the sword dance they had almost chopped off his thumb. 'Well', my company said, 'with all that beer flowing around – no wonder'. I had not known this, and it was against university rules.

Sherrill Wexler examined and danced with us in 1983. She performed *Casteltersol*, a dance from Catalonia, and a delightful dance with clogs, as well as a *Jota* from old Madrid, all with choreography by Juanjo Linares. She also gave the company a delightful solo, *Caracoles*, with choreography by Mercedes y Albano. I re-choreographed it for three women in long tail frocks and two men with suits, *trajes cortos* and *cordobes* hats, and it became our signature item.

Caracoles with, from left, Joanne Erlebacher, Diane Pisano, Ziva Cohen. Photo Vic Cohen.

John Magnus, a former student of mine from the University of Cape Town, and at that time a very fine ballet teacher at the Joffrey Ballet School in New York, came to dance with us. Another former student who came to dance was Charla Genn, who made a tremendously successful career in New York with her own ballet company.

Dancing *Boleras de la Cachucha* with John Magnus was Irena Campbell, a former soloist who had danced as Irina Monter in the Antonio company in the 1960s in Spain. She was thrilled to find out about our syllabus, and she came to learn it all and became our first examiner in America. She said she was thinking along those lines and was about to start something similar, when she heard about the Spanish Dance Society's syllabi. Her personal assessment of the Spanish Dance Society is at the end of Chapter 18.

Irena was an exquisite dancer, and she danced *Rapsodia Valenciana* into the audience's hearts, including that of the *Washington Post* dance critic Alan Kriegsman. We were so lucky to have him reporting on our performances, with his good understanding of dance and way of expressing himself. Sadly, he has passed away. The other dance critic was George Jackson, who became a dear friend, who has now retired. I still have many of his reviews. He once wrote, 'Marina Keet who thinks everyone should be doing Spanish dancing'.

I first met George when he arranged a party for the English writer and critic Kathryn Sorley Walker when she visited Washington DC. The fascinating author Victoria Huckenpahler offered me a lift to the party. As we travelled in her car, she regaled me with stories about the various scandalous goings-on in the dance world and when I looked shocked she said, 'Marina my girl, lift your mantilla'.

Paula Durbin had passed through the city from Hawaii, saw what we were doing and came to live in Washington to join us. She was to dance with Manolo Rivera, a charming person and delightful dancer who came from New York as our guest artist. Irena Campbell, because of an injury, could not join in the flamenco as planned, so I asked Paula to jump in at the last moment. She said, 'I'm not really a flamenco type but I am a good sport' – and so she danced. Manolo was to dance again with us and his choreography was innovative, bringing new life into flamenco.

In 1983 Sherrill Wexler founded the Spanish Dance Society in Malta in the ballet studios of the delightful Tanya Bayona. She agreed to become our organiser (today: Deborah Caruana), and we examined there. For my first visit, Tanya generously gave an elegant dinner party for me to meet the Spanish Ambassador. He and the young first minister stood talking to me. The young man said, 'Of course Spain is now an industrial nation, not known anymore for its dancing'. I said, 'In order to promote something, one does not need to destroy something else that is good'. The young man was shocked, but the ambassador quietly said, 'The lady is right'. I knew all about Spain wanting to rebrand itself as a modern industrial nation. A new Spanish ambassador to the United States had written a whole article about it in the *Washington Post*.

In the 1980s José Tamayo's company *Antologia de la Zarzuela* toured the USA with highlights from this special type of Spanish light opera. The choreographer Alberto Lorca's theatrical staging of his choreography in various dances highlighted the diverse regional instruments, music, costumes and dances. He was later to become a great friend of ours, and I have more to say about him in Chapter 37.

Marina Keet y la Sociedad de Baile Español

Dice Marina Keet que el baile español ha sido su vida entera, y sería difícil imaginar a otra extranjera que se haya dedicado tanto a este arte. Sus primeros contactos ocurrieron cuando ella, siendo una joven estudiante sudafricana perfeccionándose en ballet en Londres, oyó una carretilla de castañuelas, la siguió, y abrió la puerta del estudio de Elsa Brunelleschi. Reconociendo sus aptitudes, la Brunelleschi la mandó a estudiar con Emma Maleras en Barcelona, La Quica en Madrid, y Realito en Sevilla. Keet iba a volver a estas otras fuentes españolas, pero, primero regresó a Capetown donde enseñó, bailó y montó danzas españolas durante dos décadas.

Sudáfrica tiene, aunque parezca increíble, una fuerte tradición de baile español. Allí, docenas de maestros, entre ellos muchos egresados de compañías madrileñas, enseñan a miles de alumnos. Tomando como inspiración el entusiasmo que provocaron las giras de Luisillo en los años 60, Keet y sus colegas sudafricanos fundaron la Sociedad de Baile Español, cuyo objetivo era desarrollar un método para producir, fuera de España, un conjunto de bailarines disciplinados en la gran variedad de las danzas españolas. Sirviéndose de lo mejor que les legaron sus maestros españoles —entre ellos Mercedes y Albano, Juanjo Linares, Pedro Azorín, Enrique el Cojo y Juan Urbeltz— los sudafricanos produjeron un plan de estudios que consistía en una serie de ejercicios y coreografías progresivas divididas en nueve niveles, cada uno con su examen correspondiente.

Los alumnos de este plan practican la técnica básica en el ingreso y los dos primeros años, cuya duración realmente depende de la edad y de la aptitud del alumno. Como principiantes, por ejemplo, aprenden el paso de vasco español en su forma más pura. Luego, en los años siguientes lo practican con un cambio de dirección y más tarde tocando castañuelas. En el tercer año, se introducen pasos de la escuela bolera, y para el quinto año los alumnos tienen que integrar todo lo anterior para bailar el Olé de la Curra. Una progresión parecida les lleva al Fandango de Huelva de Mercedes, a la Rapsodia Valenciana de Brunelleschi, y al Sacromonte de Enrique Segovia.

La Sociedad se hizo internacional en 1977 cuando Keet dejó Sudáfrica para seguir a su marido a su nuevo puesto en Roma. Su intención en aquel momento fue abandonar la danza para dedicarse a su hogar y a sus tres hijos, pero los aficionados romanos, encabe-

"Seguidillas del candil"

Joana del Rio y Alejandro Marin

28 MONSALVAT

Paula Durbin's article commissioned by the Catalan arts magazine Monsalvat. Alejandro Marin, Reina Getz, Ziva Cohen, DeAnna Pierce in Seguidillas del Candil. Joanna Erlebacher and Alejandro Marin in Sevillanas.

32

Marcus Overton and the Smithsonian Institution, José de Udaeta and our 25th Anniversary, Joan Fosas and the Esbart Dansaire de Rubí Company

The Smithsonian in Washington is an interesting institution. It was founded from a grant by a rich English scientist called Smithson, who had never been to America but left all his money to set up this institution. It is actually a series of museums and it sponsors educational programmes. It is under the latter that we came upon the scene, doing lecture-demonstrations on Spanish dancing. They were more like illustrated performances, and the audiences loved them. We used to perform to packed houses. These took place in the Baird Auditorium at the Museum of Natural History. At one of these performances Joan Fosas and Nancy Sedgwick danced the famous historical Valencian *Bolero de Torrent.*

Our contact person at the Smithsonian was Marcus Overton, a great and unique person. When he came into our lives, he changed our whole horizon. He is sensitive and caring and so professional. He knew what the audience wanted and how to present it to them, and we had a long and very productive artistic relationship. When he left to take up a post as Executive Director and Producing Director of Spoleto Festival USA in Charleston, I could not understand how the Smithsonian could let a man of his calibre and experience leave. I missed him. He now lives in Southern California and we are still in contact. Here is one of the most moving and beautiful letters I have ever received, sent by him on 11 April 1991:

> 'What pleasure it gives me to send another contract for two wonderful performances! You are one of a small handful of artists who have that rarest of gifts: the ability to embody in your work the intangible virtues that the practice of art should increase in us. Knowing you, and working with you, has made me a better person, and brought me great happiness. Encountering you, your work and your dancers at the Smithsonian, has brought our audiences insight into the past, delight in its manifestation in the present, and the hope for the future that successful human endeavour should always leave in its passing.
>
> Thank you.
>
> With great and everlasting affection,
> Marcus'

The Spanish dancer José de Udaeta wrote to ask whether he could perform with us, as he was coming on a visit. It was a fortuitous time and we were able to fit him into two of our performances, one at the Marvin and one at the Smithsonian Baird Auditorium.

José had seen Susanne Audeoud, a tall Swiss girl, in classes when she was studying in Madrid. He had said, 'I shall wait for you'. He did, and he also trained her while rehearsing their repertoire to dance as *Susana y José* on tour. He was over six feet tall and needed a partner to suit his height. Most Spanish female dancers are petite, and he was delighted to find her. It was a happy partnership, but he was upset when years later she made a film of her teaching and made no mention of him or of their dancing together, nor that her husband had been hired by José as their pianist.

José had a delightful sense of humour. At a Washington party he told how he and his partner Susana had toured for about ten years. They had many quick changes to keep the show going slickly. He had just finished his one solo and she leapt onto the stage to join him in the next duet. He noticed that she was behaving and dancing very strangely on bent legs. She kept shaking one leg or the other. Every time he had his back to the audience he would ask in a whisper, 'What's the matter?' But she continued in that way and suddenly from under her skirt fell a coat hanger, with a terrible clatter as it landed on the stage. She had changed in such a hurry, jumping so frenziedly into her skirt that the coat hanger had remained attached, and as she stepped onto the stage it had wedged itself between her knees. As they took their bows he wondered what the audience had made of that strange dance.

It was all tremendous fun. Well, almost all the time. Some moments were bizarre. When he arrived, we went to the theatre to set the sound levels and lights for his items at the Marvin. No technician appeared to do the technical side. Eventually we just put his little tape recorder on the stage and he practised to that. Then just before the show we plotted the entire performance. Come the performance, which was a matinée, we managed to get through it all with no hitches.

We then rushed on to the Baird Auditorium, where we were doing a completely different show that night. As we drove I said to José, 'If you look to the right you can see the White House. To your right again is the Washington Monument', and that was how José did his sightseeing, at breakneck speed.

After Nancy Sedgwick finished dancing *Olé de la Curra*, the *Escuela Bolera* dance from the 1840s, I heard José shouting from the auditorium, 'What have you done to it Marina? What have you done?' My nerves were shattered by this time. I felt my knees go weak. What *had* I done? He came running to the stage. 'You have given new life to this old warhorse', he said. 'How did you do it?' I sank onto a chair with relief. What I had done was to first cut all the endless repeats except for the very first one, which sets the scene; second, I gave it an interpretation with some exciting build-up. He helped Paula Durbin with her costume, teaching us that *Peteneras Boleras Andaluzas* could be danced wearing a flamenco *cordobés* hat. I was so relieved that he had liked what I had done in this staging. Years later, talking to Maricarmen del Gordo, the knowledgeable folk dance teacher at *Coros y Danzas* in Madrid, I found out that she considered that dancing it with an exciting build-up was the way it used to be danced in Seville by the teacher Realito's pupils. She felt that the classical dances were dying a slow death because they were treated like museum pieces, instead of being showed in lively, living performances. So I had been on the right track after all.

While we were rehearsing before the night's show at the Baird Auditorium, the tape recorder chewed up the tape. I sat smoothing it out, when Marcus Overton came up and said, 'I have very bad news for you'. I said, 'Don't tell me, I have had enough'. Ziva Cohen took over smoothing out the tape. Marcus said that the whole sound and lighting system had crashed. Luckily they did not have a performance in their other auditorium, so they were able to bring the equipment from there over to us and set it up in time for the performance.

Later, in the middle of the night, I realised that the person who had done the technical work at the Marvin performance was not the one who had been at our rehearsal. How that was physically possible, I still do not know. José was staying with us, and I actually woke him to tell him the story. We collapsed laughing. It had been such a bizarre day.

Usually I wrote little notes to him because I did not want to disturb him, and put them outside his door for him to find when he came out. One night I went out of my room and there was a note from him – he wrote that he had nothing to say but did not want to be unreciprocal. I was very tired and in the morning dropped a bread roll on the floor. We both bent down to pick it up and bumped our heads together. He quickly scooped up the roll and I said, 'You can't eat that now', but he rubbed the roll and said, 'We do this all the time in Spain. It's tradition'. He was so thrilled with the company that he gave us a gift of two lovely dances and offered to host the 25th Anniversary of the Spanish Dance Society in Sitges, near Barcelona.

The year 1990 was filled with important occasions. The chairman of the society, Joanne Petrie, wrote:

Nancy Sedgwick in Olé de la Curra.

> 'Congratulations to Professor Barbara von Barghahn for her international seminar at George Washington and Georgetown Universities. We are proud of having been included. It gave us the opportunity to show some of Spain's impressive cultural heritage through our performance of the dances from Castile, Valencia, Asturia, Galicia, Salamanca, Extremadura and the Basque Country, and regional and flamenco dances from Andalusia. President Mazarrasa of the Spain '92 Foundation and Mrs Mazarrasa, and the new Deputy Cultural Counsellor Mr Alvaro Alabart, came backstage to congratulate everyone, saying, "You made us proud to be Spaniards". A very excited Professor Jesús Palomero Páramo from Seville rushed up to Marina and said, "Where are all the flowers and where are the medals you deserve?" She was able to say that she had recently been honoured with the *Orden de Dama de Isabel la Católica*. He then said excitedly, "But where are the others?"'

From the society's newsletter I quote: 'Sell-out performances at the Kennedy Center under the auspices of the Washington Performing Arts Society were booked out eight months in advance; at the Smithsonian, in which 400 people were turned away and of those 200 are already reserving seats for the next year – even though it has not been advertised; six performances sold out at the John Addison Theater at the University of Maryland, to which additional shows had to be scheduled; and then the American Museum of Natural History in New York and the Juilliard School of Performing Arts in New York.'

Kennedy Center

The Washington Performing Arts Society took us to perform at the Kennedy Center, which was at that time the only way local dance companies could get to perform there. Our first performance was in the performing arts presentation called City Dance. We were one of several local companies. It was heavily subsidised by Amy Goldstein and her husband. Amy is a lovely person, full of personality and with a delightful sense of humour. The first time she met us, she went up to one of the dancers and said, 'You must be very nice to me because I am very rich'! She and her husband lived in an apartment near us and we often gave them lifts to the theatre and back for dance performances, and I became very fond of them. It was Amy's idea to give local companies a chance to perform at the Kennedy Center.

From this we went on to do our own performances, first sharing with another Hispanic company and then several times on our own. The Kennedy Center authorities were keen on us and presented us themselves, which was unheard of for a local dance company before then. We were always dancing to sold-out performances. This was because we presented all types of dance – regional, classical and, of course, ending with flamenco. I have charming letters of appreciation from them. I had hijacked any and every musician who I thought could play the local regional Spanish instruments. This delighted the Spaniards at the embassy. It was the cherry on the top.

In Washington DC I also met Athol Fugard, the South African playwright and actor, who was performing one of his plays at the Kennedy Center. It was most heart-warming. There we were, two South Africans, and both involved in the theatres of the capital city of the USA.

The 25th Anniversary

Also in 1990 the Spanish Dance Society's 25th Anniversary was spent in Spain with José de Udaeta. It was scheduled during his summer school in Sitges, which is on the eastern coast of Spain. In his brochure, which was distributed throughout the world, he dedicated his summer school to the Spanish Dance Society. He had tailored the classes to our needs, after discussions with me. He invited special teachers: Eloy Pericet for the *Escuela Bolera* lessons; Jorje Sanchez, new to us, for *jota* classes; Pacita Tomás, Juaquin Villa and Mercedes '*Merceditas*' León for flamenco. She is the daughter of Mercedes y Albano and is fondly known as 'Itas'. She was to do us proud many years later with her praise at the *Escuela Bolera Hoy* symposium in Madrid in 2009.

Oh how proud we in the society were when the teachers were surprised at our pupils, who came from all over the world, dancing so well; they were all well-groomed and their basic technique so correct. It was a revelation to others who had been trained elsewhere. Mercedes and Albano who were the main teachers were so impressed that they immediately agreed to become our patrons. Teachers and dancers on the course wished to learn our syllabus that achieved such results. Our promised place for our classes, the theatre, had been usurped by a guest dancer, and the teachers and dancers wanted to learn. We found a venue but the police were called to stop Mavis Becker teaching on a balcony – well, it was siesta time. So we all taught our syllabus wherever we could. One day a man pointed to Mavis, Rhoda, Sherrill and me and said, 'You are the people teaching on street corners'.

There were three American Nancys among the participants: Nancy Heller and Nancy Sedgwick from the Spanish Dance Society in Washington, and Professor Nancy Ruyter from the University of California. When they arrived at class in the morning, the Spanish students greeted them with '*Hola las Nancys*'!

José gave three parties and specially invited the famous dancer Rosario from Seville to be patron of the performance and to close the proceedings. She had been the partner of Antonio, the doyen of Spanish dance, and she was a very charming person. What honours José was giving us. At the performance, which was also dedicated to us, Nancy Sedgwick and Joan Fosas performed the elegant Valencian dance *Bolero de L'Alcudia de Carlet* in the beautiful antique costumes designed by the famous Catalan artist Fabiá Puigserver, and made magnificently by hand by Rosa Fosas Juliá, the sister of Joan Fosas. I explain later how I acquired this dance.

One day during all this activity, José and I were having a meal in a nearby restaurant and we had a bizarre conversation. I was telling him how the singing of a *Seguiriyas* had been my most profound experience of flamenco. I said that I never imagined that it would be singing and not dancing that would give me such an intense flamenco experience. I said that it was by the revered old flamenco singer who was known as *El Chocolate* because he was so dark. 'Who?' asked José. '*Chocolate*', I said. '*Choc-oh-LAAH-TAY*?' questioned José, still disbelievingly. 'Yes. *Choc-oh-LAH-TAY*'. Then a waiter bellowed from the other end of the room, '*CHOC-OH-LAH-TAY*', repeating an order from a customer and shouting it as if irritated that José was doubting what I said.

SDS 25th anniversary in Sitges (Barcelona). TOP from left: Marie-Louise Ihre, Marina, Paula Durbin, José de Udaeta, Nancy Ruyter, Ziva Cohen, Irena Campbell. CENTRE: Mercedes y Albano, main flamenco teachers at the summer school. BELOW: Rosario (seated), Patron of the summer school performance, with Rhoda Rivkind, Marina, Mavis Becker and Sherrill Wexler.

It was such an unbelievable coincidence that we burst out laughing hysterically. The customers around us probably thought that we were drinking too much but I was only drinking water.

José de Udaeta in SDS T-shirt and Marina in front of part of his castanet collection. Sitges.

The singer *El Chocolate* (Antonio Nunes) was in the most exciting flamenco show I have ever seen, *Flamenco Puro*, which was presented in Washington and New York in 1987 by two Argentinians, Claudio Segovia and Hector Orezzoli, with the best Gypsy dancers from Spain. Performing in that show was also the famous dancer El Güito (Eduardo Serrano Iglesias) whom I invited to teach a class to our company in Washington DC. He taught us a terrific *bulerias* which became our party piece.

Carola Goya, Matteo and I attended another of the summer schools organised by José de Udaeta in Sitges. The heat was killing and I decided that I should leave, as I am intolerant of heat and suffer very much. It was a wise decision. Intense heat like that had killed King Baudouin of Belgium when he was holidaying one summer with his Spanish wife Fabiola on the Mediterranean coast of Spain. But Carola and Matteo stayed on, with disastrous results for Carola. She had

Marina, El Güito (guest teacher, GWU; Eduardo Serrano Iglesias) and Mavis Becker in Washington DC.

several severe strokes and it took five hours before an ambulance came from Barcelona. Matteo was such a devoted husband and looked after her so well. She once said to me, 'I am so lucky to have a husband who loves me so much'. But she too pampered and fussed over him. Most impressive. When she died some years later, he keenly felt the loss.

In José's home nearby, which is like a castle that he had restored, is his incredible castanet collection all around the walls of one room. When Margot Fonteyn was filming *The Magic of Dance*, she stayed with him and his wife Marta, and above the sink in his kitchen there is a plaque engraved with the words, 'Margot Fonteyn washed her hair here'! The film showed José's feet doing a *Zapateado*; Carmelita and Eloy Pericet stylishly dancing a *Boleras de la Cachucha* inside the historic castle and Joan Fosas and his partner dancing outside on the grass in the garden the beautiful Valencian dance *Bolero de L'Alcudia de Carlet*. When I saw this last dance in the film, I did not know where or from whom to get hold of it. I was entranced by the dance and the rich costuming – and I wanted it. So I phoned José de Udaeta. He said that it was easy, as it was danced by Joan Fosas in Rubí, near Barcelona, and was in the repertoire of the *Esbart Dansaire de Rubí* company. He said that I should write to their artistic director, Albert Sans, and ask to learn it. I did so and Sans replied asking me to come to the Catalan town of Rubí where they would teach it to me. I was to go to a certain shop in a square in Rubí and they would pick me up there. So a date and time were arranged and I set off for Rubí.

I arrived and found that that particular house in the square was under reconstruction, and the workmen just shrugged their shoulders. They directed me to a shop across the street. There they knew all about me and told me to sit down. They made a phone call to say that I had arrived. A slim small energetic man swept in and said that I was going to stay with him, but not to worry, his sister would look after me too, and he would teach me the dance.

He was Joan Fosas and we were to develop an amazing interaction between Rubí and Washington. He took me to a theatre where we were going to do the class but the humid heat was finishing me off. At last I suggested that he should dance each step and I would write them down and then teach them in Washington from my notes. This, to his bewilderment, we did. Then in the evenings he showed me wonderful videos of their company.

When I returned to Washington I thought that Joan should join us to dance these dances. I wrote to him, and he accepted. When he arrived I had taught the dance, but he had to add the final touches, and teach the company the 'mourners' dance', *Mortitxol*. His sister Rosa arrived with him. We had had the dresses made but she brought with her magnificent additions to the *Bolero de L'Alcudia* that she had made: a fichu covered in glittering paillettes, an apron similarly decorated, and sleeves for the girl and leggings for the man, crocheted by an old lady in Rubí, she said. These were the touches we could not get in Washington. Rosa had also made a frill with paillettes, which was to be added to the underskirt. They had also had a special hat made for us for the *Bolero*. Everything was white and gold. He also brought the four men's black hats for *Mortitxol*. As usual, we had problems with rehearsal space, and Mary Day of the Washington Ballet kindly lent us one of her studios. It all went well and soon everything was ship-shape. The 'old lady who crocheted the leggings and sleeves' turned out to be – young Rosa. Everything they brought were gifts for the company.

When we arrived home, Joan threw himself down on the sofa and, kicking his legs in the air, shouted, 'I'm happy, I'm happy, I'm happy!' I said, 'I'm so glad'. But he continued, saying that he could not have believed I could learn from notes and that I had come to Rubí, sat down and written words on paper and he'd had no idea whether I knew what was going on. When I had written and asked him to come and dance, he had been tempted but worried sick as to what he might be coming to in Washington. He had been so nervous that he had asked his sister to come with him to help. It was a roaring success.

Besides the show at the Kennedy Center we also had more shows at the Baird Auditorium. Joan Fosas came again with more beautiful dances and we went to the Juilliard School of Music and Dance in New York. We were most grateful to him, and we gave a certificate of appreciation to his dance company in Rubí. I also gave one to Rosa for the absolutely magnificent costumes she had provided for the dance *Bolero de L'Alcudia de Carlet*, and I called her up on the stage of the Baird Auditorium to receive it from Professor Maida Withers. She was so happy, and so were we. She said that no one had ever singled her out to thank her for her help; she was full of emotion.

Rosa and Joan had amusing stories about Rosa. She was the smallest in the Rubí company and therefore the one who led them all on to the stage in any given dance. With one programme they decided to have the music orchestrated for a full orchestra, but the music just never arrived. In the end it came so late that they had to perform without having had an orchestra rehearsal. The curtains parted and the orchestra struck up, but Rosa did not recognise the music. She peered around the curtain and shook her head at the conductor. He stopped the orchestra, looked at the music, puzzled, but decided that it was the correct music, lifted his baton and struck up again. Again Rosa peered around the curtain and shook her head, this time adding a waggling finger: 'NO'. Again the conductor stopped the orchestra, looked at the music and then decided to start again. The third time Rosa stuck her head out, he decided to ignore her and suddenly Rosa recognised that it was the correct music after all and on she danced with the rest of the company following her.

One day I received the following (here slightly abbreviated) letter from the School of Fine Arts, Department of Music and Dance, University of Kansas, inspired particularly by *Mortitxol*:

'An open letter to Dame Marina Keet (Grut), Artistic Director, Spanish Dance Society.

From Joan Stone, Professor of Dance History, University of Kansas, 24 June 1992.

This is a letter of thanks for an extraordinary program done by the Spanish Dance Society at the International Early Dance Institute at Goucher [College in Baltimore where I taught during a summer school]. I have read about legendary figures such as Carmen Amaya, and seen the films of Antonio Gades and an occasional performance of flamenco dance, but knew little about the amazing range of rich history of Spanish dance, revealed by your program and the excellent program notes.

I have pulled out my Goya book to make a better-informed search for dance forms, such as the *Seguidillas.* I suggested to a colleague in ballet that he learn to play the castanets and take on the *Escuela Bolera.* The *Passapied de España* and *Vestris Gavotte* got me thinking about the transition from French and Spanish Baroque to early ballet. I was fascinated by the dance from Galicia to bagpipe accompaniment, showing the Celtic influence, a Basque dance, *Escuela Andaluza,* a dance from Mallorca, a *bolero* for three showing Moorish influence, and a bolero… the powerful *Mortitxol* so astonishingly modern in its composition that I had to write a special response to it [see poem below]…

The dancers performed with such conviction, skill, joy, drama, understanding… switching from style to style with ease and clarity. The costumes… beautiful in color, design and materials, and very flattering on the dancers… were a feast for the eyes. I got to see peach silk, hand embroidered scarves up close and a magnificent white and gold costume with hand crocheted sleeves, confirming my notion as a viewer of the care and attention that has gone into costuming and other aspects of production.

Jaime Coronado and Nancy Sedgwick in Bolero de L'Alcudia de Carlet. Photo Vic Cohen.

> For me the program was a journey through Spanish dance in the company of a diverse group of dancers and musicians led by an ebullient, witty, irresistible storyteller. I would like my colleagues in the dance program at the University of Kansas and dancers here and elsewhere to share this experience. I hope that it will be possible to find a way of videotaping the vast repertoire of the Spanish Dance Society, so that these treasures of a tradition that is rapidly disappearing will not be lost like so much of dance history.
>
> Joan Stone'

Professor Stone also sent me her following moving poem about *Mortitxol*, choreographed by Albert Sans i Aris of the *Esbart Dansaire de Rubí* (Barcelona) dance company. This mourners' dance, performed when a child dies before the age of seven years, is a religious celebration of the passing of a pure soul into heaven. Although it is a Valencian bolero, Sans was the first choreographer to theatricalise it for the stage, and in his version it was sung in Catalan, *Mortitxol* meaning 'death of a child'. In order to reconstruct this almost extinct dance, Joan Fosas had searched throughout the region of Valencia for old people who still remembered dancing it.

'They enter two at a time
in couples
but each man and woman is alone
they walk slowly
feeling the ground
the women are in black shawls
bound in their grief
the men keep their arms close to their bodies
the gaze is down
the couples cluster like people in a room after a funeral
along the back wall
the one couple more forward
are they the parents of the dead child?
there is music playing
but the dance is silent

the couples drift apart imperceptibly
the men seek each other out
and so do the women
the men begin a rhythmic pattern in the feet
they surge forward and back
making half wheels
broken circles
with their arms
as one arm rises, the other falls
they have castanets in their hands
but the castanets are silent
the women have begun moving
not dancing

until they take off their shawls
feet come to life
torsos
arms
the gaze leaves the ground
and the castanets begin
the men dance
forward and back
forward and back
the pattern of the fields and crops
their arms pulse
up and down
up and down
the pattern growing and dying
they charge through the line of women
who twist and turn and change places
dancing from side to side
weaving
gesticulating
remembering the birth
mourning the death
of the child

a circle forms imperceptibly
men and women join imperceptibly
the dance intensifies
faster foot rhythms
bigger arm and leg gestures
more insistent clicking of the castanets
a wrenching, wheeling dance of death
around and around
an inner circle and an outer circle
death has brought people together
the community has taken on the burden of grief
now the pure soul of the dead child can pass into heaven
bodies, gaze, arms lift to the sky!'

Finale of Mortitxol by SDS's Spanish Dance Theatre, Washington DC.
Photo Vic Cohen.

This was written about a performance by our company in America, the Spanish Dance Theatre of the Spanish Dance Society. It was a remarkable group of dedicated dancers and musicians who together formed a 'family' and who loved what they were doing. Their integrity was remarked upon by many, especially at the Spanish embassy and other centres where we performed. Professor Joan Stone, a revered person in her own right, captures their devotion to the art they were disseminating with such ardour and conviction. It is also why José Greco was astonished when he wanted to tour the company and found out that they were not professionals.

Marina, José Greco, and Joan Fosas at the Smithsonian in Washington DC.

33

The Spanish National Ballet, the *Escuela Bolera* Symposium, My Book *The Bolero School,* and the Basque *Argia* Company

The Spanish National Ballet

During the years that José Antonio (Ruiz) was the artistic director of the Spanish National Ballet and patron of the Spanish Dance Society I used to watch rehearsals and performances of the company. In 1993 the National Ballet appointed a triumvirate of women as joint artistic directors: Aurora Pons most successfully put the finances of the company back on to a firm basis; Nana Lorca was responsible for rehearsing and staging the repertoire with panache and humour; and Victoria Eugenia, 'Betty', lovingly gave the company their daily classes. She based these on what she had seen of the previous day's rehearsals and performances.

One day Aurora Pons said that they were uneasy about a ballet by Mariemma, *Danza y Tronío,* which was in their repertoire, and which incidentally happened to be my favourite ballet of hers. In it she was highlighting the dance styles of the 18th century. They asked me to advise them. The ballet was structured in two sections: one based on *Escuela Bolera*, the other on a dramatic depiction of the dances of the people, led by the charismatic Antonio Marquez and beautifully sensuous Anna Gonzales. After we had watched a performance, I said that the classical costumes of the first half could not hold their own with the drama of the second half. Later I saw that the costumes had been most successfully redesigned.

Betty asked me to watch her give a class. She was a really special teacher and the women of the company adored her. After the class she asked the dancers to stay on. She told them that she was going to improvise an arm exercise and that they were to follow her. She turned to me and said, 'I am dedicating this to you, Marina'. There ensued a most beautiful and gripping series of movements which built up in emotion and ended with everyone crying, including me. It was an unforgettable experience for both the company and me.

The National Ballet of Spain is now in the good hands of talented artistic director Antonio Najarro. His ballet *Suite Sevilla,* using music of the three composers Rafael Riquenui, Miguel Rivera and Diego Losada, and with his own costume designs, achieves what was great in the past – what presentations by past choreographers had given to the world of Spain's rich variety of dance styles – and which was now lost. The sets and lighting dramatically composed with much emotional atmosphere, demonstrate artistically his wish to present the range of these dance styles. The delightful light touch with the brilliantly danced *Escuela Bolera* solo introduced a humorous glint within the drama. This is something Spain desperately needs. Enthusiastic reviews and public reaction showed that this touch of humour fell on parched ground. However, it will be an uphill battle to encourage a public that has been fed 'flamenco only' for so long, to appreciate the riches and diversity that Spain has to offer. Najarro is certainly the right man to create a company worthy of Spain, as his background includes all this in his training at the Mariemma Royal Conservatory in Madrid. Covering all aspects, as did his dance career, he performed in ballets by all the major choreographers, ending as Principal Dancer of the National Ballet which he now directs. One hopes he has peace to achieve his wishes, and I praise the wisdom of those who placed him there.

I was heartened that I had met him before in Mallorca, when I was examining the Spanish Dance Society examination session in the Balearic Isles. I had examined him and picked him out as being a particularly gifted dancer. He was also a handsome, personable young man.

Spanish Classical Dance Symposium

In 1992 I was asked to write an article about a Valencian mourners' dance from Jijona for the Spanish Ministry of Culture's symposium *Encuentro Internacional Escuela Bolera* in the Zarzuela Theatre, Madrid, on the classical school of Spanish dance, the *Escuela Bolera.* The seminar was organised by Roger Salas of the Ministry. The 19th-century French author Baron Davillier wrote about this dance, calling it a *Jota,* in his book *Travels Through Spain* with illustrations by Gustave Doré, famous for his illustrations of the Bible. Knowing the dance, I recognised at once from his illustration of the arm positions of the dancers performing it that it was not a *Jota* but a *Bolero*. Davillier toured Spain in 1862 writing articles on each province. It is from those articles and the exquisite sketches by Doré that we find out about the famous *Escuela Bolera* dancers Dolores Serral and Mariano Camprubí. The large painting of them by Manet hangs in the Phillips Collection in Washington DC, where they had no idea who the dancers were. I gave their names to the museum and also pointed out that the dancer seated in the background was Lola de Valencia.

The first dance in the video which I showed at the symposium,

Gustave Doré's drawing of the Valencian mourners' dance.

the *Bolero de L'Alcudia de Carlet* performed by Nancy Sedgwick and Joan Fosas, produced an exciting moment in the theatre. The audience applauded wildly and shouted. I think that not only the beauty of the dance gripped them, but it came as something positive amid all the talking. But when I tried to show the dance of mourning, a Valencian came up and grabbed the microphone. How could a foreigner present *his* region's dances? Fortunately the information which he prevented me from giving to the audience was in my illustrated article in the book published for the symposium. He must have been upbraided during the intermission because afterwards he apologised abjectly. To make up for his rude intervention, he came to America and taught us twelve additional dances! While he was in Washington DC we had a performance at the Kennedy Center, and by way of celebration he was planning to set off firecrackers in the audience. Luckily one of our dancers discovered this and stopped him. It would have created a panic and we would never have been allowed there again.

At the symposium a young dancer came up to me and said he hoped I would not take it amiss but the costumes were wrong. I explained that they were '*antiguo*', from a very early era, which had been brought to life by a famous Catalan artist and handmade by Rosa Fosas especially for us in Washington DC. Standing next to me was Maricarmen del Gordo. She shook her head afterwards and said, 'These youngsters know nothing'. We were about to perform those dances in Washington and New York.

At this historic symposium, Angel Pericet Blanco was scheduled to dance *La Maja y el Torero* with his sister Carmelita, the only remaining duet from that era which still used mime. However, he did not appear on the stage, but did take part in the roundtable discussion at which José de Udaeta was sitting in the front row. He rose from his chair and dramatically accused Angel's grandfather and father of having changed the precious style (to compete with the Madrid ballet teachers, so it was said). Angel hotly denied this. They exchanged heated words. De Udaeta threw his cape dramatically over his shoulder, turned to face the stunned audience, said, 'I am off to Berlin', and sailed out, cape flying, leaving a hushed silence behind. However, I personally experienced the change of style, having been taught the old style on my first Spanish visit and the changed style on my next visit. Alberto Lorca, who had studied with his beloved Luisa Pericet Jiménez, agreed with de Udaeta.

JOAN FOSAS
Y LA SPANISH DANCE SOCIETY

por Pilar Llorens, «Pastora Martos»

Joan Fosas nos dice que para él ha sido una experiencia inolvidable. Participó en un programa donde además de las danzas valencianas que interpretó figuraban otros estilos, como la «Jota Aragonesa», «Jota Asturiana», piezas clásicas como «Asturias», de Albéniz, y un «Gloria» extraído de la Misa Flamenca de Torregrosa, con coreografía de Marina Keet. En la parte flamenca «Caracoles», «Farruca» y «Alegrías». Las piezas que protagonizó Fosas fueron «Mortitxol», canto y baile fúnebres para un velatorio infantil, y «Bolero de l'Alcudia de Carlet» (Valencia, siglo XVIII).

Le preguntamos:

—¿Qué impresión traes de allí y de tu colaboración con esta compañía y su directora?.

—Marina es una persona muy documentada en baile popular español y tiene que sentirse orgullosa de dirigir una compañía como ésta, además de contar con un muy buen equipo de trabajo. Me ha llamado la atención la seriedad y la disciplina que existe en este grupo. Creo que es la misma que en una compañía profesional. A mí me hicieron sentir como pez en el agua, y aunque no soy profesional, en

En el Kennedy Center se agotaron las localidades. La Spanish Dance Society se presentaba con el bailarín catalán Joan Fosas, procedente del Esbart de Rubí en calidad de artísta invitado. Marina Keet, directora de la compañía, es una de las principales investigadoras del mundo sobre los bailes populares en España.

En la fotografía: Joan Fosas y Nancy Sedgwick en el «Bolero de L'Alcudia de Carlet» (foto Victor Cohen).

MONSALVAT

España

Article from *Monsalvat* about the Spanish Dance Society, with photo by Vic Cohen of Joan Fosas and Nancy Sedgwick dancing the *Bolero de L'Alcudia de Carlet* in Washington DC.

My Book and DVD on *The Bolero School*

I tried to persuade Eloy Pericet to publish all the steps in writing and on a DVD but he was not keen, although he assisted when Conchita del Campo and I went to him in April 2002 to verify all the *Escuela Bolera* steps and dances for my book *The Bolero School*. He allowed my husband to film our classes, and called him 'Fellini' after the famous film director. I thought he would be upset when the book and the DVD were published. Instead I received the following letter of congratulations:

'Madrid 10 Junio de 2002

Querida amiga Marina:

El libro me ha gustado muchísimo, es una verdadera joya. La información bibliografía interesantísima, las ilustraciones preciosas y lo más importante el método de enseñanza de nuestra *Escuela Bolera* perfectamente detallado y clarísimo. Es un gran aporte a la cultura de la danza Española.
Mi sincera enhorabuena por su maravillosa obra – un gran trabajo.Yo lo he recomendado a todos mis alumnos y profesionales.

El éxito es seguro.

Espero vernos pronto. Un cordial saludo a su esposo, un abrazo,

(Eloy Pericet)'

TRANSLATION

'My dear friend Marina,

I liked your book very much, it is a real jewel. The really interesting bibliographic information, the beautiful illustrations and, most importantly, the method of teaching our *Escuela Bolera* perfectly detailed and so clear. It is a great contribution to the culture of Spanish dancing.

My sincerest congratulations for your marvellous work – a great work. I have recommended it to all my pupils and professionals. An assured success.

Hoping that we will meet soon, a cordial greeting to your husband. Warm wishes,

(Eloy Pericet)'

Conchita del Campo, Mikael, Eloy Pericet and Marina in Madrid, 2002.

From Mr Antonio Álvarez Cañibano, director of the Centre for Documentation of Music and Dance in the Spanish Ministry of Education and Culture, I received the following letter (translated extract) about my book:

'I am contacting you at the suggestion of Mrs Martin-Asin to congratulate you on the publication of *The Bolero School*. We have bought the book for our library and can see that it

> is an important work for the international dissemination of this type of Spanish dance.... It would be very important for the community of university teachers, researchers and *Escuela Bolera* dancers if your marvellous [*estupenda*] work could be translated into Spanish, for its effect not only here but also in other Spanish-speaking countries.'

Professor Rosa Ruiz at the Royal Conservatoire of Dance in Madrid wrote: 'Su libro es una autentica joya. Lo he recomendado y mostrado a todos.' ('Your book is a real jewel. I have recommended it and shown it to everyone.') She translated it for her students while teaching them.

Oliver Busch, the German editor of my book *Royal Swedish Ballet* later said that my *The Bolero School*, published by David Leonard's Dance Books Ltd, was the best printed book that he had seen for years. He said that each language requires a different typography and production, and he was very excited about the way the Bolero book had been published. For the book cover, I had given my son Nicolai a picture which was suitable but dreary, and I said, 'I want an old master please', which he then miraculously produced.

Nicolai was the editor when we made the *Escuela Bolera* DVD. He made many invaluable suggestions, such as starting with a storyboard, and filming against a grey background which was very hard to find when all the theatres were closed for refurbishing in the summer when we would be filming. Most important was to pre-record the castanet-playing on the recorded music before filming, and then play the recorded version to dance to. Nicolai said that this avoided picking up extraneous noises during the filming. What was tricky was that the machine on which this music was replayed differed from the one on which the recording had been done, and Nicolai spent many weeks in his studio re-recording and refitting the music to the dances – gruelling work. Also, the dancer Paul Rooney's waistcoat had gone missing and the only one I had left did not fit him. His shirt kept escaping from under the waistcoat as he danced. At last we just had to accept one of the takes. Again Nicolai went beyond the call of duty and sat for hours 'painting out', slide by slide, portions of the 'escaped' shirt on each section of the film. I said, 'You are so professional'; he laughed and said, 'Mamma, I *am* a professional'. Mothers!

Cover of Marina's book about the bolero school.
Cover design by Nicolai Grut.

Conchita del Campo, Francesca Fröhlich, Gillian Hurst and Claire Matthews, who were performing in the DVD, impressed and amazed me by their thorough approach to the pre-recording of the castanets. They had individually notated the music, each one using a different method, and they read the notation from a music stand while Richard Rabe (the music director) recorded. They are all members of the Spanish Dance Society, and they donated their work. The two male dancers Paul Rooney and Rhys George were from Elmhurst School, where Sherrill Wexler taught.

Dancers in the bolero school DVD from left: Gillian Hurst; Francesca Fröhlich and Rhys George; Conchita del Campo and Paul Rooney; Francesca Fröhlich and Paul Rooney; Marina Lorca. Photo by Chris Boyce.

Nicolai also suggested that the DVD should have bonus performances offered by professional guest artists. These items were kindly given to me by Marina Lorca and Joan Fosas, and my pupils from America Nancy Sedgwick, Lourdes Elias and Jaime Coronado, joined by Conchita del Campo and Francesca Fröhlich. All exciting performers. I donated the income from the sales of the DVD to the Spanish Dance Society, from where it can be obtained (www.spanishdancesociety.org, then 'Shop'). The society has received a goodly income from these sales. So my thanks go to all participants. My husband also contributed much work to both the book and the DVD.

When I went to check the stage the night before the only two days we had for filming with Chris Boyce, I found the grey backcloth torn near the centre. I worked on my knees until 5am trying to rearrange it before the morning's filming. I managed, but we were left with a minute stage area and the performers had to dance so carefully so as not to stray beyond the confined space. They were troopers and there were many retakes as dresses swirled out of camera range. We all struggled in a heat of 35 degrees. I fed everyone each day. Conchita's help with both the book and the DVD was unstinting. My motto was once again proved correct: 'Nothing in life is easy'.

During our last few fraught hours of filming, the secretary of the dance school came to me to say that the 'Queen of Bulgaria' was visiting them, and could she please bring her to watch the filming? 'Yes, yes,' I said in a hurry, and went on with the filming, but we all wondered, 'Queen of *Bulgaria*'? Then entered the Queen of *Buganda* (a small traditional kingdom within the Republic of Uganda) with her African retinue. My husband explained *sotto voce* to her what it was all about. One particularly successful take, with a spectacular jump by Paul Rooney, which I would have included in the DVD, was ruined when a member of the retinue took a flash photo. However, they were all very polite and quiet, and they thanked us very much when they left.

Chris Dance played the music on a fortepiano, giving the delicate sound of the era of the *Escuela Bolera*. Some dances were accompanied on guitar and bandurrias by the Grupo de Danzas Adolfo de Castro from Cadiz, who played for Saura's film *Sevillanas*. They had asked me to teach them some regional dances to perform at a competition, and when I was making my Bolero DVD I asked them what the fee would be to use their music. The reply was, 'There is no fee, the music is yours to use. You helped us, and now we return your kindness'.

Back to Madrid and the Pericets. On one of my study visits to Eloy in Madrid he had double-booked himself and had to go to Andalusia. Because I had come from so far he said that his brother, on a visit to Madrid, would come instead. This would be a lesson with the gorgeous Angel Pericet Jiménez, 'lord of the *Escuela Bolera* dance', who danced like a dream. I was delighted and not a little intimidated.

When we started the class he said, 'I am not a teacher, so I suggest we dance together the dances you wish to study'. I felt so privileged. However, I was to learn that there were differences between what he danced and what I had learnt from Eloy. I asked why and he said, 'Because I am a dancer and I adapt the dance to make it more theatrical'. There were many moments when we went off in different directions – much hilarity. This knowledge would prove useful later.

I first met Angel when he was in charge of the Spanish National Ballet's visit to America in 1983, invited by María de Avila to join as her assistant director. He left two years later in disappointment. He felt that he had achieved nothing of his high expectations of bringing the correct classical *Escuela Bolera* style to the company. Angel was only allowed to do one choreography and not much else.

The Basque Company *Argia* Visits Washington

Each year Juan Urbeltz and his Basque dance company *Argia*, mentioned in Chapter 15, travel to Boise, Idaho, to give a course to the dance companies there. They also take their costumes and props, and present performances. One year they let me know that they would be coming via Washington DC and would like to make contact with me. I replied, asking them whether the stopover could be long enough to do a lunch-hour performance in the large Lisner Auditorium; they agreed. We were very excited and planned a party for them afterwards. They duly phoned me from the airport to say that they had arrived. We went to the Lisner, and the audience was already filing in. We waited and waited and waited.

We then received a message that there was a delay. So I went on stage to make the announcement, and said that I would tell them about the Basques and their dances while we waited. When after an hour I had reached their blood groups, I knew I was in trouble. Some of the lunch-hour audience began to leave. From backstage I was told that the company had arrived. I went to them and was told that at the airport some of the skips containing their costumes and props had disappeared. While they were taking their luggage from the transport belt, the skips had been whisked away. They did not seem to understand the urgency of getting the performance started. The girls were quietly sitting in the changing rooms plaiting their hair. I said nervously, 'The audience has been waiting for two hours, you must dance *now*'. They seemed surprised, so I added, 'Send someone to dance, even if it is only a *Pas de Basque'*. To them, all their steps were *Pas de Basques.* One man then went on to the stage, followed by a *Txistu* player and a drummer. He danced up a storm and brought the house down. The audience clapped, stamped and shouted, 'Wonderful!' By then the others were ready. They gave a show-stopping performance and we had a lovely party afterwards.

34

New York

The Museum of Natural History in New York

Sheila Greenberg of the Museum of Natural History in New York contacted us to perform there several times. Neither we nor they had funding, so we subsidised part of it and she gave what they could afford.

We would hire a bus and leave at the crack of dawn, 4:30am to be exact. Ziva Cohen, who was our organiser, used to bring funny videos for us to watch on the long trip to New York. Then Ziva's dancer side came to the fore and she decided we could make better use of our time by watching the video of our last performance and improve on it in our minds. We arrived at the theatre and sneaked in backstage to unload our costumes, working quietly because they still had film shows until 5pm.

This museum has the largest cinema screen in the USA, set up in the museum's lovely old historic theatre. For performances, which usually start at 7:30pm, they lower the screen down below the stage and then build the floor over the space into which it has sunk. This took to 5:30pm.

At 5:30pm the dancers started to put on their makeup and I went in to do the staging and lighting with the wonderful man there. When I said, 'How do we manage to do this each time?', he replied, 'Because we're two old pros!' How right he was. I had every detail written out for what we were to perform and what lighting I wanted but I could trust him to play around with the lights during the actual performance to get the best effects. His crew were also real professionals. Without my training with Dulcie Howes I could *never* have done those shows.

By this time the dancers were ready and we did a run-through of as much of the show as we could, before the audience had to be let in. By then the sweat was pouring down me, and one time I was so wet that I could not get my arms into the long sleeves of the dress in which I was going to give my lecture.

The dancers were indomitable. Backstage there was just no space at all. As each item ended, we would dump the costumes in big rubbish bags and they would be stashed on the bus to give us room. Every dress rail had to be planned to be efficient and have the next set of costumes ready. At 7:30pm the audience streamed in and the show had to start.

Caracoles. Lourdes Elias, Jaime Coronado, Ziva Cohen, Nelson Sitton, Mary Anne Shelton. Photo Vic Cohen.

The first performance overwhelmed us. We had not experienced the intensity of a New York audience before. As I went onstage after our first item, always with live musicians playing the instruments from the Spanish regions, I was totally unprepared for the tumultuous applause. New York audiences usually saw only flamenco and they loved the regional dances. I stood stunned at the podium while wave after wave of cheering and clapping poured over me. Then I knew what pop stars must experience. I finally had to hold up my hand to be able to speak, and said that there was more to come. They just loved us and we were invited to return again and again, but at last the company just could not cope. The performances had to take place on a Thursday. This meant that everyone went to work exhausted on Friday after arriving home in Washington DC at 4:30am. The remarkable founder of the Washington Performing Arts, Patrick Hayes, asked a famous singer, 'How would you judge success?' The answer was, 'To be asked back'.

Jota Aragonesa. From left: Mary Anne Shelton, Nancy Heller, Nelson Sitton, Nancy Sedgwick, Lourdes Elias. Photo Vic Cohen.

After that first show ended I went back to the podium to collect my notes and there, to my utter amazement, was the entire audience still seated, patiently waiting in silence. 'It's over', I said. 'That's the end; there is no more'. 'We know,' they shouted back, 'but we want more!' 'Tell us more', they shouted. It was so exhilarating. So I asked them to ask questions, which I answered. As I write, the feeling of excitement that ran through me returns. It was an incredibly uplifting experience.

After each performance in New York, people came up to me to chat. One night a man introduced himself. 'I'm Michael Lorimer', he said. I said I was delighted to meet him, but I had no idea who he was. He could see that. Other people were chatting and suddenly he was gone, only to turn up a little later. He thrust a cassette tape in my hand and said, 'I happened to have this in my car. Please keep it, and when you have some time, listen to it'. I went home and played it, and the most divine music came forth. He was the famous Baroque guitarist Michael Lorimer. I phoned him to apologise for my stupidity and asked him to do a performance at the Smithsonian Baird Auditorium with us. He came and it was so successful. With him came Alan Tjaarda-Jones, who performed historic Spanish dances in a mask. This association led to other performances. The world is so rich in talented artists. We were to repeat this cooperation in New York when Marina Lorca joined us once more. That is the theatre life that I miss, now that I am retired in London.

Michael Lorimer also discovered a lost book of music by the Spanish Baroque composer Murciana. It turned up in Mexico in the ownership of a man called Saldívar. It was bound in the same way as another book of Murciana's and contained the collected dances of this famous Spanish guitarist and composer. Everyone always wondered how it was that he had never composed any dance music, and there it was, bound in red-tooled leather with gold leaf on the edges of the pages. He was given permission by Saldívar's widow to publish the music and add his introduction on how, having seen Murciana's other manuscript, he could recognise this as coming from the same pen and being the twin book. The music is most beautifully and distinctively written out, so there can be no mistaking the authorship.

Michael Lorimer is a delightful person. When we visited New York, Michael chatted to Mikael and me until 4am. When he was with us in Washington, his wife would phone and say, 'Have you any idea where Michael is?', because he would wander off, start talking to people he met and forget to go back to where he was supposed to be.

One day, when we had lived in London for a year or so, the phone rang. I answered it and a voice said, 'Do you recognise this?', and a Basque tune played on a guitar floated across the wires. It was Michael, and he thought I might just like to hear it. How right he was.

Invited to the Juilliard School in New York by Hector Zaraspe

We had been invited the Juilliard School of music, dance and drama by Hector Zaraspe, who is very well-known in the dance world and who is such a delightful and kind person. He welcomed us warmly. To get to New York we repeated the same process as with the Museum of Natural History, hiring a smaller bus this time because we were taking a smaller company. We had Joan Fosas with us and also his brother-in-law Pere (Pedro) Juliá who had come along to experience America.

We performed to a peer group of dancers, musicians and faculty staff. We did wondrous regional dances from Salamanca, Valencia, Catalonia, Aragon, etc., and received thunderous applause. Afterwards the excited students and faculty members chatted to us. A man and woman came up to me. She, a well-known modern dancer, said, 'Why aren't you performing at the Joyce Theater? They have never, ever had anything like this – never'. I explained that we did not have the funds for a week-long stay in New York. The man was Michael Maule, and I said, 'Oh yes, you are from Durban; I know all about you'. He was stunned to hear that he featured in my book *The History of Ballet in South Africa*, especially the story about him rending his shirt in anger after one performance.

It was for us most gratifying to get so much appreciation from such knowledgeable people. The Juilliard students were overawed at the height the dancers had jumped in the Jota. Our dancers said, 'Never before have we had such a well-sprung floor. We just wanted to keep on dancing and never stop'. Another unforgettable experience to treasure.

In May 2017 the Spanish Dance Society in the USA was presented with the prestigious Fidelio Award in Washington DC for its major contribution and dedication to the Washington DC arts community and beyond.

Fandango de Verdiales. Nancy Sedgwick, Jaime Coronado, Ziva Cohen.
Photo Vic Cohen.

Alegrías. Joanne Erlebacher, Diane Pisano, Ziva Cohen and DeAnna Pierce.
Photo Vic Cohen.

Asturian. Antonio Saldaña, Paul Shelton, Eric Rice-Johnston.
Photo Vic Cohen.

Danza Estilizada. Jaime Coronado with the SDS company. Photo Vic Cohen.

Charrada. Renée Iannuzzi, Jaime Coronado.
Photo Vic Cohen.

Galician. Antonio Saldaña, Orlando Vargas, Nancy Heller, Ziva Cohen.
Photo Vic Cohen.

Seguidillas del Candil. Alejandro Marin, Reina Getz,
Ziva Cohen, De Anna Pierce.
Photo Vic Cohen.

Bulerias. Mary Anne Shelton, Lourdes Elias, Nelson Sitton. Photo Vic Cohen.

Guajiras. Danielle Polen, Nelson Sitton, Lourdes Elias and, in background, Nancy Sedgwick.

Spanish Dance Theatre members. BACK ROW: Concha Egea, Nancy Heller, Lourdes Elias, Carol Sanders, Mary Ann Sheltorn, Ziva Cohen, Joan Fosas (guest artist), Marina (artistic director), Manolo Leiva (guest flamenco singer), Nancy Sedgwick, Annette Smith (stage manager), Jorge Porta (singer), Danielle Polen, Triana d'Orazio, Marla Bush, Alan Tjaarda-Jones (guest artist), Eric Rice-Johnston (gaita/bagpipe player), and Pepita Pagán (*jota singe*r). FRONT ROW: Jaime Coronado, Antonio Saldaña, John O'Loughlin, Juan Pagán, Larry Robinson, Henry Jova, Ralph Pemberton, Orlando Vargas, Michael Perez (obscured) and Nelson Sitton. Photo RT Regan.

35

Adjudicating With Olga Vasilievska Lepeshinskaya, 1993

In 1993 I was asked to adjudicate the first choreographic competition in a certain European country. I do not normally adjudicate because I find it cruel to choose one amongst many talented dancers. But because I love that country and its people, I decided to go there, and I accepted the offer. There I met the very famous Russian dancer from the Bolshoi, Olga Lepeshinskaya. She was limping, and so was I – an injury from playing soccer with my grandchildren. The specialist called it 'the oldest soccer injury he had ever dealt with', as I was in my late fifties. The nurse said that it should go into the *Guinness Book of Records*. Olga's first words were directed to me, 'Which leg?' Her bright eyes twinkled with charm. 'The left', I replied. 'Oh good; mine is the right,', she said. 'Then we have a good pair between us'. Much laughter ensued and she kissed me on both cheeks. She was to be fun all the way. Her next words were, 'I was married to a four-star general, you know, *four* stars,' she said, stabbing her left shoulder with her right forefinger. 'One, two, three, four. He was a very important man, you know'. I assured her that I was impressed.

On arriving at the hotel, I sat waiting in the lobby. A man dressed in black walked past and glanced at me through his very dark sunglasses. I was immediately wary. He returned, sat down at the window and shot surreptitious glances at me. I felt very uncomfortable. This went on until they came to fetch us to meet the committee, and he turned out to be the third adjudicator, an Italian, and he was charming. He was to represent contemporary and jazz dance, I the Spanish dance, and Olga the classical ballet. Olga was an amazing technical and expressive Principal Dancer at the Bolshoi in Moscow, according to Natalia Roslavleva in her book *Era of the Russian Ballet*, which Mary Clarke lent to me while I was writing my *History of the Royal Swedish Ballet*.

Even as a child she showed remarkable dance talent. Born in 1916, she went from the Bolshoi school, which she joined in 1925, to her first performance in the Bolshoi Ballet company as Cupid in the following year, 1926. Even then she had stage presence and personality, for which she was to be known in her later career. Because of her determination to perfect every step, she stayed on in the studio after class to practise, and early on was marked for a great future as a dancer. Even before her graduation in 1933, she was mentioned as a future ballerina. That was the year before I was born.

Her technique was flawless and formidable when leaping and turning, helped by her short, compact stature. Olga told me that she could do ninety-six *fouettés* with ease. She said that once she got going, it was not difficult to keep going. At one performance her fellow dancers in the wings dared her to ignore the conductor and just continue to turn after the required thirty-two *fouettés* in *Swan Lake* Act 3. Her mischievousness got the better of her and she performed sixty-four of them and finished with a triple turn. 'People still talk about it. It is a legend', she laughed. However, it was her ability to act and project her presence that made her so lovable to the audience.

At that first meeting she had a charming young local Russian girl sitting beside her, who translated everything. Putting her head on one side, like a little bird, the pen poised by her cheek, she gazed at the interpreter with intense concentration, before making a note in the booklet in front of her, nodding as though in agreement. She spoke no English during the meeting, working only through the interpreter. Afterwards, when we were alone, she nattered away in perfect English, seeming comfortable with the language, with her bright eyes twinkling. She said sadly, 'I weep for my Russia. Life is so hard for the young and the old. If I can give some work to this young girl, I am happy'. I shall give Lepeshinskaya the benefit of the doubt because she was very careful and she wanted to be sure to get all the information precisely.

During the competition, the young Italian judge and I were of exactly the same opinion. This surprised me. Olga had very different opinions from ours, but she was so good about it. When it came to decision-making she accepted our judgement and we gave over the ballet-judging entirely to her. This she authoritatively took on as her right.

There were delightful entries and the standard was very high. A Chinese ballet was announced and this excited Olga. 'I love Chinese dancing', she commented. I knew that that was not what it was going to be, and tried to explain to her that it would be the choreographer's interpretation of what Chinese dancing was to him. She just smiled and settled down to enjoy herself. Unfortunately I was right and she was disappointed. Turning to me she said, 'We weel keel that 'Chinaman'!'

There are always problems with such events, and on one decision we needed her support. The outcome can be obvious when one item rises above all the others, but generally it is better to put the competitors into three groups of good, better and best. That is never done.

The problem came with the contemporary/jazz entries. Two were neck and neck at the same level. One, however, was more tasteful in costuming, whereas the other one was rather brash. The Italian and I favoured the former. The problem was that we would be massacred by the other group's vociferous supporters. Contrary to the rules, they yelled and clapped throughout their favourite group's performance. Looking up at where we were seated, they made sure that we knew their priority.

After much agonising, we decided to have a draw and consulted with the organisers. They were horrified. That was out of the question. It was a money prize, enabling the group to costume and stage a new production. After much wrangling, they had to accept our decision, supported by Olga. I had a sneaking suspicion she rather preferred the brashness. When the winners were announced and the prize did not go entirely as the supporters wanted it, there was a howl of protest and almost a riot. We survived it and went back to the hotel. The Italian went out on the town to get a drink and unfortunately ran into the howling mob. He had to run for it, as they wanted to lynch him.

The following morning Olga invited me to go to Moscow to adjudicate there, at a big international competition which she was organising. I was so upset that I could not accept her invitation, as we were going to be in South Africa. How I would have loved that experience. We kept in touch and I phoned Lepeshinskaya in Moscow from time to time and chatted. She was trying to give her cultural treasures to various museums but they would not accept them as they did not have the staff to look after them. She repeated again, 'I cry for my Russia'. Then one day I phoned her and was told that she was very ill. She could hardly speak. I sent a card and when I phoned again to find out how she was, there was just silence. Olga disappeared out of my life. She died of a heart attack in 2008, at the age of ninety-two. A brief but wonderfully bright flame in my life was extinguished.

36

The Spanish Dance Society's Intellectual Property

Intellectual property is the most precious commodity in today's information age, and the syllabus of the Spanish Dance Society (SDS) is like gold. I had hardly arrived in London in 1993 when one of the largest societies of dance teachers approached Sherrill Wexler, asking the SDS to join them. Our chairperson Maisie Louden-Carter, Sherrill and I went to meet their chairman about what their thoughts were. After a long discussion came the fatal words in answer to my question, 'Of course the syllabus will then belong to our organisation'. There the discussion ended, as we would never relinquish our well-thought-out work to others to 'fiddle with'. We three were of one mind, and in shock.

I had also been approached by an organisation in America to join them, but as an Afrikaans saying goes, 'I am old where the dog bit me', so I wrote to the now-deceased chairman of the society in Johannesburg, Fred Ziegler, asking for permission to copyright the SDS syllabus in the society's name in America, to protect it. He wrote back asking me to do so, and saying that I was free to do anything I deemed necessary to protect our intellectual property. One of the lawyer members of our society in America, Paula Durbin, set to work to start the process.

Ivy Conmee, our president, came from South Africa to the USA to visit her sister and asked me for a meeting in Washington DC. We were joined by our chairperson Joanne Petrie. Conmee was critical of me having copyrighted the syllabus in America but I showed her the letter from the South African chairman asking me to do so. She was not aware of it, so I made a copy of the letter for her and another one to take to the committee in Johannesburg. I suggested that the South African committee should copyright the syllabus there, where it had originated. Years later another committee member visited me from South Africa; she also seemed to have no idea about the letter. Once again I repeated that the committee in South Africa should copyright the syllabus and music etc. I gave Sherrill Wexler a copy of the letter to keep on file.

On another occasion Luisillo phoned to tell me that he had been given the position of overseeing Spanish dancing in the schools of Madrid. He proposed that I come to live in Madrid for several months, teach the syllabus, film it with beautiful Spanish dancers performing it, using the appropriate ages for each examination, and he would then introduce it into the schools in Madrid. When I asked who the syllabus and the films would belong to, I was told, 'With the cost of it all, of course to the government of Madrid'. They would then spread it throughout the schools of Spain. Again the idea that others would then be able to do what they wanted with our carefully worked-out syllabus was certainly out of the question. We would never ever consider this, and I hope that future guardians of the society's valuable intellectual property will respect it and not tamper and abuse the aims and ideas of the founders. It is a great responsibility for the future members of the Spanish Dance Society.

37

Roberto Ximénez, Alberto Lorca and Reminiscing About Old Madrid and Seville

In the early 1990s, when I was living in the USA, I received a phone call from a woman, unknown to me, who said that she had heard I was going to Spain (the Vikings used to say, 'The world knows what three people know'), and would I please contact the famous dancer Roberto Ximénez and try to get him to do a workshop with my company in Washington DC. I told her that I doubted we could afford him, but she pleaded and I said I would try my best. She said, 'We were once very close friends and I would love to see him just one more time. I am unable to go to Spain, but it would be of benefit to both you and me if he came'. Roberto Ximénez and Manolo Vargas were two of the famous male dancers trained by Pilar López in her company. Later these two brilliant performers of Spanish dance, both Mexicans, formed their own company.

On arrival in Madrid, I contacted Ximénez and we arranged to meet. An elegantly dressed man introduced himself. I asked if he would give a week's seminar to my company in America but he said that he could only achieve something significant if he worked with the company for not less than three months. I totally agreed with him, but that was beyond our resources. However, we became totally immersed in discussing dance, and he appreciated that I agreed with his decision.

Sitting in front of the oldest bar in Madrid in the Plaza Santa Ana, the sun faded and died and the moon rose, slowly peering over at us. To our right was the *Teatro Español*, the theatre where the dancer and choreographer Alberto Lorca had made his debut. Still further down the road was the fascinating antiquarian bookshop of the knowledgeable José Blas Vega, author of many books and the two-volume *Diccionario Enciclopedico Illustrado del Flamenco*. It was co-authored with Manuel Rios Ruiz. Through the years José Blas Vega and I had become friends and he gave me many of his fascinating research papers and gifts of books, and I gave him mine, and information about Mavis Becker (Marina Lorca), who is in his dictionary. He once showed me the most enticingly beautiful copy he had for sale of the drawings by Gustave Doré of the *Escuela Bolera* dancers that I used in my *Bolero* book, enlarged and excellently produced. It broke my heart not to have the money to buy them.

This was a truly historic and fascinating part of old Madrid, where I had come to study the rich bounty of Spanish dance. One could just visualise the *Manolos* and *Manolas* walking there in the 19th century, their sumptuous clothing copied more flashily by the *Majos* and *Majas* of Goya fame; their naming came from the Arabic *maho*, 'glitter'. Goya painted them dancing each Sunday on the meadow, *Prado*, where the museum of that name is situated today. I asked José to write about the other dancers in a book like his for flamenco. He said he had written it already but that there was no money to publish it. What a loss to the Spanish dance world. Flamenco always takes preference.

The old areas of Madrid used to be divided into *madriles*, or *barrios* (boroughs), as the locals called them. Three of the most historic areas denoted the social level of the people who lived there. The richest were at the top of the hill, going down to the poorest by the river. Everywhere, many dance studios are and were situated, such as that of Mercedes y Albano in the middle block. We all studied with them and they became patrons of the society. This is where dancers such as Alberto Lorca and José de Udaeta were taught that famous flamenco dance that everyone wants to know, *Zapateado de las Campanas*. This was the choreography of Estampio (1879-1957), which he taught in Calle Relatores 20, two floors up the broad staircase. In his youth he had been a bullfighter, and became a legend. He was known as '*El Feo*', 'The Ugly One'. The descriptions were nothing if not explicit. Enrique '*El Cojo*', 'The Lame', another sought-after teacher, taught me in Seville.

In his old age, Estampio gave his classes sitting on a chair with his back to the window, dressed in his pyjamas and slippers. Alberto wrote in my Bolero book that the slippers had rubber soles and that he did not know how he managed to learn anything. Udaeta said that he was taught a few steps and then off went teacher and guitarist to drink coffee in a bar, while he was told to practise. This he did for hours, doing the same steps over and over till they deigned to return. He maintained that this was what gave him his strength and stamina! Ximénez can be seen dancing the famous Estampío *Zapateado* – cleverly adapted to be performed in a tavern, starting on a table and moving to other surfaces like a chair and a barrel – in that great film by Edgar Neville of the famous dancers of a bygone era, *Duende y Misterio del Flamenco*. There is a very special duet with Pilar López and one of her 'products', the exciting Alejandro Vega, who I believe died young. Also appearing are Manolo Vargas, Pacita Tomás and Alberto Lorca, whose asthma cut short his dancing career. He became Pilar's assistant and then worked as a choreographer in films where Ava Gardner became enamoured of him, absorbing his time. One famous item is of Antonio dancing in the open air beside the pillars of the Roman aqueduct outside Toledo, the striking of the iron *martinete* accompaniment echoing around him. I had heard of this dance, yet nowhere could I find the film to see it. Then there it was listed in the films at the Lincoln Center library in New York. It was so old it had a snowstorm of falling pixels to see through. There I sat determinedly, squinting, bent forward to see, while passers-by stopped, peered at the screen, shook their heads and walked on. When Alberto heard this, he immediately bought a copy and sent it to me.

I remember those old Madrid studios well, with a broad wooden staircase, the worn-down stairs winding their way upward with flat easy-to-tread steps, well-worn in the centre portion. The last person I visited there was Mercedes and Albano's daughter, María Mercedes León, nicknamed 'Itas', whom I mentioned in Chapter 3. Her newly furbished, pleasant studios were situated there. There were people milling around, and all types of dancing were represented. She was a great supporter of the Spanish Dance Society, admired our work, and contributed dances.

Alberto Lorca told me how he was creating a choreography in one of those studios when the door opened and Pilar López, who was rehearsing her company in another studio, put her head around the door, asking permission to watch him working. After a while she rose and left, saying nothing more than *gracias* (thank you). A few days later she phoned and asked him to hasten to her company to replace a dancer who had let her down. And that was his entrance into her company and a lifelong, close friendship, with mutual respect and adoration.

His stage name was Alberto Lorca but he had been christened Albrecht Nicol van Aerssen, born in 1924 of an aristocratic family, and he grew up in Seville. He was a baron but being very unassuming he never mentioned this. He wrote in the Prologue to my book *The Bolero School* that I had asked him to write down his experiences because he was the last living 'mammoth' of Spanish classical dancing, the *Escuela Bolera*. 'It all began in September 1944. I was twenty years old.... At that time I was an extremely handsome (young) mammoth, with a very impressive body, built up by all sorts of sporting activities... and I had a fine ear for music'. A friend took him to the earlier mentioned *Teatro Español* and once he'd stepped onto the stage with youngsters to do dances, he learned quickly. 'I realised that my life had changed forever. I had to live in the theatre and on the stage'. He later founded the *Ballet Nacional Festivales de España*, which became the *Ballet Nacional de España*.

The area of Madrid where he studied dance stretched from Puerta del Sol through Plaza de Santa Ana to where Luisillo's studio was later situated in Calle de las Huertas. It is now the area where guitarists and dancers from all over the world flock. He helped so many of them. Spanish dancing spread across the world and enriched it. Nearby was the picturesque area called *Lavapies,* 'wash feet', an obviously Catholic area but with the old Jewish quarter situated close by. Also close to Luisillo's studio were the studios in the minute street called *Amor de Dios*, 'Love of God', where Marta Carrasco and I first met. We knocked ourselves out leaping around with gorgeous Azorín (Ibañes), the *jota* king, dancing vigorous *jotas* and also endearing ones. It was also where I once waited for my lesson with María Magdalena, while a German girl hit her head against the wall exclaiming on each bang, '*Nunca, Nunca,*

Nunca!' – 'never' was she ever going to learn that dance. María had also danced in a Basque company. She of flamenco fame chortled as she told me this unknown fact. Now the studios have been moved to more 'clinical' quarters, the atmosphere is gone and the after-class trips to the bar with Azorín are all but forgotten, except for the memory of his magnificent smile and his good humour.

My friend Susan also knew Alberto Lorca whom she had met in 1983 in Mallorca, where she and José were performing. Alberto was there to teach his choreographies to a group of young dancers performing in a theatre. Susan watched while they danced. She asked whether she could join the daily ballet class he was giving them. He soon saw that she had been a ballet dancer. They became friends and he went to watch Susan and José perform. We had never discussed him, and only discovered when he died that he was a mutual friend, as adored by her as by me.

In 2002, Alberto, his charming partner Manolo Gutiérrez, Mikael and I went to the palace of *La Granja* in Aranjuez together because he wanted to share this beloved place with us. It was an unforgettable outing. The beauty of the palace and gardens stand out in my memory as though it was yesterday. We were celebrating our wedding anniversary and had arrived at the hotel in Madrid to a room full of the most gorgeous, enormous, pink, long-stemmed roses. What a delightful surprise from this real gentleman. I said, 'Alberto, how could you do such a thing?!' He replied as usual, 'But of course. What else?'

He also wanted me to see HIS Seville. So I went there with him. We walked all over the town. He showed me the Pericet School, where he had studied *Escuela Bolera* with Luisa Pericet, the daughter of Angel Pericet Carmona. He loved her dearly. It was closed, and had been for years. Alberto, lost in his memories, looked entranced at the studio at the end of the road, with grass growing out of its roof, glowing as though in a sunlit spotlight, while we looked down the darkened street leading up to it, in shadow. An unforgettable sight.

In the evening we went to a performance because Alberto wanted to show me that the *Cuadro Bolero* was still in existence in Seville, danced together with a *Cuadro Flamenco*, although the former had disappeared elsewhere in Spain. In my book on the Bolero school I mention that as a child Antonio Ruiz Soler recalled seeing *Cuadro Boleros* being danced in the café in Seville where he performed in the *Cuadro Flamenco*. We went to a restaurant where Marta Carrasco Benítes, the charismatic writer and critic, joined us for a hilarious lunch. We were old friends.

Manolo Gutiérrez's kindness knows no bounds. In 2009, a year after Alberto had passed away, I was trying to buy a magnificent book with commemorative stamps of each Spanish region's dances, with their history, descriptions and incredible colour illustrations. It was issued by the post office with the title *Los Bailes Populares de España*. I could not find it. Asking Manolo about it, and fully intending to pay for it, he went to incredible lengths to find four copies, because my friends also wanted one when they heard of it. Rhoda, Mavis, Sherrill and I were each given a copy as a gift. What kindness and generosity, and a pleasure for life. It is difficult to describe the beauty, taste, perfection, and production quality of the volumes, each in its own case. We thank you and treasure them, Manolo.

Mikael, Marina, Alberto Lorca and Monolo Gutiérrez
at La Granja palace near Aranjuez.

I knew that Luisillo, someone who presented Spain's regional riches theatrically, dearly wanted the post of artistic director of the Spanish National Ballet, but he never achieved that. I was invited to go with a group of dancers squashed in a small car to a faraway theatre in another town to see his *Don Quijote* with the National Ballet. It was not well positioned in the programme. Several ballets were put on before his and by the time it was staged both the company and the audience were falling over with exhaustion. We drove back to Madrid feeling deeply sorry for him. The dancers felt it was done on purpose to thwart his bid for the directorship. Antonio was leaving the company, I believe. I did not tell Luisillo that I had seen the performance. He was very withdrawn.

It was sheer serendipity that I happened to be in Madrid and was able to see Luisillo's swansong, a repeat of his 1994 masterpiece, *La Malquerida,* 'The Disliked (one)'. It was given rave reviews and I was put in the front row, so the intensity of it overwhelmed me and almost blew me away at the final dramatic moment. He was looking drawn and was walking about in his usual restless, pensive way. It was our last meeting before he died of cancer.

The ballet was set in a rural community devoid of flamenco, with music by Luis Pontini. Earlier, while working on it, Luisillo had told me that he was very excited by some of the music he had discovered – Castilian folk music, and especially one hauntingly beautiful ancient song, long forgotten. It set the pathos of the story of the stepfather totally obsessed by his stepdaughter, and the villagers conscious of it. This play by the writer Jacinto Benavente is set in the home of the richest family in a Castilian village, with all the problems of small communities – scandals, jealousies and disasters. Luisillo went with the ultimate theatrical way of mixing theatre and dance, with the dancers reciting the author's words as well as dancing. The two principal dancers were Emilio Fernández and Lola Zambrano. He researched all the old customs, now confined to history, to use as his story unfolded.

It is a loss that Luisillo's choreographies are not in the repertoire of any company. They are probably lost forever. His talent received recognition in his lifetime and he was rewarded with many medals. Because he was a very religious man, the one he valued most was from the Pope, given after the performance of his ballet commissioned for a world gathering of Gypsies at the Vatican. It was the first time any such event had been held at the Vatican. It made him very proud.

38

Settling in London, 1993: Working President of the Spanish Dance Society; Council for Dance Education and Training; Clement Crisp

At the World Bank, where my husband worked, the staff had to retire at the age of sixty-two. Although I had been blissfully happy in Washington, we decided to go to London, for family reasons. The move was in October 1993. The Spanish Dance Society in Washington gave us a wonderful farewell party in the home of Evelyn Woolston-May. The charismatic Spanish Ambassador, Jaime Ojeda, could not come but he sent me a handwritten farewell letter ending with the words: 'This city will not be the same without you'.

When we left the party, Joanne Petrie was standing by the door waiting patiently for her Russian husband Vladimir Ankudinov, who had been saying goodbye to his friends for about half an hour but who was still lingering. We said to Joanne that we had not said goodbye because we did not want to break up the party, so she said, 'The English [that is what people outside Britain call my husband and me] leave without saying goodbye and the Russians say goodbye without leaving!'

Farewell and honouring parties in Washington DC. TOP row: Jaime Coronado, Lourdes Elias, Marina, Nancy Sedgwick, Danielle Polen; Marina, Nancy Heller, Lourdes Elias, Maida Withers. CENTRE row: Norma Sedgwick, her daughter Nancy Sedgwick, Evelyn Woolston May; Nat Deutsch, Nancy Heller, Marco Caceres. BELOW: Joanne Petrie, Maida Withers, Mary Day, Elvi Moore, Nancy Sedgwick, and unknown.

In England we bought a flat in Wimbledon on the south-western outskirts of London, on the fourth floor of a high-rise building, with a lovely view of trees, sky and spectacular sunsets. We have been here twenty-four years now. Our immediate neighbour is the All England Tennis Club. One year during the tennis championships there was a dramatic fire on the ninth floor of our building; the cameras which were filming the matches from above swung around to film our building, and the BBC announcer said that there was drama not only on the tennis court. Friends in South Africa, America and Canada who had visited us, wrote that they had seen our burning building on their television screens.

Our whole family meets once a year for a week, and in the early days we used to go during the children's and grandchildren's Christmas and New Year holiday. In the year when we came from Washington, we met in Puerto de Mazarron in south-east Spain. My grandchildren Oscar and Josephine, both under two, woke at 5am and I looked after them to allow their parents to lie in. I turned on the TV and hoped for the best. Oscar, aged two, looked at me and said repeatedly, 'I want CBBC' – this was Children's BBC, which we could not get. He said to his mother later, very upset, 'They talk a 'linguidge'. We still meet once a year, but now we are nineteen, with children, grandchildren and in-laws, and now we meet in summer, the last four years in the beautiful little town of Sigtuna on Lake Mälaren, near Stockholm; this year in Eastbourne on the south coast of England, which we are also very much looking forward to.

A Working President

Living in London brought me closer to Europe where I examined, studied and often visited my Spanish 'family' the Fosas in Sitges, Barcelona. However, once established in London, I was asked to become president of the Spanish Dance Society (SDS) in Europe. None of my predecessors had shown any interest in participating in the society so I decided to be the first 'working' president. I joined the committee where Maisie Louden-Carter was chairperson (present chair: Sue Hilton) and

3 pictures together. TOP: Rosa Fosas Julià, Marina, Pere Julià, Luis (friend), Joan Fosas. CENTRE: Marina, Mavis Becker, Sherrill Wexler, Rhoda Rivkind. BELOW: Standing – Mavis Becker, Sherrill Wexler, María Jesús García, Geoffrey Neiman, Marina, Sue Hilton, Helena Montoya, Mandy, Gabriella Cutrupi. Seated – Sue Arkle, Conchita del Campo, Rhoda Rivkind, Nancy Sedgwick, Maria Papadakis.

Sherrill Wexler was executive administrator. The three of us worked well together. Sherrill and I were also on the International Board of the society together with Rhoda Rivkind as secretary, Geoffrey Neiman as chairman, Mavis Becker from South Africa and Nancy Sedgwick from America. A valuable Spanish member is Isabel Baquero. One of my first tasks was to attend a meeting of the Council for Dance Education and Training, the CDET.

The Council for Dance Education and Training (CDET)

I quote from CDET's own description of the aims of their organisation: 'In 1979, alarmed at the indifferent quality of what was being presented as appropriate education and professional training in dance and musical theatre, a number of eminent artists met with representatives of the leading dance and performing arts organisations to discuss how the industry could work together *to ensure high standards of provision* [my italics].'

It is an excellent organisation but it was constricted by bureaucracy and government interference. My assessment of the situation is that the government should have recognised the older ballet societies as they were constituted, having so successfully trained superb dancers and teachers for almost 100 years in Britain and the Commonwealth. The examination systems of those societies are based on tried and true methods, centuries old, known in important ballet countries like Russia, France, Italy and Denmark. That wisdom was not given credit. Other societies not in this situation could have received assistance, instead of a blanket-covering for all. The old established dance societies were so well organised that they could easily have handed the results directly to the government. Instead, the government insisted on external monitoring.

I shall never forget my first CDET meeting to represent the Spanish Dance Society, being faced with all the problems of setting the simplest norms in order to get all the societies, at various levels of development, to conform to the same procedures. It continues endlessly. One size doesn't fit all. I was told that once the CDET was created, the board decided it was not possible for them to do what was required. They handed over the accreditation of dance to the music societies as 'awarding bodies', with dance societies paying them to assure their validity and to pass on their marks to the government. Arriving in England from abroad in the mid-1990s and having experienced the freedom given to dance elsewhere, I was mortified to see the bureaucracy being imposed on the dance societies, totally unnecessarily.

Lack of Feedback to Students

The biggest problem turned out to be two bureaucrats representing two societies, who decided that feedback to examination candidates, other than marks, should not be allowed in societies that sought government recognition. For example, if a candidate fails an examination, he or she should not be told why! There should be no detailed remarks or explanations on the 'report' card, only a general one. One reason given for this was that it would avoid challenges from disappointed examination candidates, but marks can be challenged as much as remarks. In fact, the only such challenge we had in the Spanish Dance Society when we wrote marks and remarks, concerned a *mark*. Another reason given for no longer writing remarks was that they would be cumbersome to send to, and be processed by, the government. However, the government is not interested in remarks, but can be sent the marks for their digitised records, if they want them, while the candidates and their teachers can be sent the feedback remarks.

Schoolchildren are given feedback, so why shouldn't dance school students? Often it is the same examiner who writes dance examination reports for schoolchildren but is forbidden to do it for the students of a dance society or a private teacher. Remarks are written on the report cards of dance students in other countries, so why not in England? (Education in the United Kingdom has been devolved, so Scotland, Wales and Northern Ireland do not have to follow the rules set in England. Similarly, those rules result in government recognition only in England.) The music and drama examiners include written remarks on their report cards, so why shouldn't the dance examiners? How could such an insane decision be taken at a meeting of an organisation which was supposed to be dedicated to the *improvement* of dance education and training?

I happened to be present when the momentous decision was taken to no longer write on the report cards of examination candidates in dance societies seeking government accreditation. Such societies should be more, not less, quality-conscious. The decision was very harmful to dance training in England, and I expressed my dismay. However, there was no dissent from the other dance society representatives at the meeting. Afterwards two teachers said that I was trying to take them back to the Stone Age. Perhaps the bureaucracy made them feel important.

Richard Glasstone and I had been writing in the *Dancing Times*, deploring the dearth of feedback to exam candidates. The Cecchetti teacher Jacqueline Davenport in Germany supported us in another letter to the *Dancing Times*. The situation today is described below in a letter from Rosie Watson, Bristol, to the *Dancing Times* in August 2013. It is reprinted here by kind permission of the *Dancing Times* and Rosie Watson. It was published under the heading 'Bureaucracy stifles dance teaching'. The explanatory words in square brackets are mine.

'Dear Editor,

> I was very glad to read Jacqueline Davenport's letter in the July issue of *Dancing Times* regarding numbers for results in students' exams. I have long considered writing to your page on the very same matter, but was reluctant to do so for fear of seeming controversial or that it was "just me".
>
> I am the parent of a daughter who has enjoyed learning ballet for a few years now and is working her way through her RAD [Royal Academy of Dance] grades. The first time she took an exam (primary, some 7 or so years ago), I was surprised and disappointed to see that her report contained an impersonal and unspecific series of marks out of 10 which meant nothing to either of us. Now at grade 5, we still have no idea how she has really done in her exams or how the marks/results are arrived at.
>
> When I was learning ballet as a child (more years ago than I care to remember) and took both ISTD [Cecchetti method]

and latterly RAD exams, all my reports had personally written or typed comments pertaining to each section (barre, ports de bras, adage, allegro, etc.), indicating what I had done well and what I needed to work on in the next grade. It made me feel that the examiner at least had acknowledged me, had encouraged me and helped with improvements. Now, all my daughter receives are meaningless numbers, based on unknown criteria, and relating to vague sections such as 'Technique 1, Technique 2, etc.'. What do these headings mean? How are we, or her teacher, to know what the examiner really thinks of her? I expect it is all intended as a cost-cutting measure, to save examiners' time in putting together detailed reports, but isn't that a rather sad state of affairs when these children work so hard for their exams, deal with their nerves and then receive nothing in the way of personal encouragement or guidance?. Exam fees are not cheap these days, so it is a shame that, for all we pay, we then wait often up to 3 months for a series of numbers. Numbers cannot praise or guide – surely students deserve at least a little of that for their efforts. Maybe the exam boards can explain their thinking behind this and consider even a partial return to the good old days of the personal touch?

Yours sincerely,

Rosie Watson'

This is indeed an extremely important matter. The Spanish Dance Society (SDS) examiners always wrote comments on reports, and I wrote in Chapter 18 about the importance of this. SDS still writes on reports outside Europe (the European branch is administered from England and follows English rules): careful comments to aid the dancers on how to improve; and praise given when it is due. In Europe the SDS examination candidates now request a choice between the bureaucratic English system and the original syllabus.

Mary Clarke, the former editor of *Dancing Times*, was deeply troubled by the drop in standards which she witnessed. She, Clement Crisp and I were to write an article discussing this state of affairs but this was interrupted by her sudden death in 2015. Until her retirement in 2013, she went to dance studio performances to write reports for the magazine. She considered it her duty to follow dance education. She had written about ballet since the 1950s. I said that she was the 'institutional memory of dance', and when she died I quoted an African saying that 'when an old person dies in the village, a library burns'.

From the start, we in the SDS had been accepted by the prestigious international Trinity Music Society. We worked happily together for many years, steered by Mark Stringer and Glyndwr Jones, until government cuts took hold and Trinity could no longer accommodate us. When I asked whether Trinity writes feedback remarks on its reports, the reply was, 'Of course. That is what examining is all about. We thought that the SDS had been given special dispensation not to'.

The CDET is now a validating body, which was the original intention at its founding, so societies can now claim recognition from the government or from the CDET. Some societies prefer CDET recognition to the government alternative. The syllabus of the Spanish Dance Society is recognised by both the government and the CDET.

Spanish Dance Society examiners and teachers in South Africa soon opted out of the overly bureaucratic English examination system and returned to the one they had created in 1965. Astute Commonwealth ballet societies also opted out. They are now flourishing, whereas their former London-based mother societies were deprived of their membership fees and lost some of their best talents.

In the newspaper *i* of 10 April 2015 there was an article under the heading 'Choreographers step outside Britain for talent' by their arts correspondent Nick Clark in which he wrote: 'Three of the leading dance choreographers in Britain have launched an attack on the UK's contemporary dance schools, saying that they were "dismayed" at the declining standards among graduates that forced them to look overseas for talent'. I am convinced that one reason for this decline is the lack of feedback to the students at many dance schools.

In *The Dancing Times* of August 2016 Daniel Pratt wrote: 'Most shocking to me… was the suggestion that the general European view is that the British dance training falls short. This warrants serious thought. If this perception is true, we must change it.'

An exception to this decline in the standard of teaching at several major dance societies in England is the excellent teaching at the Royal Ballet School (RBS). I had the pleasure of attending several performances by the students at the RBS school in White Lodge, Richmond Park, where the principal was Diane van Schoor, trained under Dulcie Howes at the University of Cape Town Ballet School. When she left to become an independent Cecchetti master teacher, working as a consultant on an international level, she won high praise in a speech from Monica Mason, artistic director of the Royal Ballet. One of van Schoor's tasks at the moment is to make a DVD of the Cecchetti Final Diploma work, to be demonstrated by professional dancers. Another exception is the excellent teaching at the English National Ballet School under the directorship of Samira Saidi, where contemporary dance is taught by Nuno Campos. Both the school and the company are under the exciting artistic directorship of Tamara Rojo, who has breathed life back into dance. She is a patron of the Spanish Dance Society.

Increased 'Academisation' of Dance Teaching

Another problem, other than the lack of feedback for the students of the dance societies, is that in dance teaching all over the world, but more especially in England, the accent is now placed more and more on the academic side. This may be good for those who are academically inclined but not necessarily good for all those who want to become dancers or dance teachers. Carmen Amaya was the most famous of Spanish dancers and yet she could neither read nor write. Academic qualifications are now in vogue everywhere. Soon only those with degrees will get teaching posts. They will be able to write about dance but not impart it.

Disappearance of Style in Dance Teaching and Dance Companies

Clement Crisp, the esteemed author of dance books and articles, and *The Financial Times*' dance critic, wrote as follows to me, published here with his kind permission. He worries about the disappearance in British dance teaching of style, which only the personal touch can impart:

> 'If we do not know about our past – as members of a family, as a nation, as artists in whatever discipline – we are rootless and incomplete. In dancing, and especially in classical ballet, it is vital to know, and indeed to feel in our bodies, the physical past which is our ancestry and which gives us our physical and spiritual self in no matter what role we dance. For our British classical dancers, it is vital to understand Ashton and de Valois and MacMillan through their choreographies, and surely as beneficial to know those forces – technical and creative – which in their turn had shaped them. An understanding of Bournonville, of Petipa, of Fokine and Nijinska and Balanchine, of the great teachings that educated and inspired them – the Italian/Milanese school, supremely found in Maestro Cecchetti's teachings; the older French style from Auguste Vestris which shaped Bournonville; the great developments in late 19th century St Petersburg which formed such pedagogues as Preobrajenskaya and Vaganova: all this is still significant, valuable, artistically essential for dancers today. Not to know it is to be hobbled and hampered as a theatre artist and a performer.'

Today some ballet companies are unfortunately losing their characteristic style, perhaps because they employ so many foreign dancers – another victim of globalisation. It is exciting for the dancers and the audiences but not good for the personality of the companies.

Globalisation has brought about a levelling of the ballet companies, who strive for excitement with a polished technical excellence at the cost of an individual style that made them great. They end up looking similar. It was Tennyson who wrote, 'The old order changeth, yielding place to new', but is that really always necessary? Is there not room for both the old and the new in the established companies?

39

Honoured by the Society in the USA and by the Mayor of Washington DC, 1997

In 1997 Nancy Sedgwick contacted me in London on behalf of the Spanish Dance Society in Washington and said that they needed me in Washington on 27 April. Although I maintained that it was not possible, she wrote that they had arranged a flight for me and I had to please come to Washington DC on that date. So I arranged to go. It almost ended there at Heathrow Airport in London. The clerk at the check-in desk looked at my ticket and then my passport and said that she could not possibly let me on board because the ticket was made out to 'Keet' but my passport said 'Grut'. I nearly passed out. Then I asked, 'Please phone my husband at home and ask him to fax our wedding certificate. Will that allow me to go?' She confirmed that it would. She phoned, he faxed, and I left! Later I realised what a disaster it would have been if I had missed that plane.

Why I was going was a dark well-kept secret. They were to honour me at the Arts Club with a Lifetime Achievement Award, but until I walked in at the Arts Club Theatre door the next night, I had no idea what was to happen.

My family always came first. What I did not know was that my family would grow so much when I went to Washington DC. It was this dance family that has overwhelmed me with so much love, first when my husband was so very ill – I felt it reach out and sustain me through that very difficult time; and again recently when I returned to be honoured with so many awards, not least that of everyone's love. Lou Elias said that I was like a 'mother' to my students. I am a very proud mother. My husband said that my teaching had fallen on very fertile ground and after seeing the lovely show they presented on Sunday 27 April at the Arts Club for me, I know that he is right. I also know how hard it is for all of them to do these shows, but they bring so much joy to people that it is worth suffering for. They are all so beautiful and so talented. I also really appreciated Jaime Coronado's choreography. Lou looked so elegant in her beautiful black lace *bata de cola*. The two share the artistic direction of the Spanish Dance Theatre company. Danielle Polen danced so well. I really appreciated the time and energy they all donated in preparing this amazing performance for me, and I am deeply grateful for the honour of a day in my name, 27 April 1997, bestowed by Washington DC Mayor Marion Barry ('Dame Marina Keet Day').

The effort that goes into such a gala is very draining and I hope that they did not take too long to recover from it. Everyone thought of all my needs. Nancy Sedgwick planned my visit down to the tissues and needle and thread in my room. As usual it was all done so elegantly and tastefully. She also kept the secret of all the awards very well. Jaime Coronado, Lou Elias, Nancy Heller (vice chairman and archivist of the SDS) and Nancy Sedgwick (chief executive administrator of the SDS) spoke so eloquently and looked so beautiful and 'did me proud'. Evelyn Woolston-May, the chairperson of the board after Joanne Petrie passed away, was elegant and impressive, and she and her husband Bob were delightful hosts. Manolo Leiva and Maríja Temo provided true flamenco flavour with their singing and guitar playing – and, in Maríja's case, dancing. What a memorable and truly impressive occasion it was. The first to arrive at the Arts Club were Marla Bush and Nancy Heller and it was a heart-warming reunion. Nathaniel Deutsch was there doing his impression of me! Mary-Ann Shelton said, 'Don't go. Stay here with us in Washington!' 'My cup runneth over'; thank you, everyone.

My World Bank friends also came to the party – beautiful Carmen de Perignat and erudite Ralph Pemberton, our guitarist and music, history and language adviser. He not only entertained me to lunch, but ensured, with his wife Anne's good advice, that my beautiful engraved glass award arrived safely packed and in one piece. Anne has become somewhat of a celebrity with her glass artwork and Ralph always helps us with so much knowledge and good advice.

When I returned home to London, I was met by our daughter Vicky, her husband Bill and son Oscar, with so much love, beautiful long-stemmed white roses and a welcome-home gift. They all spoil me.

Some years later, in London, there was a knock on my door, and the postman handed me a square parcel. It was an 'Outstanding Service Award' from the International Association of Blacks in Dance, 'In appreciation for your many years of service to dance in Metropolitan Washington DC, *Given this 15th day of January in the year 2003*'. It was signed by Dr Sherrill Berryman Johnson, IABD Chairperson, Conference Host 2003. I made it my business to find out who had proposed me for this great honour, and I asked her why. She said that although many years had passed since she saw our performances, she had never forgotten them.

40

35th Anniversary of the Spanish Dance Society at the Clore Studio in the Royal Opera House, London, 2000

In London, on Sunday 23 July 2000, at the Royal Opera House's Clore Studio Upstairs, we celebrated the 35th anniversary of the Spanish Dance Society (SDS). The guests from Spain attending the performance were the choreographer, teacher and founder of the Spanish National Ballet Alberto Lorca, and Professor Rosa Ruiz from the *Conservatorio* in Madrid. They attended the performance, which I had dedicated to Alberto Lorca, as is the Spanish custom when honouring an artist. The event took place with the kind permission of Monica Mason, artistic director of the Royal Ballet. Professor Ruiz said afterwards that she was so moved that foreigners could present the range of dances from her country so perfectly and beautifully costumed and with the different styles performed so correctly. She pointed to her tear-stained cheeks saying, 'I am feeling so emotional. I never expected to see anything of this standard of presentation outside of Spain – as a Spaniard I feel greatly honoured'.

The performance was presented by Deborah Bull as the Artists Development Initiative director. I called it *Beyond Flamenco* because it showed a whole range of regional dances performed by my former company members and their students from the Spanish Dance Society in Washington DC. They were led by Nancy Sedgwick, Lourdes Elias and Jaime Coronado from my Spanish Dance Theatre company, of which they were now the artistic directors. Their pupils were the dancers Christina Conrad, Carla de la Torre, Heidi Kershaw, Kumi Kitamori and Renee Lamont, joined by the singer Peter Burroughs who also came from Washington DC to London to take part in the performance. From London were Conchita del Campo and Gillian Hurst, demonstrating ballet's inheritance from the connection between the classical *Escuela Bolera,* or Bolero School, and the Cecchetti classical ballet respectively. I found it so significant that those two and the Danish Bournonville style were all connected to the early French style of the 18th century, all delicately poised to fall into the abyss of 'modernisation'. The Americans were joined by Francesca Fröhlich, Nuno Campos, Sandra Doling, Hugh Rathbone and Fenella Barker, demonstrating classical and regional dances, other than those danced by the American guest dancers. The performance ended with a flamenco scene led by guest artist Marina Lorca from South Africa and Carlos Robles from Spain. The pianists were Judith Binding and Carlos Rodriguez; the flamenco singer Jasmine, together with guitarists Juan Ramires and Angus Cruickshank, presented the flamenco accompaniment, while I narrated the proceedings. Jaime and Lourdes danced the *Jarabe Tapatio*, known as the 'Mexican hat dance', to show an example of Latin America's connection to Spain's dance heritage through the music of the *Seguidillas*.

From South Africa came the founder of the society Rhoda Rivkind and one of the co-founders Theo Dantes, who now lives in London. The executive administrator and founder of the society in Europe, Sherrill Wexler, thanked everyone for coming such a distance to perform, contributing to the occasion and celebrating the society's anniversary with us in England.

TOP PHOTO: Jarabe Tapatio or "Mexican Hat Dance". Lourdes Elias and Jaime Coronado, London 2000. CENTRE PHOTO: SDS 35th anniversary performance at the Royal Opera House, London, 2000. Front row: Jaime Coronado, Professor Rosa Ruiz from the Conservatorio in Madrid; Nancy Sedgwick, Marina, Carlos Robles (guest flamenco dancer from Seville), Peter Burroughs (singer, USA). Back (top) row: Lourdes Elias, Penny Whiting, Christina, Tracy Bernhardt, Renee Lamont, Kumi Kitamon, Heidi Kershaw. BOTTOM PHOTO: Lourdes Elias, Marina, Alberto Lorca, Jaime Coronado and Conchita del Campo in our home in Wimbledon, July 2000, after the performance.

41

Louisiana Purchase Anniversary, New Orleans, 2003

In New Orleans, Louisiana, I was to meet Luisillo's Teresa. More about that below. It was July 2003 at the symposium organised by the intrepid Olga de Smoak for the 200th celebration of the Louisiana Purchase from France. I had been asked to present a lecture-demonstration and teach the *Escuela Bolera*, and Nancy Sedgwick, Lourdes Elias and Jaime Coronado joined me to dance.

As my plane started to descend and I looked down on this scene of water and small knolls of land, I wondered where they had found a space broad enough for a town and an airport. But they had. As I stepped onto the awaiting bus on arrival, I heard, 'Well he-llo, Marina Keet!' It was Sandra Noll Hammond, the historic dance researcher and teacher. It was she who had danced the *Vestris Gavotte* so exquisitely at Goucher College in the USA, clad like a miniature porcelain doll. She was to help so much with my article on the *Vestris Gavotte* and the Basque connection for the *Dancing Times,* with illustrations by Heather Magoon (see Chapter 15). *What an occasion this is going to be*, I thought; and it was.

The event was to be a gathering of the glitterati, among them George Zoros of Diaghilev days, to be seen in the wonderful film *Ballets Russes,* a brilliant documentary about those times, available on

DVD – as well as Ivor Guest of ballet books fame whom I had first met in London in 1955 and who had asked me to contribute to his book on *La Fille Mal Gardée* published by *The Dancing Times* in 1960. He also launched in London my book on the *Royal Swedish Ballet History from 1692 to 1962*. Also at this event was Professor Alkis Raftis, president of *Conseil International de la Danse* (CID), whose business card I kept losing until he gave me a pack of them saying, 'Here you are, Marina. Now you can lose them one at a time and not worry'. What a good friend he has become. We exchange books, among them his enticing anthology *Dance in Poetry*. We keep in touch through all the lovely ladies at the CID in Greece. The executive secretary Lambrini Raikou and secretary Magda Terzidou, together with Tanya Bayona from Malta, 'kidnapped' me at the airport and we sat eating a famous New Orleans delicacy, with icing sugar pouring down on us. It acted as decoration all over me on the flight home – apparently a must-eat if you visit New Orleans.

It was a really magical time among the places where jazz was born, with a party to end all parties held by a generous, delightful benefactor in his home, an old mansion surrounded by flowers. Inside was great food, and Jaime and Lou danced to incredible jazz musicians who just casually sauntered in. We were in the heart of voodoo country and I saw some awesome people who could make anyone believe in black magic.

The *Escuela Bolera* class with Nancy Sedgwick and my lecture went well. The enthusiastic, knowledgeable international audience generated such enjoyable discussions about classical Spanish dancing, of which little was known because it is so rarely seen. They were fascinated and wanted to learn more facts. Also the music on a fortepiano intrigued them with its delicate sound, as played by Chris Dance. It was most stimulating. The dancers demonstrating were given enthusiastic applause. A lovely experience for all of us, including Marina Lorca, who had come all the way from South Africa to dance the *Peteneras* in a regional style, differing from the classical and flamenco versions. Because of the trade routes, dances were influenced across borders, and this dance can be seen in classical, regional and flamenco styles.

I went on a trip through the city of New Orleans and was shown the basin where the boats turned around to go home, which was where the *Basin Street Blues* originated. There was also a street with tall, narrow, double-storey houses from an era long past, lined with beautiful red-flowering trees. Thinking of the clothing of the time and the intense humid heat and malaria, one wonders that anyone survived. And, most historic of all, I was shown by the guide where the flooding would occur one day and which of the barriers, or 'levees', would break. When the disaster happened and an aeroplane showed the overhead view on television, it was exactly as she had said. For decades the residents had begged successive governments for it to be reinforced.

At the sumptuous closing banquet I felt a touch on my shoulder. Looking round I saw the charming and beautiful Teresa, Luisillo's first dancing partner and wife. She had just received a full-length painting of herself in a Spanish dress, commissioned decades ago by Luisillo. He had kept it by his side. She said quietly, 'He wants me to have it'. He was prepared to relinquish it, obviously aware of his approaching death from cancer in Madrid in 2007. She said they were in constant touch by phone and her bright eyes glistened as she said, 'We talk about you, and I know all about your interesting life, so it is such serendipity to meet you here'. I did not doubt his bid to acquire our syllabus was one of the subjects. She is now married to an Italian conductor and is leading a very happy life in Louisiana.

42

Flamenco Festival at Sadler's Wells and *Beyond Flamenco* at the Lilian Baylis Theatre, 2007

'That performance was the best part of the whole Flamenco Festival', wrote one critic. 'That' was the performance when Sherrill Wexler asked me to join her at the Flamenco Festival at Sadler's Wells to present a lecture-demonstration in its Lilian Baylis Theatre. We again called it *Beyond Flamenco* because we dealt with Spanish dance in general, not only with flamenco. Sherrill's charming regional dances, beautifully costumed, performed by her pupils from the Central School of Ballet in London, and my explanations of the regional, classical and flamenco dances, were both extremely well received. The audience leapt to their feet at the end of the performance to applaud and shout. People I did not know rushed on stage afterwards to express their excitement.

A couple pushed through the people surrounding me to say, 'We just have to talk to you'. The man said that he and his wife had decided not to go to the festival anymore as flamenco was totally un-understandable to him. They decided to come and listen to my lecture to see whether they could learn something. He said, 'I am so grateful to you for explaining the musical structure and the way it was counted, because it had made no sense to me at all. Now we are going to buy tickets to all the shows because we will now be able to follow what is going on'. Others came to say that they had found it enlightening and had especially enjoyed the types of Spanish dance other than flamenco, with all the dancers dressed in beautiful costumes.

The dance critic Robert Harrold wrote of our performance in *Dance Expression,* May 2007, that 'some said that they had no idea that Spain was so rich in dance', and that it 'could have filled the Baylis two or three times over'. That is the reaction when people see more than just flamenco. What a pity Sadler's Wells did not return to us for more, even though the organiser of our performance at the theatre had said, 'We had no idea you were so good'.

The classical *Escuela Bolera* was performed in *Beyond Flamenco* by the lovely Conchita del Campo, whose delicate classical style of arms and feet was so representative of the 19th century. She is one of London's most accomplished dancers, having been a soloist with the Ballet Rambert company. She is very knowledgeable, having also danced since childhood all the various types and styles in her mother Margarita's and father Doroteo's Spanish dance company *Los del Campo*. One day I came across one of my programmes of a gala performance I had seen on a visit to London in the 1960s. There were the *Los del Campo* family company, mother and father and their two children, Conchita and her brother Dorio. I had not realised who she was when I met her many years later after I had settled in London, although we worked so happily together and she had been invaluable in proofreading my Bolero book and helping put the computer's complications to rights. She is so knowledgeable about so much, including Pilates and health matters, saving my life when twice I contracted double pneumonia and she visited constantly with lotions and potions to get me on my feet again. She is a caring 'friend indeed' and beloved by all her pupils. A very rare breed of goodness in a harsh world.

Conchita had studied with the multitalented Lucille Armstrong, whose colour sketches record the regional and other dances she taught. They remain for posterity, the costumes showing so clearly the movements and styles of many dances. That period also heralded the arrival of the celebrated guitarist Paco Peña to London. Still performing and touring his shows, Peña has also created a centre for flamenco studies in Córdoba. In his shows he brings with him each year that charismatic, exciting dancer Angel Muñoz, who means so much to the Spanish Dance Society, together with his wife Charo Espino, and Miguel Espino and his wife Inmaculada Ortega. They brighten up our lives in the spacious Peacock Theatre in Portugal Street. The atmosphere in this old London theatre is perfect, with its comfort and good sightlines taking us back to the 'good old days'. Speaking of the word '*peña*' reminds me of the Spanish dance *peñas* (clubs) of London, especially the *Peña Flamenca de Londres* which is expertly run by the erudite and gentle Vera King, who also publishes their newsletter.

Maisie Loudon-Carter was chairperson of our Spanish Dance Society's committee in England at the time of *Beyond Flamenco*. She said that a grey-haired gentleman sitting in front of her during the performance was nodding all the time while I spoke, as though in agreement. She said, 'I thought his head would fall off'. Maisie and I shared much laughter on our trips to meetings at Sherrill's home in Staines. We met at Clapham Junction station and travelled together from there. There were hilarious times, such as when I stood on the platform refusing to get into the carriage with her because I thought she was on the wrong train, and she saying, 'Get on, get on', and I replying, 'No, you get off, get off', until the conductor joined the chorus and said, 'Ladies, ladies! Make up your minds; get on or get off'. Good that I leapt on because Maisie was right.

43

Carina Ari Foundation, Bengt Häger, *Royal Swedish Ballet History from 1592 to 1962,* and Carina Ari Gold Medal 2008

Carina Ari was born in poverty in Stockholm in 1897 and died a millionairess in Buenos Aires in 1970. As a child she was placed in the Royal Swedish Ballet school by her mother. She was a bright child in many ways. On her own initiative, aged ten, she made posies of flowers which she sold on the street and in the shops to augment their finances. Who could doubt that with her cheerful personality and beauty she would succeed in her chosen career?

Her talent was quickly realised by Fokine on his first visit to the Royal Swedish Ballet in 1913, when he made the unprecedented move of placing her, aged only sixteen, straight from the school into the *corps de ballet* of his productions, passing over company dancers. She was also included later in Rolf de Maré's company of *Les Ballets Suédois* in the 1920s. Her charisma was so strong that she outshone others in performances. While under contract with Rolf de Maré's Swedish company, outside of the Royal Ballet, he refused to allow her a reprieve from the company during her holiday to choreograph, dance and act in a German film. It would have changed her life by bringing her instant international fame. Instead the role went to Pola Negri. It happened because she did not understand that de

Maré, unlike others, paid his dancers all year round. She was clearly mortified. Balanchine asked her to become his partner but instead she engaged Boris Kniaseff, who was considered a good partner.

Carina Ari had left the company in frustrated anger for a life as a soloist, given encouragement by the conductor Desiré-Emile Inghelbrecht, Debussy's favourite student and the greatest French conductor of the 20th century, whom she married. He had been the conductor for *Les Ballets Suédois*, and was the conductor for the forty-piece orchestra at the Paris *Théâtre National de l'Opéra-Comique*, where he accompanied her solo recitals. His friends in the music and art world contributed without charge with music and décor for her recitals. After choreographing her successful ballet *Ode to a Rose* in 1927 for celebrations in the presidential palace, she was commissioned to create a ballet for the Paris opera in the hope of raising its declining standard of ballet, which was used as a filler in opera programmes. In 1928 she staged her ballet *Moonbeams,* 'a choreographic poem' on the very well-trained dancers; it was about dancers in search of a choreographer. Then, from 1929, Lifar started to organise the opera ballet and asked her to dance as his partner in his 1938 ballet *Cantique des Cantiques* (Song of Songs) to Honegger's percussive music. During a performance, in the *pas de deux,* Lifar began to improvise, and she angrily retaliated, causing a battle. Defeated, Lifar withdrew it after eight performances. Her *Scènes dansées,* staged in 1938 at the *Opéra Comique*, was her grand finale as a dancer.

Because of Swedish impresario and writer Professor Bengt Häger's interest in ballet, he became great friends with Carina Ari and she relied on his advice. In 1951 her happy marriage to the Dutch Bols liqueur millionaire Jan Moltzer ended when he died. She was devastated. She consulted Bengt Häger on what she should do with the fortune she had inherited; she had no children to bequeath it to. Häger advised her to establish a foundation in her name, which would be of use to many dancers and historians in the future. She took his advice. It became the largest dance fund in northern Europe, from which I too was to benefit.

Her memorial foundation was set up in 1963. It started to function from 1973, a little over two years after she died, with 12 million Swedish crowns, and is today worth about 100 million crowns[3]. Swedish dance is so well served by it because she took great care to ensure that it was well set up. For advice she went to a personal friend, Herman Kling, the then government minister for justice. She had benefited from help to study with Fokine; so scholarships are available for dancers to further their studies abroad. She knew the fear of a penniless old age which had haunted her; so she supported deserving elderly dancers, especially in connection with illness. Funds also go to dance research. Carina Ari also founded a dance library just a year before she died. This is well-served by the excellent collection that Bengt Häger looked after and continued to stock with paintings and photographs documenting the past and present of dance, until his death at the age of ninety-five. The library also receives rare and valuable manuscripts which it publishes. The members of the foundation boards are carefully selected from dancers, scholars and other people knowledgeable in the field of dance.

In these turbulent times the Carina Ari Foundation is like a sea of calm and stability. In the dance world it represents not just Sweden, but it is international, something which is very important for those who wish to do research. The staff are amazingly knowledgeable on many levels, and always most helpful. The kingpin around which everything revolves is the librarian and manager Satu Mariia Harjanne, who was the whole world to Bengt Häger. Peter Bohlin, who works there occasionally, is also a great asset and dear friend. His knowledge of Russian is very useful in cataloguing and translating. He translated many important papers for my book *Royal Swedish Ballet History from 1592 to 1962* (Olms Verlag, Hildesheim, 2007).

The great ballet historian Ivor Guest did me the honour of introducing my book *Royal Swedish Ballet History from 1592 to 1962* to the guests at the book launch in London, hosted by the Carina Ari Foundations of Sweden. It took place in December 2007 at the Royal Overseas League in London. Eleanore Fitzpatrick, the archive and records manager of the Royal Academy of Dance, was also very helpful in assisting at the launch.

---

3 Corresponds to £8.95m, EUR 10.3m, US$11.5m and ZAR 147m according to May 2017 exchange rates.

Cover of Marina's book on the Royal Swedish Ballet history.

London book launch 2007. *Top photo,* from left: Marina with Ivor Guest (ballet author) who introduced the launch. *Centre photo*: Ann Hutchinson Guest (Laban notation centre), Heather Magoon (artist) and her husband Richard Glasstone (MBE, Cecchetti Society), and Diane van Schoor (Principal of the Royal Ballet Junior School). *Third photo*: John Travis (BBO), Dick Matchett (MBE), Diane van Schoor and her husband Roland Thompson (Music Director).

First photo: Marina, David Leonard (Director, Dance Books Ltd), Jane Pritchard (Victoria and Albert Museum), Vicky Grut (writer) and Maisie Louden-Carter (SDS Chairman). Second photo: Mikael Grut (doctor of forest science, former World Bank staff member), Eleanor Fitzpatrick (RAD Archives and Records Manager), Marina, Conchita del Campo (SDS Examiner, Cechetti and Pilates), Diane van Schoor, Maggie Foyer (dance journalist). Third photo: Richard Holland (Man. Director, Dance Books), Conchita del Campo, Basil Hoare, Maisie Louden-Carter, Marina, Robert Harrold (ISTD).

Each year the bequeathing of the Carina Ari Gold Medal, designed by her, is a big international event held in the Gold Foyer, *Guldfoyén,* at the Opera House, where artists such as Mikhail Baryshnikov, Birgit Åkesson, Ivo Cramér, Mats Ek, Margot Fonteyn, Erik Bruhn and Vladimir Vasiliev have been brought to the public's attention, together with international choreographers who have influenced Swedish dance, such as Martha Graham, Kurt Jooss, Merce Cunningham and Antony Tudor. This shows the wide choice of international artists. The multitalented Carina Ari not only designed her own medal, but also made sculptures of the famous, including one of Dag Hammarskjöld which is today in the UN headquarters in New York.

It therefore came as such a surprise when I was awarded the Carina Ari Gold Medal in 2008 for my book on the history of the Royal Swedish Ballet. This great honour was bestowed upon me by the first established of the three Carina Ari foundations, the Carina Ari 'medal' Foundation, and its then board of directors: Ellen Rasch, former prima ballerina of the Royal Swedish Ballet; Mariane Orlando, former prima ballerina; Gunilla Jensen, dance critic and dramaturge; and Professor Ana Laguna, Royal Court dancer. I received the award in the Gold Foyer of the Royal Opera House in Stockholm, from the hand of Princess Christina of Sweden, a great balletomane. In connection with the medal presentation I also gave a talk about the book at the Carina Ari Foundation.

My first contact with the foundation was when I asked for a grant so that I could publish my book to conserve the almost lost classical Spanish dance, *The Bolero School* (Dance Books Ltd, London, 2002). It was approved, and Bengt asked me to complete my book on the Royal Swedish Ballet history which Mary Skeaping had encouraged me to research and write, having begun it already in 1959. Satu Mariia was the one I turned to for any help that I needed. Her calm and unruffled manner is very confidence-inspiring. I watched how she and Bengt steered enormous conferences and individual needs with no fuss or bother. By the time I finished writing my book on the Swedish Ballet, Carina Ari had died, on Christmas Eve 1970, after her broken thigh caused by a fall failed to heal because of her diabetes.

THE CARINA ARI MEDAL 2008

Princess Christina of Sweden, Marina, and Bengt Häger at the 2008 Gold Medal presentation.

Marina introducing her book on the Swedish ballet, watched by Satu Mariia Harjanne, Carina Ari Foundations Administrator and Librarian. This and the two following photographs were taken at the Carina Ari reception in April 2008.

From left: Magnus Blomkvist (retired head of Drottningholm's Library), Peter Bohlin (formerly with Dansmuséet), Grete Hallberg, Marina, Anna-Karin Ståhle at a reception by the Carina Ari Foundations in 2008. Behind Anna-Karin is Anders Jörlén (critic).

From left: Inger Pålsson, her husband Roland Pålsson (formerly head of the Culture Department at the Swedish Ministry of Education), and Solveig Svalberg.

When setting up her foundations, her trust in Häger was such that she made him the lifetime director to look after them carefully for her. That was a good decision, as they have expanded their benefits to Swedish dance. He had worked in so many fields of dance – impresario, writer, critic, and manager of companies at home such as Cullberg's, and abroad with Celia Franca at Ballet International. He was also constantly organising ballet presentations with foreign guests in Stockholm and Copenhagen. He co-founded the Dance Museum in Stockholm with Rolf de Maré, becoming its director from 1950 to 1989. He was appointed professor and dean of the Swedish College for Dance, and was awarded an honorary doctorate. Endless other international roles, such as president of the *Conseil International de la Danse* in Paris, were placed in his capable hands. All this brought him many accolades and honours in his long life.

The 'on and off' gestation period of my book had covered forty-seven years. Churchill was so right when he said something to the effect that to start a book was like acquiring a mistress but by the end she has become a tyrant. But a book like that was greatly needed to show Sweden's position in the world of dance. One day I said to my friend the dance librarian, researcher and writer Magnus Blomkvist, 'Nobody knows how hard it has been for me to write this book'. He said, 'Marina, I know'. He had been through it all and helped me for many years with not a murmur of complaint and far beyond the very onerous call of duty. For example, he and Peter Bohlin spent an inordinate amount of time searching for the original hotel register which my husband's Aunt Margit, a librarian at the Royal Library, had found there in 1959. It showed Filippo Taglioni's signature from when he signed in himself, Marie Taglioni and their daughter. They had come to visit her grandmother for an emotional series of performances where, because of her poor eyesight, she watched her granddaughter dance from backstage so that she could see her clearly. Peter Bohlin eventually traced the inaccessibly stored hotel register.

However, we never again found the historic letter from Gustav III, Sweden's theatre and dance king, which my husband's Aunt Margit had also found at the Royal Library. It was written from Likala in Finland during a war with Russia, demanding that Charles Didelot return home immediately to Stockholm and dance for the king, as he was paying him a salary. To the king's chagrin, he was dancing all over Europe and not in Sweden. There followed a hilarious chase from country to country to pin him down. It is recorded in the king's correspondence. What is intriguing is that Gustav III was at war, at the front in Finland, but dance was his main concern. He wrote in French. I held the letter in my hand in 1960 but by the time I returned years later Aunt Margit had passed away and no trace of the letter was found; documents had been moved around. It was said about Mary Skeaping: 'Be careful not to get her talking about Gustav III because she will never stop'.

Without the publication grants from the Carina Ari Memorial Foundation, neither of my books *Royal Swedish Ballet* and *Bolero School* would have been published. Nor would the privately owned historic paintings of Marie Taglioni and Per Christian Johansson performing Filippo Taglioni's ballets in Stockholm have been seen, but now they are in the book about the Swedish Ballet. It has always been thought that Marie Taglioni took Johansson to St Petersburg where he then remained, but my book shows that she had seen him dance there on an earlier Russian sojourn and that when she was to perform in Stockholm she asked him to partner her there, after which they both went to St Petersburg, after a horrendously dangerous winter journey.

The same paintings also show the intimate touches of the grandmother watching her granddaughter from the wings, as well as the crowds around her carriage on her arrival and departure. Historic moments have been immortalised for posterity. I am eternally grateful to the Carina Ari Foundation for having enabled me to publish my books on the classical Spanish dance and on the history of the Royal Swedish Ballet because both contain the results of gruelling research which I hope is of benefit to the world of dance. I was so touched when Stephanie Jordan, a Dance Research Professor at the University of Roehampton in London, called my book on the Royal Swedish Ballet 'your wonderful book'.

Bengt and I had mutual interests. We knew the same dancers, ranging from the Danes to the Spaniards, whom he could discuss. He revered especially the choreographic talent of South African Frank Staff. He had watched him create his ballets for the International Ballet in North America. Once, a long time ago, he presented in Stockholm one of the most talked about dancers of the time. Bengt was asked to book a room for him in the most prestigious hotel in Stockholm, with a bed large enough for *three* people. The surprised hotel manager complied. But it was a step too far when they started cooking on their own gas stove on the bedroom floor.

Once Bengt Häger had to vacate his flat for six months while the water pipes in his building were replaced, and during that time he lived in a hotel. I was in Stockholm doing final research for my book, and we sat on the balcony having lunch. There was a constant stream of young dancers studying with Carina Ari grants who came up to consult him. He gave them his time, and good advice. It was an enlightening and happy experience.

I became friends with Bengt and his lovely dancer wife Lilavati. Her exquisite performances delighted Stockholm audiences and me. He once said to me, when she offered me the use of her flat across the street from their apartment during my research visits, that I was favoured. He said he knew of no one else, except their son, to whom she would extend such an invitation. They took me to performances, and dinners afterwards with endless conversations about dance. They told me how the Chinese foreign minister Chou En Lai (Zhou Enlai) had put his aeroplane at Lilavati's disposal to transport them during their visit to China. This led to exchange trips between the Chinese and Swedish companies. Skeaping was to benefit from this. On their China tour the ballerina Ellen Rasch shared a train compartment with her – and her embrocations.

Oh Ellen! Now she too has passed away. She was another of my Stockholm delights. She was a prima ballerina to her fingertips, and a dear friend with a delightful sense of humour. And my ever-helpful friend Grete Hallberg – also passed away.

There are still the knowledgeable balletomanes Anders Jörlén writing for the online *Dansportalen,* and Eric Näslund, author and (1989-2016) director of the Dance Museum, *Dansmuseet,* which presents fascinating exhibitions and other informative attractions. It was so suitably situated in one of the last Gustavian buildings surrounding Gustav Adolf's Square, where one could sit on the terrace at Café de Maré, looking across the rushing water at the Royal Palace on the island of *Gamla Sta'n* – the 'old town'. The balletomane Swedish king Gustav III had designed the square for beauty, which he looked at from his carriage on his way out of town to his stunningly beautiful Drottningholm Palace, which today has the oldest functioning 18th-century theatre in the world (see Chapter 12). Unfortunately the historic venue for *Dansmuseet* has been turned over to government offices. Lost is the former close proximity of the museum to the Opera House next door. Visitors could go to the ballet or opera after doing research at the museum, and then end a fruitful time with a bite to eat in the restaurant *Bakfickan*, the 'Back Pocket', attached to the Opera House. What a loss. The takeover was fought, I joined in, but the bureaucrats won – as always.

44

Summary of my Husband's Speech at my 70th Birthday in 2004

Marina says that she is past her 'use-by' date but I say that she still has a long 'shelf-life'. She is what the French call a 'force of nature'. By the time I get out of bed at about eight o'clock every morning, she has already been up for several hours, written a book or two, listened to news broadcasts, and written letters to prime ministers to protest against the latest war of aggression. Whenever I consult one of her three main books I am astonished: so much useful information, so much hard work.

If you told Marina that she had to clean all the streets of London with a toothbrush, she would just say, 'Give me the toothbrush' and she would finish the job. One reason for this prodigious energy is perhaps that she is a 'colonial' or 'new-worlder'. We Europeans *talk* about doing things but the colonials actually *do* them. Another reason: she is a dancer. They are so tough, so hardworking, so disciplined, and have so much courage. Goethe said: 'Money lost, something lost. Honour lost, much lost. Courage lost, everything lost'.

There are enormous problems in connection with the video that Marina is now doing for the Spanish Dance Society (SDS) of part of its syllabus, namely on the Spanish classical dances: the rehearsals all winter long, the dancers not being paid, even having to pay the transport out of their own pockets; setting up the stage; sitting on the pavement waiting for Conchita to open the building, surrounded by plastic bags with costumes, food (because Marina also fed everyone during each day of filming) etc.; we looked every inch like homeless people. Conchita said to the taxi driver: 'There sits a Dame of the Spanish Empire'. The taxi driver looked very worried. He seemed to think:*How the mighty have fallen. One day that could be me.*

I always suspected Marina to be a 'closet' or crypto Latin, and when I did the children's family tree I found a lot of south French Huguenot ancestry on her side. I, on the other hand, am very much a northerner. We complement each other. If I see that she has written to a prime minister, 'You are a despicable warmonger', I change it to, 'Sir, I strongly disagree with your foreign policy'. She provides the fireworks and I keep her out of prison.

King Gustav II Adolf of Sweden and his chancellor Axel Oxenstierna also complemented each other. The king said impatiently: 'If things depended on you, they would freeze to ice'. Oxenstierna replied coolly: 'And, Your Majesty, if they depended on you, they would burn up'.

We are so grateful that our three children and their spouses made it here today, some with considerable difficulty regarding work and children.

Marina, there has never been a dull moment since we married forty-five years ago. I suggest that we drink a toast: 'To Marina, with love and best wishes for the future'!

Mikael and Marina,
Wimbledon 2012.

Our daughter Vicky (Vibeke), her husband Bill (Alun), and their sons Oscar and Dylan. London 2012.

Our son Edmund (3rd fr. left), his wife Pernille (5th fr. left), and their children Josephine, Sebastian, Theo, Victoria, Alexander and Julius. Copenhagen 2012.

Our son Nicolai and his wife Lorraine, Toronto, 2012.

Bibliography

This book is an autobiography, not a book based on other books, so the Bibliography is short.

Bourio, Juan María. *Coleccion Juan María Bourio. Archivo de Baile Español.* Madrid Capital Europea de la Cultura, 1992. Depósito legal M-28.342-1992.

Grut, Marina. *The History of Ballet in South Africa*. Human & Rousseau, Cape Town, 1981. ISBN 0 7981 1089 9.

Grut, Marina. *The Bolero School. An illustrated history of the Bolero, the Seguidillas and the Escuela Bolera: syllabus and dances.* Dance Books Ltd, London, 2002. ISBN 1 85273 081 1.

Grut, Marina. *Royal Swedish Ballet History from 1592 to 1962.* Georg Olms Verlag, Hildesheim, 2007. ISBN 978 3 487 13494 9.

Huertas, Eduardo. *Teatro Musical Español en el Madrid Illustrado.* El Avapies SA, Madrid, 1989. ISBN 84-86280-38-9.

Instituto Nacional de las Artes Escénicas y la Música, Ministerio de Cultura, Madrid. *Encuentro Internacional La Escuela Bolera.* Madrid, 1992. ISBN 84-8773105-8.

Koegler, Horst. *The Concise Oxford Dictionary of Ballet.* Oxford University Press, London, 1977. ISBN 0 19 311314 7.

Shearing, D and van Heerden, K. *South African Wild Flower Guide 6: Karoo.* Botanical Society of South Africa, Cape Town, 1997. ISBN 1-874999-04-X.

Wilson, GBL. *A Dictionary of Ballet.* Adam & Charles Black, London, third edition, 1974. ISBN 0 7136 1395 5.

Annex 1

Officials at the Spanish Dance Society in Washington DC, 1989

The Spanish Dance Society in Washington DC had an incredible list of high-powered people supporting it.

Patrons

His Excellency the Ambassador of Spain and Mrs Julián Santamaría; Dr Ramon Remacha, Minister for Cultural Affairs, Embassy of Spain; Carola Goya and Honorary President Matteo.

Advisory Members

Lala Custodio de Aza, wife of the Spanish Ambassador to the Organisation of American States; Margaret Ferry, Cultural Alliance; Patrick Hayes, Emeritus Director, Washington Performing Arts; Abel López, GALA Hispanic Theatre; Jack Perlmutter, Emeritus Professor, Corcoran Gallery; Susanne Roschwalb, American University; Leila Smith, Cultural Alliance.

Board

Chermine de Chillaz, Marina Keet (chairman), Sandra and Jordan Laby, Joanne Petrie, Diane Pisano, Evelyn Woolston May.

Committee

Joanne Petrie (chairman), Nancy Heller (vice chairman), Ziva Cohen (treasurer), Mary Anne Shelton (secretary).

Annex 2

Spanish Dance Theatre of the Spanish Dance Society, Washington DC: Repertoire and Members, c.1984-1990

By Spanish Dance Theatre member and Archivist Nancy G Heller,
Professor of Art History, The University of the Arts,
Philadelphia, PA, USA
(Information from 1982 and 1983 added later.)

Alegrías Antiguas [chor. La Quica; also Irena Campbell], *Alegrías Contemporáneas* [Mercedes y Albano], *Arín-Arín* [Rhoda Rivkind and Geoffrey Neiman], *Baile de las Nacres* [Marina Keet], *Ball dels Nans* [Joan (Juan) Fosas], *Benamor* [Theodoro Dantes and Marina Keet], *La Boda de Luis Alonso* [Paco Alonso], *Boleras de la Cachucha* [Elsa Brunelleschi / Keet], *Bolero de L'Alcudia de Carlet* [Joan Fosas], *Bolero de Algodre* [Keet y Casa Zamora, Madrid], *Bolero Buñyola* [Joan Fosas], *Bolero de Caspe* [Marina Keet/Pedro Azorin Ibañez], Bolero de Torrent [Valencia; Joan Fosas], *Bolero Plá* [Enric Marti i Mora, Valencia], *Bulerías* [El Güito], *Bolero Robado* [Alan Tjaarda Jones], *Bulerías* [Tomás de Madrid], *El Café de Chinitas* [Mercedes y Albano/Marina Keet], *Caña* [Mercedes and Albano], *Caracoles* [Mercedes y Albano/Marina Keet], *Careado Asturiano* [Antonio Saldaña], *Celebration* [Manolo Rivera], *La Charrada*

[Marina Keet], *The Choice (?), Colombianas* [Chelo Jacobo], *Córdoba* [Elsa Brunelleschi/Keet], *Corri-Corri* [Marta Padilla/Keet, Madrid], *Los Cuatro Muleros* [Marta Padilla/Keet, Madrid], *(Ereverencia Vasca/ Reverencia* [Juan Urbeltz/Keet], *Ezpata Dantza* [Basque, María Isabel Matos, daughter/M García Matos/Keet], *Fandango del Candil* [Coros y Danzas Madrid Carmen Gordo/Keet], *Fandango de Comares* [Andalusia, Marta Padilla/Keet], *Fandango de Hortunaz* [Valencia, Enric Marti i Mora], *Fandango de Huelva* [Mercedes y Albano], *Fandango de Verdiales* [Juanjo Linares/Sherrill Wexler], *Flamenco Actual* [José de Udaeta], *Flamenco Con-Tiempo* [Charo Linares and Marina Lorca], *Farruca* [Marina Keet and Jaime Coronado], *Galop de Panderetas* [Valencia, Joan Fosas], *Garrotín* [Vicki Kurland Ramos], *Garrotín Antiguo* [Elsa Brunelleschi/Keet], *Gloria* [from *Misa Flamenca*, Keet], *Godaleta Dantza* [Juan Urbeltz/Keet: San Sebastian], *Guajiras* [La Tati], *Jota Aragonesa* [Pedro Azorín Ibañez/Keet], *Jota Asturiana* [Antonio Saldaña], *Jota de Huesca* [Zaragoza: Jordi Sanchez], *Jota Montrové* [Galicia: Celsa Cainzos/ Keet], *Jota Navarra* [Concha Egéa], *Jota de la Pradera* [Coros y Danzas, Carmen Gordo/Keet Madrid], *Jota de la Uva* [Marta Padilla/Keet, Madrid], *Malagueña* [Elsa Brunelleschi/Keet], *Mateixes* [Marta Padilla/ Keet, Madrid], *Martinete* [various contributors], *Mortitxol* [Valencia, Joan Fosas. Choreography: Albert Sans], *Mozárabe* [Marina Keet], *Muñeira Asturiana* [Antonio Saldaña], *Muñeira* [Galicia, Celsa Cainzos], *Nosotros Somos* [Marina Lorca], *Olé de la Curra* [Elsa Brunelleschi/Keet], *Panaderos de la Flamenca* [Elsa Brunelleschi/Marina Keet], *Pandeirada Galician:* [Celsa Cainzos/Keet, Madrid], *Parado de Valldemos* [Joan Fosas], *Parranda Murciana* [Antonio Saldaña], *Peteneras* [Roberto Lorca], *El Polo* [Hazel Acosta], *El Ramilletillo* [Marta Padilla/Keet], *Rapsodia Valenciana* [Keet], *Missing* [Juan Urbeltz/Keet], *Ritmos de Bulerías* [El Güito], *Ritual Fire Dance* [Keet], *Romeras* and *Rumba Flamenca* [Daniel de Córdoba], *Sacromonte* [Enrique Segovia], *(Salinas?) Segoviana* [Theodoro Dantes], *Seguidillas del Candil* [Coros y Danzas, Madrid, Carmen Gordo/Keet], *Seguidillas de Carlet* [Joan Fosas], *Seguidillas Manchegas* [Eloy Pericet], *Seguiríyas* [Marina Lorca and Carlos], *Sevillanas* [Keet and many versions], *Sevillanas Boleras* [Keet], *Soleares* [group; La Quica], *Soleares del Maestro Arcas* [Luisa Pericet/Paula Durbin], *Street Scene* [Keet], *Tangos* [La Tati], *Tanguillo de Cádiz* [Enrique *El Cojo* Jemenez/Keet], *Tanguillo de Málaga* [Enrique *El Cojo* Jimenez/Keet], *Tientos* [Luisa Pericet],

Tientos [Mercedes y Albano], *Tirana del Zarandilla* [Coros y Danzas/ Keet], *Triana* [Roberto Amaral], *Uztai Txikiak* [Juan Urbeltz/Keet, San Sebastian], *Uztai Aundiak* [Juan Urbeltz/Keet, San Sebastian], *Makilla Txipiak* [Juan Urbeltz/Keet, San Sebastian], *Makilla Aundiakikoa* [Juan Urbeltz/Keet, San Sebastian], *El Vito* [Marina Lorca], *Xiringüelo Asturiano* [Antonio Saldana], *Zambra; Zapateado* [various], *Zapateado de María Cristina* [Eloy Pericet/Keet], *Zorongo* [María Rosa], *Zortzico* [Juan Urbeltz/Keet, San Sebastian], *Pasapie de España* and *The Vestris Gavotte* [Nancy Sedgwick and Alan Tjaarda Jones; Marina Keet's 'suites' – *Gran Vía*, etc.]

COMPARATIVE MATERIAL

Latin American

Las Bicicletas (Mexican polka) [Antonio Saldaña], *Cumbia*; *Danza de los Viejitos* [Antonio Saldana], *Tilingolingo* [Antoñio Saldaña], *Jarabe Tapatío* (Mexican hat dance) [Jaime Coronado], *Mexican Zapateado* [Jaime Coronado], *Malambo* (Argentinian Zapateado) [Nestor Epifanio/ Marina Keet], *Zamba del Grillo* (Argentina) [Eloy Pericet/Keet], *El Gato* (Argentinian) [Nestor Epifanio/Keet]

PERFORMERS

DANCERS (IN ALPHABETIC ORDER BY SURNAME)

César Aquino, Roslin Arington, Paul Bade, Jeff Bailey, Brian Baltrop, Bambi, Debra Belo, Marla Bush, Virginia Campbell, Jordi Chalezquer, Chung-Jung Chun, Ziva Cohen, Iver Cooper, Jaime Coronado, Nicole Corrieri, Véronique Dang-Tran, Nathaniel Deutsch, Monica Diggle, Paula Durbin, Concha Egéa, Lourdes Elias, Antonio Fernández, Tatiana Figueroa, Carlos Fondeur, Steve Gerstein, Elisabeth Gettins, Reina Getz, Deborah Gómez, Orlando González, Larry Graves, Karen Green, Chuck Hanclich, Nancy Heller, Tom Hinds, Ben Hole, Renée Iannuzzi, John Jacobin, George James, Peter Leeds, Susana Lorenzo,

Alejandro Marin, Trish McClean, Jacques Oberto, Triana d'Orazio, Isabel Otero, Nancy Parenti, Joaquin Perez, Joanne Petrie, Deanna Pierce, Diane Pisano, Danielle Polen, Joana del Río, Dennis Rodríguez, Diane Rowe, Antonio Saldaña, Carol Sanders, Nancy Sedgwick, Mary Ann Shelton, Nelson Sitton, Robert Teri, Indri Tjandrasuwita, Tom Truss, Orlando Vargas.

GUITARISTS AND OTHER MUSICIANS

Henry Jova, Charlie Moser, Eric Nothman, Ralph Pemberton, Miguelito Pérez, Tom Stefanic.

Domenico Caro, William Christie, Maricarmen Ciccone, Carmen de Perignat, Flory Jagoda (Ladino singer), Los Amigos (mariachi band), John O'Loughlin, Juan Pagán, Jorge Porta, Eric Rice-Johnston, Larry Robinson, Manuel Rocca, Manuel Romero Pedrera, Paul Shelton,

GUEST ARTISTS

DANCERS: Carola Goya and Matteo, José de Udaeta, Irena Campbell, Marina Lorca, Roberto Amaral, Margarita Jova, Joan Fosas, Emilio Acosta, Michael Lorimer, Charo Linares, Manolo Rivera, Ricardo Villa, Alan Tjaarda Jones,

GUEST TEACHERS: El Güito, Enric Marti i Mora, Theodoro Dantes (choreographies),

SINGERS AND GUITARISTS: Manolo Leiva (*cantaor*), Paco de Málaga (guitarist) Maríja Temo (singer and guitarist), Benito Palacios (guitarist), Luis Primitivo (*cantaor*).

BENEFACTORS

Spanish Ambassadors to Washington DC, His Excellency Jaime Ojeda, His Excellency Julián Santa Mari Rosa, His Excellency Alberto and Mrs Aza, Cultural Minister of the Spanish Embassy Dr Ramon Remacha, Founder of the Washington Performing Arts Patrick Hayes,

Costumier Rosa Fosas from Barcelona, the GWU Professors Chairman Nancy Johnson and Maida Withers, Artistic Director Mary Day of the Washington Ballet, Sandy and Jordan Laby, our Chairman Evelyn Woolston-May, Costume Designers: Prof.William Pucilowsky of the GWU Theater Dept., Peter Cazalet of the CAPAB Ballet Co., and Costume Reseacher Carolina de Weinberg, Prof. Carl Gudenius and Prof. Bradley Sabelli of the GWU Theater Dept.

HELPERS (OF ALL KINDS)

Marco Cáceres, Renata Klingenberg, Abel López, Enric Marti i Mora, Kathie Somerville; among many others.

Index

(Annexes only partially covered)